The

DISSENTING

ACADEMY

The

DISSENTING

PANTHEON

ACADEMY

~ Edited by Theodore Roszak

BOOKS *A Division of Random House, New York*

Preface

AS THIS BOOK GOES TO PRESS, THE AMER-
ican academic world finds itself more agitated and agonized
by political discussion than perhaps at any time in its history. The Vietnam war has inspired a range of resistance
on the part of teachers and students that extends from conventional petitioning to the practice of mass civil disobedience. While those involved in this resistance are still a
strict minority of the total academic community, since the
1965 teach-ins no single group in our society has been as
persistent and vocal in its opposition to official policy as
the professors and students. For those who reject the
Vietnam war as fundamentally ill-conceived and immoral,
and for those who believe that it is a responsibility of the
academic to participate in the discussion of vital public
issues, this remarkable show of active concern on the campuses is bound to be encouraging. It may, indeed, be the
most hopeful event in postwar American history, for it
may mean that at last there will be a significant injection
of intellect and of conscience into our society's politics. It
may mean that, finally, we stand the chance to have done
with living inertly off the political capital of New Deal
policy and the antiquated orthodoxies of cold-war diplomacy. It may mean that the universities are about to cease
functioning as the handmaidens of whatever political,

military, paramilitary, or economic elite happens to be financing their operations, and to become an independent source of knowledge, value, and criticism. If indeed this is true, then government in America may yet become an art instead of a shabby form of social engineering based on conditioned reflexes and institutionalized cynicism.

But if this long-overdue return to a substantive democracy is to take place, we must recognize the more dismal truth the Vietnam war has to teach us: namely, that the war is very largely a product of the academic community's own cultural default. It has been called the "liberal's war" —and so it is, to a very large degree. The advisers who have moved both the Kennedy and the Johnson administrations toward that war are, for the most part, prestigious and conventionally liberal academics from our best schools. The rhetoric and the rationale for the war, as well as a deal of the expertise that has gone into organizing the various Saigon regimes, have come from what Mary McCarthy has called "the paramilitary intellectuals." Further, the very fact that the war has been able to creep steadily and without significant debate from a marginal commitment to a major preoccupation of our society has much to do with the silence and caution that characterized our universities prior to 1965. Those who might have asked the vital questions and formulated the feasible alternatives did not do so.

In this sense Vietnam is as much a measure of the failure of the academics as it is now becoming a gauge of their conscience. If *this* Vietnam is not to be followed by another and still another—if, indeed, the next Vietnam is not already imperceptibly taking shape by the same processes in some other quarter of the world—then it may be necessary for academics to do a great deal more than simply protest ad hoc against the war at hand. One may justifiably ask: Does the business-as-usual of the American academic community do more to assist in the production of Vietnams than it does to examine, resist, and correct policy that leads to such moral disaster?

It is that question to which this book addresses itself. The contributors were selected as socially engaged intellectuals each of whom, in addition to serving his chosen field of knowledge as a teacher and scholar, has entered significantly into the discussion of public policy. Eight of the contributors are here as representatives of the standard disciplines of the social sciences and humanities. In addition, Gordon C. Zahn has contributed a special chapter on the role of the Catholic university and Noam Chomsky has done a concluding statement on the part academics have played in the formulation of current public policy. Perhaps it should be mentioned that the field of sociology is absent because an excellent and extensive critique of the discipline already exists in C. Wright Mills's *The Sociological Imagination.*

The contributors share a common polemical ground. They accept as given the fact that we live in a world where civilized values are gravely menaced. It is not the object of this volume to argue or prove that point all over again. Rather, the writers argue that the learned professions of our society, confronted with the protracted emergency in which our civilization finds itself, have been grossly remiss in meeting any defensible standard of intellectual conscience. Beyond the polemic, they seek to formulate a conception of intellect that would make the professions and higher education as a whole relevant to the task of creating an active and enlightened citizenry. The charge that was put to the contributors was the question: How has your

profession, and the academic community generally, fulfilled its social responsibility, and how ought it to dis-
charge the educational obligation it bears?

In answering that question, the writers have taken a
variety of approaches. There would be, one suspects, a deal
of controversy among them on many points of analysis and
value. But what emerges clearly is the conviction of all that
the proper and central business of the academy is the public examination of man's life with respect to its moral quality. It is, from first to last, the spirit of Socrates that broods
over the "dissenting academy" this volume comprises.

One last word. This book confines itself to the social
sciences and humanities partly for the arbitrary reason that
space is limited. But there is also the fact that the social
responsibility of the natural scientists has already received
a good deal of critical attention in the years since Hiroshima. A publication like the *Bulletin of the Atomic Scientists,* an organization like the Society for Social Responsibility in Science, make it clear enough that the moral
agony of the natural scientists, while far from achieving a
resolution, is at least very much a matter of public record;
that of the humanists and the social scientists has only
begun to find significant discussion. It is, then, to the character of academic life and work in these fields that this
book devotes its investigation.

CONTENTS

CONTENTS

The

DISSENTING

ACADEMY

ON ACADEMIC

DELINQUENCY

∽ Theodore Roszak

THERE WAS A TIME WHEN MEN OF INTEL-
lect described the purpose of their lives in ways that
stirred the souls of the noble and chilled the blood of
the base . . .

If those of us who teach in the universities today were to
observe this fact, how many of our students would believe
or understand us? And of those who did believe and understand, how many would have learned what they knew
from the lessons and examples we have set for them?

"Dare to know!" So Kant defined the function of intellect in a day which pursued the critical examination of life
and society neither as an amusing pastime nor as a lucrative career, but rather as an act of defiance and of risk. It
was a day in which men of intellect carried banners as if to
battle and on them inscribed mottoes of impudent and
hazardous intention. "Everything," Diderot insisted,
"must be examined, everything must be shaken up, with-

out exception and without circumspection." And *"écrasez l'infâme!"* Voltaire commanded. These were marked men and they knew it. With Jefferson, their intellectuality was an oath sworn upon an altar against enemies who were many and mighty. Denouncing the *Encyclopédie* on the eve of its suppression, the Attorney General of France drew the line between official authority and the free intellect with menacing precision.

> Society, Religion, and the State present themselves today at the tribunal of justice in order to submit their complaints. . . . Impiety walks with head held high. . . . Humanity shudders, the citizenry is alarmed. . . .
>
> It is with grief that we are forced to say it: can one conceal from oneself that there is a project formed, a Society organized, to propagate materialism, to destroy Religion, to inspire a spirit of independence, and to nourish the corruption of morals? . . .[1]

But the great project went forward nonetheless, though its authors were driven to desperation and ruin.

That was one age . . . and this is another. And what are the imperatives our students would find inscribed upon their teachers' lives? "Secure the grant!" "Update the bibliography!" "Publish or perish!" The academic life may be busy and anxious, but it is the business and anxiety of careerist competition that fills it, not that of a dangerous venture. So it is by and large outside the boundaries of the academic profession that our students must look for the defiant minds of the time.

But then let us admit that the academy has very rarely been a place of daring. One might perhaps count on the fingers of one hand the eras in which the university has been anything better than the handmaiden of official society: the social club of ruling elites, the training school of whatever functionaries the status quo required. The great minds of the Enlightenment—and especially the French *philosophes*—were not, of course, academics. They preferred to think of themselves as "men of letters." Most contemporary studies identify them by the more generic and free-wheeling term "intellectuals": non-university-related thinkers and writers. The distinction is historically correct, but too often it becomes, for the academic, a convenient moral barricade. *"They were intellectuals; I am an academic. Theirs is not my tradition. Their ideals place no claim upon me."* But why weren't the *philosophes* university men? Because the universities of their day proved to be inhospitable to the most advanced, critical thought of the time. Important intellectual history *had* to be made outside the oppressive environment of the academic establishment. The *philosophes* were not academics, because to be an academic in their age required that one be a petty and irrelevant mind, thus a "safe" mind from the viewpoint of the authorities. The contemporary academic who connects himself with the tradition such minds represent, claims a pedigree that is historically legitimate but not, alas, ethically ennobling.

The American university has been no exception to the historical rule. It has offered its academics little opportunity to disconnect from this dismal tradition of official conformity. No doubt if Jefferson had had his way, things would have been different. For Jefferson, the purpose of the academy—as he outlined it in his plans for the University of Virginia—was to exercise an independent criticism of those forces of church or state which "fear every change, as endangering the comforts they now hold." The university was to "unmask their usurpation, and monopolies of honors, wealth, and power."[2] But Jefferson's influence was limited to one school and to his own lifetime. While his controversial ideals of nonsectarianism and the teaching of practical knowledge were eventually picked up later in the nineteenth century by the great state universities, his ideal of independent criticism never proved acceptable to the forces of church, state, or corporate wealth which were to dominate the funding of higher education.

Interestingly enough, it was, in the early nineteenth century as it is now, very largely the students who exercised initiative in demanding that a critical social relevance should be an integral part of their education. The medium which the students chose for this objective was the extracurricular literary (or debating) societies. These societies, which sprang up in the wake of the Revolution, were by far the most vital element in American education through the first third of the nineteenth century. Their purpose was to study and debate the issues of the day, very much in the tradition of the *philosophes*.

> . . . the propagation of dogma was not the purpose of the literary societies. They, instead, respected reason, nurtured intellect, and subjected much that was established to scrutiny and debate. . . .[3]

The clubs also served to bring controversial speakers to the campus (like Rufus Choate and Ralph Waldo Emerson; the latter was frequently denied the use of college buildings on campuses where he spoke), produced literary magazines, and assembled the best libraries of current literature available.[4] As one might imagine, the clubs were never well accepted by college authorities.

But with the weakening of the debate tradition (mainly before the advance of the fraternities) it is only at exceptional schools like the early Oberlin that we find the ideal of dissent being honored. Oberlin was consecrated from its beginning to an activist Christianity that rapidly led to a dissenting position on the issue of slavery. The resistance of the campus and the students to the often violent dislike of the surrounding community was quite heroic.[5] But by the end of the century, when the modern academic establishment had fully "arrived," the closest any of the major universities cared to come to exercising an independent critical function was in providing expert advice to state legislative committees and personnel for the regulatory agencies that were becoming a feature of industrial America. The University of Wisconsin probably went furthest in formulating this type of service into a doctrine—especially during the presidency of Charles Van Hise. But even at Wisconsin, the administration decided to put the patriotic screws on once the First World War began: expert criticism, yes; radical dissent, no.

Since that time American higher education has been dominated by and divided between traditions that have had nothing to do with the socially aggressive inquisitiveness which Voltaire and Jefferson took to be the essential feature of intellect. This is not to say the dominant traditions have been totally lacking in a certain initial worthiness of intention. But despite that intention, they have corrupted fast, mainly because they have insisted on evaluating the academic, not as a whole personality, but rather as the receptacle of specialized and seemingly detachable talents. But as Socrates long ago warned the Sophists, to partition the personality is the first step away from wisdom. To isolate any human skill (as the Sophists isolated the skill of rhetoric), to cultivate and assess it apart from the total person in whom it resides, is to trivialize the skill and diminish the person.

The traditions of higher education I speak of here may be called those of "service" and "scholarship." "Service" is that catchphrase which designates a peculiarly American interpretation of the higher learning. The ideal was most clearly embodied in the Morrill Land Grant Act of 1862, which declared that the American public universities should be an integral part of the community and serve its needs. There was—and still is—an obvious democratic idealism about this conception of the university. But how was "service to the community" to be construed? The question is a classic one and it was raised by Socrates:

> To which sort of treatment of our city do you urge me? Is it to combat the Athenians until they become as virtuous as possible, prescribing for them like a physician; or is it to be their servant and cater to their pleasure?

Inevitably, the administrative and financial forces that came to govern American higher education chose to be catered to, not combatted. And so service came to mean the indiscriminate adaptation of the university to every demand that monied interests and the general public could imagine making. It meant, for example, offering "professional study" and even baccalaureates in boy-scouting, fire insurance, home economics, and hotel management. (Such were available—even from schools of the caliber of Cornell, Chicago, and Wisconsin.) It meant, in brief, cloaking in all the glamour and prestige of the higher learning whatever form of low-level training or ordinary entertainment the "community" felt it "needed."

But at the same time that the university was being turned into an emporium of marketable skills, other Americans were discovering a very different and very exciting vision of the higher learning. These were the young scholars and scientists who, in the immediate post-Civil War period, began flocking to the German universities, there to experience the intellectual vitality of the lecture method, the seminar, the laboratory, the rigorous Teutonic ideal of *Wissenschaft*. Here, they felt certain, they had found what higher education was all about—or *ought* to be all about. The German university was the academic New Jerusalem, and they brought home its style and standards like exotic treasure.

Nietzsche, far more perceptive than the German or American scholars of his day, could discern the dross beneath the treasure and he raised one of his typically abrasive questions.

> Now Pascal thinks that men pursue their business and their sciences with such single-mindedness in order to escape the most important questions which every moment of loneliness and true leisure would urge upon them—questions concerning the Why, Whence, and Whither of life. But curiously enough, not even the most obvious question occurs to our scholars: what benefit their labor, their haste, and their painful ecstasies can possibly have? . . . But if, as men of science, you go about science in the same manner in which workers go about tasks which life's daily necessities impose upon them, then what is to become of a culture condemned to await the hour of its birth and its salvation amidst this excited, breathless, aimless, fidgeting infatuation with science and learning?[6]

But who was there to ponder such questions a century ago? The "service station" ideal of education was rapidly vulgarizing the American university, and the German-bred scholars and scientists of that generation (they were to become the creators of the graduate school, of aristocratic scholarly communities like Johns Hopkins and Clark, and of the American learned societies) had their hands full with fighting the philistine. The battle was—originally—a real one and the lines were militantly drawn. Thorstein Veblen, offering the classic statement of the academicians' position in his *The Higher Learning in America,* plumped for a standard by which only the original Johns Hopkins would ever have qualified as a true "university."

The conflict between service and scholarship in higher education, between the technician and the academic, was not destined to be resolved wholly in favor of either side— at least not at the vast majority of America's more important state and private universities. Instead the conflict has gradually worked itself into an impasse. And, in a typically "pragmatic" American way, the impasse has been given a name and has become a substitute for a solution. The name is "the multiversity": the school which teaches, in Robert Hutchins' words, "anything we can get anybody to pay for." Including, let it be said, valid subjects. For if the "service station" conception of higher education has survived and, indeed, prospered over the past three generations, the dedicated scholar has at least managed to carve out a fortified niche for himself in the busy labyrinth of the contemporary campus. Such was the compromise the scholar and the liberally educated intellectual finally settled for in the major state and private universities. In the graduate school, in the colleges of arts and letters, in their portion of the general education requirements, the academics have achieved a kind of disgruntled coexistence with the home economists, the educationists, the engineers, the business administrators, and the vast contingent of those who train and entertain in the guise of educating.[7]

This turn-of-the-century quarrel between competing elite and vulgar conceptions of higher education has continued to smolder in the multiversities—but rather at the level of a peeve than a real issue. Nevertheless, it continues to structure much of whatever small amount of discussion transpires in the schools about the ideals of education—as well as a much greater amount of intramural politics on the campuses. The proponents of the multiversity parade the "democracy" of their ideal; the scholars proudly champion the aristocratic virtues of pure intellect. But the truth is that their dialogue has become a corrupted one, a debate between half-men who have lost touch with the essential meaning of both "democracy" and "intellect" and who are equally guilty of a cultural default that transcends the comprehension of both.

For where, at last, have these two supposedly irreconcilable traditions led American higher education? On the one hand, the ideal of service has matured into a collaboration between the universities, the corporate world, and the government, so indiscriminate that the American warfare state has had no greater difficulty finding academic hirelings for any project—bar none—than its totalitarian opposite numbers. Ranking physicists and engineers at the "best schools" unquestioningly pursue classified research in the refinement of the thermonuclear arsenal (schools like MIT and the University of California-Berkeley derive a major part of their budget from "service" of this kind). Biologists at the University of Pennsylvania work under secret contracts to develop chemical-biological weaponry.[8] As part of the Army's Project Camelot, leading social scientists have pooled their expertise in order to help the American military plan counterinsurgency activities in Latin America.[9] In order to provide the United States Information Agency and the military with cold-war propaganda of a scholarly cut, the University of Southern California sets up, with the generous support of a radical right-wing industrialist, a Research Institute on Communist Strategy and Propaganda.[10]

And so on. And so on.

A full listing of such activities—including the prestigious employment academics have sought at military think-tanks like the RAND Corporation—could go on for dozens of pages. And it would have to include the government's use of scholarly "names" like Arthur Schlesinger, Jr., for the purpose of authoring cover stories in support of policies secretly devised for the most cynical and unworthy purposes. But the picture is clear enough: in the name of service (and of course in return for handsome fees and cushy appointments) universities and university men have been prepared to collaborate in genocide, espionage, deceit, and all the corruptions our government's sense of omnipotence has led us to. "Service," by becoming a blanket willingness to do whatever society will pay for, has led the university to surrender the indispensable characteristic of wisdom: moral discrimination. So it is that the multiversity progressively comes to resemble nothing so much as the highly refined, all-purpose brothel Jean Genet describes in his play *The Balcony*.

But if this is what the ideal of service has come to, what, on the other hand, has become of Nietzsche's "excited, breathless, aimless, fidgeting" scholars? All the archive hunting, the document mongering and statistical surveying, all the burgeoning bodies of fact and speculation, the bulging barnloads of dissertations, monographs, learned journals, definitive editions, bibliographies, all the new interpretations, revised interpretations, and revised revisions of interpretations: what has it all totaled up to—precisely? The answer is equally melancholy. For until the recent rash of campus protest related to the Vietnam war, nothing has so characterized the American academic as a condition of entrenched social irrelevance, so highly developed that it would be comic if it were not sufficiently serious in its implications to stand condemned as an act of criminal delinquency.

The cultural default of American scholarship is much less easy to account for than that of the service tradition. Given the fact that American academics draw so heavily on the German scholarly tradition, one might have expected that the cultural disaster Germany has experienced in our time would have led to a long, hard rethinking of that tradition in this country. One might have anticipated a deepening agony of conscience—especially among American academics in the humanities and social sciences—and a growing insistence that the scholarly obsession with "disinterested research" and "pure knowledge" yield to critical examination. If, after all, the homeland of *Wissenschaft* and *Lehrfreiheit* could experience such a reversion to barbarism with so little resistance from its universities, should it not have been clear that even such careful students of higher education as Abraham Flexner were utterly and tragically wrong in contending (as Flexner did right up to the brink of the Nazi revolution) that it was the German academics who "in theory and in practice come nearest to giving higher education its due position"?[11]

One might have expected such a deep stirring of conscience among American scholars. There has been none. The "balance of terror"—which is nothing but an exquisitely rationalized social commitment to a policy of genocide—has entrenched itself in the economy, the morality, and the psychology of our society; the threadbare ideals and shoddy rhetoric of anachronistic nationalism continue to dominate the politics of the time; the war-prone imbalance of wealth between the world's rich and

poor nations continues to increase; the control of democratic institutions over decision-making elites continues to
weaken . . . and to all these familiar vices that threaten the
spiritual and physical survival of that precious thing we
call "civilization," scholars have had nothing to say. A
quarter-century after Logan Wilson made the first full-
scale sociological analysis of "academic man," the normal
career of the American scholar—from lowly instructor to
prestigious professor—can still be described as Wilson described it, without including any reference to citizenly
conduct. The pace and mobility of the academic life have
vastly increased, and so too the scale of competitive rewards. But Caplow and McGee, in their more recent examination of the intrigue and economics of the "academic
marketplace," are still talking about men whose professional calling has no relationship to social responsibility.
Professional politicking and scholarly publication are all
that academic success requires. And there would seem to
be little prospect of change. In the most detailed recent
survey and criticism of graduate education in America,
Bernard Berelson never once finds occasion to suggest that
the preparation of an apprentice academic ought properly
to include an enlivening of the social conscience, a serious
and systematic confrontation with Robert Lynd's classic
challenge: "Knowledge for *what?*"[12]

Or let us take another remarkable phenomenon of the
academic community which may serve as a convenient
measure of the professional standard of intellectuality. At
least once every year each of the learned societies that control the careers and standards of professional academics
holds a regional or a national conference. Very rarely do
these conferences gain any public visibility. Very rarely do
they seek such visibility. This is not because the press is

unwilling to give coverage. On the contrary; a paper like the *New York Times,* which troubles itself to report most of the national conferences, clearly goes out of its way to find publicly relevant activity at the meetings. But all it ever turns up in its search is an occasional paper delivered in one of the subcommittees of the conferences. Thus, at the 1965 meeting of the American Historical Association, the *Times* managed to find a paper dealing with the problem of violence in the civil rights struggle and another dealing with Pope Pius XII's relations with anti-Nazi conspirators—and reported them. Indeed, it gave the Pope Pius paper and discussion two full columns of coverage. At the 1965 meeting of the American Political Science Association, a *Times* reporter, clearly scraping the barrel, went about the corridors pressing political scientists for their opinions on the Johnson administration—only to come up with a modicum of cautious, pedestrian, and remarkably amateurish opinions. Following the 1965 conference of the American Sociological Association, the *Times* even ran an editorial ("Sociology for What?"), picking up on some critical remarks of the Association's president and chiding the sociologists for offering so little that had any relevance to the problems of our times. Does one pursue sociology, the *Times* asked, "to get particular individuals academic positions, profitable grants of doubtful use, or is it to make pioneering contributions to the understanding of the nature and operation of a complex society undergoing rapid change?"[13] What is one to make of a profession that cannot even meet the intellectual standards of the society's journalists?

It was not until the 1966 conferences that two of the professions (anthropology and the Eastern Division of the American Philosophical Association) saw fit to address

themselves critically to the war in Vietnam. "The traditions of our vocation," the philosophers explained—but it
should have gone without saying—"make it appropriate
that we express our concern on issues of great moral urgency."[14] Their concern and that of the anthropologists
was not shared in any collective capacity by the other professions. Despite the pressure the war was putting upon
male students, despite the fact that a presidential commission was scheduled to make crucial recommendations on
the draft only one month after the conferences convened,
none of the professions even troubled to debate a resolution on conscription. None raised any question of the
propriety of using grade records as a basis for selective service classification. The failure is not surprising. The conferences, being august assemblies of professional scholars,
place teaching and students in their proper perspective:
out of sight and out of mind.

Clearly, the conferences of learned societies are simply
not understood to be public events. They serve other functions than that of communicating with the greater society.
Normally they provide for an exchange of new and specialized knowledge; beyond that, the conferences are a social
occasion—a chance for old colleagues to get together—and,
more importantly, they are "flesh markets" where academics and jobs are put in touch with each other. Thus,
the conferences of learned societies are, in structure and
intention, identical with trade conventions—like those, let
us say, of the Association of Plumbing Contractors or the
Association of Hotel Managers. At those conferences, too,
new and specialized knowledge is passed about, old friends
get together, and valuable commercial contacts are made.

Now it is, to say the least, odd that the conferences of
learned societies should convene and transpire so unob-

trusively in our society. There is, after all, not a single one of the learned professions that is not ultimately connected with that aggregation of ideals which defines civilized life from barbarism: the free market of ideas, the dignity of the individual, the pursuit of intellectual and aesthetic excellence, the value of moral courage. There is surely not a single academic that has not, in the course of his career, studied and probably expounded upon the life and work of the great teachers who often enough struggled and suffered in behalf of those ideals. Indeed, none of us who teach in the universities would want to consider a student fully educated who had not been asked to ponder the examples of Socrates and Abelard, Galileo and Spinoza, Voltaire and Pasteur . . . and all the others who fought to dignify the life of the mind and to assert the preeminence of the moral virtues. But what do the examples of these great forebears mean to academics themselves? What does it imply when those who are peculiarly charged with the cultivation and defense of civilized values come together year after year ostensibly to make a collective assertion of their identity as teachers and scholars, but in reality with no more socially significant purpose in mind than an assembly of plumbers or hotel managers? Does it suggest that civilized values in our day require no special cultivation or defense? that all is well—and there are other and better things to do than to use these assemblies as forums for the vigorous and public discussion of social questions? Or does it suggest that, whatever may be wrong with the world, it is not the academic's peculiar responsibility to address himself to its correction? How is one to account for the remarkable fact that the annual assemblies of professional academics have come to rank among the most irrelevant and inconsequential events in our society's calendar?

Let us examine a contrasting situation. The matters discussed and voted upon at the yearly convention of the AFL-CIO are apt to be front-page news of considerable impact. No presidential administration would dare let a convention of organized labor meet without entering thickly into the politics of the meeting and attempting to influence the convention's resolutions. One takes it for granted that there *will* be publicly relevant politics at the convention; one *expects* there to be resolutions on public questions. So it becomes important for official Washington to compete for influence in this forum. But has official Washington ever troubled itself to send representatives to meetings of the American Historical Association or the Modern Language Association—with a view to "winning over" the conference? The prospect is absurd.

One can anticipate an immediate objection to this comparison: the AFL-CIO is after all a voting bloc of immense size and is courted as such by political leaders. The learned societies are inconsequential in their voting strength, so of course they receive no political attention. But the objection will not do. Obviously, the learned societies are in no position to compete as a "bloc vote" with other forces in our society. Nor would that be an appropriate form of competition for them. But they *are* societies of opinion makers—or at least potentially so. They are composed of learned and articulate men whose words and deeds could be of considerable influence upon the voting public. Their opinions, if not their votes, should carry weight with official society. The embarrassment of official Washington in response to the poet Robert Lowell's refusal in 1965 to accept a White House award is an example of how sensitive our leaders can be to the thoughtful dissent of one intellectual. If official society does not trouble itself for the opinions of academics, it is simply because the opinions are not there in the first place. Academic societies do not enter public debate. No one expects them to. They are politically irrelevant, and so everybody—official leaders, the press, the public—treats them as irrelevant. What academic societies do and say is . . . "academic."

It is this public irrelevance, this esoteric professionalism of scholarship in the humanities and social sciences, that makes it so very difficult to take seriously much of the conventional campus competition between "academics" and "nonacademics," between "technicians" and "humanists." For is not the scholar's lack of moral responsiveness really equivalent to the technician's lack of moral discrimination? Why is the scholar who indulges in the fastidious but morally undirected handling of Shakespearean sonnets or nineteenth-century European diplomatic history any less of a mere technician than the typical electronics engineer? For what is it that significantly distinguishes the true humanist from the technician, if not the willingness to ask: What is it that knowledge is *for?* Where does it lead, and why is it desirable to go there?

Since it is not any more fashionable to raise questions of purpose, direction, and value among scholars than among technicians, it is no wonder that, whatever surface tensions exist among them, academics and the service-oriented henchmen of the warfare state have by and large been able to arrange a subtle and pervasive *entente* among themselves on the campuses. Ultimately, the antagonism between them runs no deeper than the bickering that existed between the Whigs and Tories of eighteenth-century England: rivals who always finally collaborated to maintain a regime of privilege beneficial to both. In the academic world it has become abundantly clear that it is "service"

—mainly in the form of war-oriented research contracts—
that brings in the money, the students, and the prestige
that are rapidly making higher education one of the country's largest industries. The name of the federal government's largest single, general commitment to the support
of higher education is, after all, the National *Defense* Education Act—and it came in the wake of *sputnik*. The intention of NDEA has never been ambiguous; it is "to insure
trained manpower of sufficient quality and quantity to
meet the national defense needs of the United States."
Such federal support is a technician's gravy train not many
fellow-traveling scholars would really care to see derailed,
for fear of losing any number of lucrative by-products. It
is, for example, a common practice these days to siphon off
the "overhead charges" of National Science Foundation
grants and to distribute them as research support to the
humanities and social sciences: some attractive morsels fall
off those hundred-thousand-dollar servings.[15]

The world-as-it-is is becoming increasingly generous
with its academics. So it is that academics, like technicians,
agree to prepare and equip the young to take their places
in the world-as-it-is. The baccalaureate and doctorate become passports into the skilled ranks of a growingly cyber-
nated society: the corporation, the military, the government bureaucracy. What the "humanities" add to the
technical competence of the university graduate is, perhaps, a finer taste in music, literature, art, films . . . a little
cultural icing for the economic cake. Both humanist and
technician can take pride in their share of the typical
product: let us say, he is an AEROSPACE computer pro-
grammer. Off the job, he is a man of easy culture. He
listens only to his local FM good-music station; his library
is stocked with paperback classics . . . Plato, Tolstoy,

Shakespeare; his walls are graced with Modigliani and Braque prints. No philistine he: he remembers his Humanities 1A and his English Lit. 44B, and they decorate his life. But on the job, he ingeniously perfects the technology of genocide.

Such is the condition of academic life that the corrupted ideals of service and scholarship have produced. They have reduced the American academic to being either a henchman of the military-industrial complex or a recluse in an apolitical ivory tower. And even now, while the issue of social responsibility is beginning to receive attention on the campus, the serious discussion is transpiring mainly at the student, graduate-student, and junior-faculty levels. It is difficult to see that the commanding heights of the learned professions are doing more than cautiously prowling about the margins of a question that is at least twenty years overdue for urgent and constant consideration—and contenting themselves, finally, with that strange kind of pride academics seem to be able to take in "recognizing" a problem . . . but not in solving it.

Writing in the late fifties of the academic community, C. Wright Mills charged:

> They live and work in a benumbing society without living and working in protest and in tension with its moral and cultural insensibilities. They use the liberal rhetoric to cover the conservative default. They do not make available the knowledge and the sensibility required by publics, if publics are to hold responsible those who make decisions "in the name of the nation." They do not set forth reasons for human anger and give to it suitable targets.[16]

There are many more academics now who would associate themselves with that accusation than there were when Mills wrote it. But the accusation remains in force; the cultural default Mills attacked persists. And the reason for its persistence still requires close study. For despite the fact that more academics now than perhaps ever before in American history are beginning to respond to the tug of social conscience, the problem we are confronted with is not simply a matter of overcoming a certain timidity or sluggishness on the part of individual scholars. It goes deeper. The problem has an *institutional* dimension; it has to do with the total configuration of relationships in which the individual academic finds himself: his training, his habits of work, his patterns of friendship and allegiance. Which is to say: it has to do with the fact that academic man belongs to a professional context.

In a recent critique of higher education, Paul Goodman chided the universities for failing to be "communities of scholars" and the academics for yielding control of the schools to superimposed administrators of the usual organization-man mentality. The situation Goodman describes smacks of usurpation and despotism. But in fact it is not experienced as such by most academics. Why not? Because what the administrators have taken over—actually with the full consent of most academics—is simply the running of the particular campuses on which academics work. But the campus is *not* understood to be the "community" to which scholars belong. Rather they belong to the several learned professions. It is in the professions that scholars make their careers; it is this professional audience before which every "serious" scholar performs and by which he is judged.

In reality, a "profession" such as history is simply the sum total of all the history departments at all the colleges and universities of the country—though, of course, influence within the profession is weighted hierarchically in favor of departments at "big league" schools. The profession really has no national organization of any significance —beyond, perhaps, the editorial board of its leading learned journal. Nonetheless—in the best spirit of anarchist voluntarism—these informal networks of information, evaluation, and employment exist and make their standards count in the career of every academic who wants to succeed. For success *means* professional recognition and advancement. In the mind of the academic man there exists a vision rather like Jacob's ladder: a great *cursus honorum* which runs from an instructorship at Punxatowney State Teacher's Normal up to the dizzying heights of a full professorship at Harvard, Columbia, Berkeley . . . and a handful of the big-time schools. With remarkably keen discrimination, a knowledgeable academic can probably peg the relative standing on that ladder of every one of his colleagues.

Thus it is that for most academics the locus of their allegiance is the department—and beyond the department, the profession. Everything in between, which includes the coordination and running of the campuses on which departments are encamped, is very largely left to the administrators—and gladly. For, given the prevailing standards of the learned professions, what the administrators are concerned with—mainly local and "interdepartmental" affairs —has relatively little influence on the career of the academic. It is therefore common enough that a man working in, say, political science, will know nothing of what his "colleagues" in history or economics or art are doing on his own campus. He would no more look into the affairs of *their* departments—which may be right across the hall— than he would bother reading *their* learned journals . . .

or, God knows! attending *their* yearly conferences. But he may know, in intimate detail, what is going on in other political science departments thousands of miles away.

This is the reason why academics, especially ambitious academics at the "best" schools, have so much trouble with the bothersome business of education. Students belong to the particular campus on which they are studying. Educating them has no professional visibility—again, given the prevailing standards of the professions. Designing an educational environment for the students is left, therefore, primarily to the administrators.

As with education, so too with the obligation of the campus to its community: unless this can give rise to professionally visible research, the academic will treat it as a local problem with no relevance to the professional network. While academics may become seriously concerned with these local matters, that concern has no professional importance—and departments, which are primarily professional entities, may pay very little attention to what a man does in the way of education or community activity. So, for example, when the English department at, let us say, the University of California is making its decisions about hiring and firing and promotions and tenure, what the department will be very largely concerned about is the impression its appointments will create in the department at Harvard, not with the influence they may have on the local student body or in the local community. This is what the "community of scholars" means as most academics understand that term.[17]

From the moment that a student decides upon an academic career and undertakes graduate work, he becomes part of *this* "community." And so he must play the game by the profession's rules—or he must abandon the board.

His graduate studies, his dissertation, his ability to find a position at a "name" school: all of these are tokens in the game on which his teachers have gambled a certain amount of their professional prestige. If he is to find a job (indeed, in many cases, if he is ever to be made aware that a prospective job exists), if he is to achieve tenure and promotions, if he is to survive and prosper, and especially if he is to acquire any amount of glory, then he must be obedient to the expectations of the professional powers that control these rewards. And he, in turn, will finish by enforcing the same expectations on the apprentices he ushers into the guild.

How, one wonders, have the professions managed to establish their authority so persuasively in the American university? David Riesman offers one illuminating answer. He reminds us that the academic life can very rapidly declass those who enter it, drawing them out of family, region, and ethnic background. This is bound to be the case with the student who comes from lower-class origins, from a minority group, or from a rural community. For those who are thus dislocated, the profession becomes "the scholar's country"—replete with its own jealous "nationalism." "The fervency of this nationalism reflects the sacrifices the scholar has made to become a scholar, what he has had to surrender of earlier social-class origins and ambitions."[18] The profession becomes, then, an anchorage, a place to belong. But if academic life *de*classes, it can also *re*class—into something that feels like and often even pays like the great American upper middle class, from which many of the scholar's students (at the "better" schools at least) are apt to come.

The declassing capacity of academic life (what Riesman calls its "universalizing quality") is, I think, a desirable feature. It is, potentially, a liberating experience. But the reclassing that usually follows is apt to be disastrous. It is at this point that the academic is integrated into the higher levels of the national society, with all that this means in the way of conformity to parochial loyalties. The universities, governed so ponderously by government and corporate wealth, finance and enforce the integration, and, as we have already seen, few academics, whether scholars or technicians, exert themselves to avoid the tempting rewards. The American upper middle class is a comfortable place in which to find oneself, especially when one adds just the right admixture of jet-set elegance for the highly successful academic: research grants with foreign travel, visiting lectureships, prestigious conferences, and even perhaps invitations to help out in Washington. It is a marvelous institution that can offer a young man who may have started with nothing but brains such an opportunity to rise so high in the Great Society.

Undoubtedly the social forces that structure the academic professions are powerful. But the fact that a temptation is offered does not excuse the acceptance of it. Nor does the fact that a social pressure is very strong mean that those it acts upon are totally without the freedom to resist it. It would be pathetic indeed if those who have given themselves to the life of the mind were to plead that they were powerless to reform their own professional environment, powerless even to save their own souls by the brave attempt to achieve reform. But the plea becomes outrageous when the forces to which men surrender exert their greatest power, not by terror or repression, but by offering the bribes of prestige and comfort.

There is, I believe, a deal to be said against the wisdom of organizing universities along departmental-professional lines. Robert Hutchins, for example, has observed that "liberal education cannot flourish in a university in which liberal education is under departmental control." But I suspect it would be difficult for many academics to imagine higher education taking place without the departmental arrangement. They forget how newly hatched both department and profession are—and how intellectually flimsy were many of the motives that originally spawned the various departments that are now often revered as though, indeed, God himself had designed them on the second day of creation.[19] But let us, for the present, ignore this question and agree that *some* form of professionalization among teachers and scholars is probably desirable and certainly inevitable. Let us accept the existing professions in that spirit and insist that if they are beset by vices, they must be reformed.

Clearly, the prerequisite for such reform is the development of a deeper ideal of intellect—and a more exciting one—than that which currently dominates the academic professions. It should be clear by now that I feel this ideal exists in the work of the French *philosophes.* It is there, awaiting elaboration and application to the needs of our time. Doubtless it is all but ludicrous at this point to imagine American academics following in the footsteps of Diderot or D'Alembert. But why should they not? What are the well-considered and morally persuasive reasons for abandoning that conception of intellectual responsibility? This, I submit, should rank as the foremost subject of debate in the learned professions.

For what the *philosophes* bequeathed to our society is an ideal that possesses far greater character than the traditions of service and scholarship offer. It is, indeed, an ideal that synthesizes these two seemingly irreconcilable traditions by drawing from them both what is most vital in them. The principle of that synthesis centers in the *philosophes'* conception of "citizenship": citizenship not simply as a legal status, but as a *moral vocation*. This is frequently overlooked, especially by those who are prepared to depreciate the *philosophes* as "popularizers" rather than "real" philosophers or scholars. Such an interpretation misses the crucial point: that the practice of citizenship must necessarily be a "popular" activity. It must have to do with influencing and educating people, with shaping knowledge into a basis for action. For the *philosophe*, it was a necessary characteristic of *real* knowledge, of *real* philosophy, that it should make a difference. To be an intellectually vital man of letters during the Enlightenment, therefore, implied citizenship. It implied exercising what Peter Gay has called "the sovereign rights of criticism," which in turn implied calling into question all authority, privilege, and tradition.[20]

For the *philosophe*, intellectuality began at the point where one undertook to make knowledge work. The intellectual was one who intervened in society for the defense of civilized values: free speech, free thought, free inquiry for the sake of reform. He was one who sought to clarify reality so that his fellow citizens could apply reason to the solution of their problems. And if one never arrived at this point, then one might be an enthusiast, an antiquarian, an authority—but not an intellectual.

The intellectual prowess of the French *philosophes* scarcely needs to be proven or defended. It is doubtful that many contemporary scholars will ever contribute as richly to our stock of knowledge or our literature as they. But one sees that the ideal of service is involved here also. Not service, however, as the word is understood within the multiversity. For the service the *philosophe* rendered did not mean indiscriminately assisting society in every project it might undertake, whether it be improving agriculture or perfecting genocide, advancing medical science or improving biological weaponry. It meant performing the service of criticizing, clarifying, dissenting, resisting, deriding, exposing: in brief, *educating* in the fullest sense of the word as a member of the "party of humanity." At one and the same time, the *philosophes* were keener minds, better servants of their society, and more effective educators than our contemporary academics manage to be. They held the balance that gracefully blended what has since been sundered in our universities into mindless collaboration on the one hand and irrelevant research on the other.

The issue raised here for debate has been raised before in America, briefly but intensely. When, in 1915, the fledgling American Association of University Professors was created, it was precisely to inaugurate and establish an ideal of intellect that descended from the *philosophes*. This, though it is too often forgotten, is what the struggle for "academic freedom" was supposed to be all about: to make the academy hospitable to the *philosophe*'s brand of "humanitarian meddling," to borrow still another phrase from Peter Gay. It was out of the struggles between politically engaged academics like Richard T. Ely and John R. Commons and Edward Ross that the AAUP's conception of academic freedom evolved. It is likely, however, that many unengaged academics did not understand then, as they do not now, the liberty *and* the responsibility conferred by the ideal. Let us remind them here:

> The responsibility of the university teacher is primarily to the public itself, and to the judgment of his own

profession; . . . in the essentials of his professional activity his duty is to the wider public to which the institution itself is morally amenable. . . . the university should be an intellectual experiment station, where new ideas may germinate and where their fruit, though still distasteful to the community as a whole, may be allowed to ripen until finally, perchance, it may become a part of the accepted intellectual food of the nation or the world. . . . One of the university's most characteristic functions in a democratic society is to help make public opinion more self-critical and more circumspect, to check the more hasty and unconsidered impulses of popular feeling, to train the democracy to the habit of looking before and after. It is precisely this function of the university which is most injured by any restriction upon academic freedom; . . .[21]

Needless to say, one does not require such noble rhetoric, nor the defense of special organizations like the AAUP, if one's "new ideas" are confined to esoteric research in politically irrelevant areas. If one values academic freedom in any meaningful sense, one should recognize that such research has never been an exercise of the ideal. The scholarly "disinterestedness" the AAUP General Report of 1915 speaks of was never intended to be "indifference" to the fate of man and society.

It is unhappily the fact that when the AAUP was put to its first major test as the definer and defender of academic freedom, it failed sadly. In response to the widespread and often ruthless repressiveness of university administrations during the First World War, the Association, after a deal of pathetic soul-searching, agreed that dissent may legitimately be silenced on the campuses in the face of whatever the government declares to be a national emergency. The AAUP's 1915 code of academic freedom had been a major achievement in American higher education. But the Asso-

ciation's "Committee on Academic Freedom *in Wartime"*
decided, in 1918, to convert that milestone into a tomb-
stone.

> When . . . a democracy finds itself forced into war in
> defense of its rights, . . . it will, if it has any practical
> wisdom, temporarily adapt its methods of political action
> and of governmental procedure to the necessities of the
> grave and perilous business immediately at hand.[22]

If academics were still to enter prominently into the political life of the New Deal period, the 1918 statement nevertheless prefigured the willingness to compromise, retreat,
and conform that has characterized the universities during
and after the Second World War. Once so much had been
conceded to "practical wisdom," the government—or a
Senator McCarthy—would have little trouble providing
the "grave and perilous business" that justified the loyalty
oath, the security check, and all the overt and subtle techniques of regimentation which have descended upon us in
the past two decades. As a result, the ideal of academic
freedom has, by way of diminishing exercise, been saved
the need of strenuous defense.

Now, it would be little better than philistine to suggest
that all scholarly research be abandoned unless it relates
immediately to contemporary issues. There are clearly
many perfectly valid fields of knowledge which cannot
very gracefully or directly be related to the problems of
the day. Just as there are others—like economics, political
science, and sociology—which have very little business
being anywhere but in the thick of public controversy.
There is, however, an *indirect* way in which *all* work in the
humanities and social sciences can be related to the needs
of the time—all work, that is, which possesses any maturity

and wisdom. And that is by way of the *personal character* of the scholar.

The pursuit and communication of knowledge, whether it be concerned with the sociology of the Pentagon or the aesthetic analysis of Chaucer, is, or ought to be, a noble enterprise. The rhetoric academics are in the habit of expending on this point is, indeed, almost dizzying. I suspect every academic carries around a fat selection of favorite clichés concerning the "beauty," the "moral worth," and the "dignity," etc., etc., of the "search for truth." (For example, Carl Becker's remark: "The value of history is, indeed, not scientific, but moral; . . . it prepares us to live more humanely in the present, and to meet, rather than to foretell, the future.") Such sentiments come in handy for various public occasions—such as commencement addresses. And, especially for those in the humanities and social sciences, they provide a way of holding one's own against the natural scientists, the football coach, and the Bus. Ad. Department in the ongoing competition for money and privilege on campus.

Very well, then: if the quest for knowledge *is* a noble enterprise and so ennobles those who undertake it, what are we to take as the measure of a man's nobility? Does this not have a great deal to do with his sensitivity to what is ignoble—to all that is base, false, ugly, barbaric? Does it not involve his willingness to speak out bravely against those forces that debase our lives and threaten the survival of civilized life?

Let us take some hypothetical examples of what I am proposing here.

Suppose an instructor in American history takes an active part in organizing a thoroughly thoughtful, thoroughly well-conceived campaign against capital punishment in his state. He musters the students to the cause and succeeds in engaging public officials and people generally in a searching debate of crime and punishment. Now has he or has he not made a more real intellectual contribution than if he had authored a definitive study on the decline of cotton factorage in the American South for the period of 1865–1894? What should our "professional" assessment of him be?

Suppose a psychology instructor, feeling that the politics of his community has gone slack, undertakes to run for Congress, with an eye to stimulating serious public discussion of civil rights or foreign policy? His campaign is intellectually responsible from start to finish and he forces his opposing candidates to take clear-cut stands they would otherwise have avoided like the plague. How shall we assess the man's contribution? Is it more or less valuable than an exhaustive study of olfaction in the unrestrained rat?

Suppose a philosophy instructor leads a civil-disobedience exercise against a germ-warfare laboratory. He does so after having thoroughly researched the laboratory's work and after formulating for public consumption a well-argued statement of his ethical principles. How many articles in the *Journal of Philosophy* on descriptivism, supervenience, and universalizability is his action worth?

Suppose an English instructor devotes a large amount of his time to organizing "freedom schools" for underprivileged kids—and perhaps even working the picket lines for CORE. Should we, for purposes of promotion and tenure, count his efforts as highly as those required to produce a critical study of Golding's translation of Ovid's *Metamorphoses*?

Suppose an anthropology instructor busies himself organizing a teach-in on the Vietnam war. Perhaps he even travels to Vietnam for the Inter-University Committee and then writes on the effect the war is having on village life and on American moral character for the *Atlantic* or the *New Republic*. Is his work worth more or less—intellectually speaking—than a study of unity and diversity in the celebration of cattle-curing rites in a north Indian village?

Perhaps we should anticipate a question with respect to the examples we offer here. Since our hypothetical instructors are all involved in what many academics might take to be "action'" as distinct from "thought," do they deserve any academic consideration at all? Isn't the academic's function to "think" rather than "act"? This is the question I remember arising frequently in the discussions that took place among the members of the now defunct Council for Correspondence, which was probably the most significant single postwar effort that has been made to organize academics into a political force.[23] The question invokes the conventional dichotomy between "thinking" and "doing" which seems to be an occupational disease among academics. The reply to it is, I think, to ask what the sense is of treating "thinking" and "doing" as separate if not indeed incompatible activities. Analysis and discussion, where they are politically relevant, become political *acts*— and it is this that we have specified as the peculiar social responsibility of intellectuals. To think, to speak, to teach, to write: all these *are* forms of doing. They ought properly to be seen as integral components of action and as an indispensable part of the political process. Without going any further, an academic may help make the life of his society richer and nobler. But what if he does go further? If a man's thought should carry over into more overt forms of action such as those we mention above, are we to regard it as somehow automatically debased? Surely not. For in a healthy personality, thought and action merge gracefully along a single spectrum and there is no artificial barrier that prevents a man from undertaking some task of leadership or organization in order to realize in fact what his understanding tells him must be done. Indeed, let us recognize that action—say, in the dramatic form of civil disobedience—may in many cases be the only way of forcing an intellectual dialogue upon reluctant and secretive authorities. In such situations, an unwillingness to act, to "make trouble," may imply that a man is less than entirely serious about the intellectual position he holds. Perhaps he simply doesn't care whether the values he asserts are engaged in a meaningful dialogue.

In the examples we give above, then, let us assume that we are dealing with men who can make a decent intellectual defense of their activity: their action grows out of thought and their thought is enhanced by their action. What shall we say about their value as members of their respective professions? There is of course a limited amount one can say about any hypothetical example.[24] One can imagine all sorts of questions being raised about our selection of instructors before any decision could be made about hiring or promoting them. But the fact is, at no more than the barest handful of schools in America today would the citizenly conduct of instructors like these be given *any weight whatever* in making "professional" decisions about them. No matter how intellectually sound or morally courageous that conduct, no matter of what benefit it might be to students or community, it would normally be discounted out of hand in evaluating the man. And that is the measure of how far removed the modern academic conception of intellect is from that of the *philosophes*.

Why should this be? Is it because one feels that *just anybody* can "be political"—and so it isn't much of an achievement to do these things? Nonsense. There are wise and foolish ways to "be political"; there are profound and superficial ways to "talk politics"—just as there are wise and foolish, profound and superficial exercises in scholarship. A Warren Harding might indeed be a fool. But a Thomas Jefferson, a Norman Thomas, an A. J. Muste, or an H. Stuart Hughes (running for the Senate in Massachusetts) has made intellect central to his politics. To be deeply and wisely political is a rare and commendable achievement—and one that often takes a very great deal more courage than "pure research."

Should citizenly conduct be discounted because one fears that politically engaged academics won't know how to train graduate students in scholarly techniques and may fail in their duty of discovering knowledge? But if one accepts that it is the function of intellectuality to make knowledge work in the defense of civilized values, then we may be dealing here with men who are indeed capable of "training" intellectuals. They may be able to do precisely what our present forms of graduate instruction never do: namely, to force a man to reflect on the function and deep purpose of his professional commitment.

For what I contend here is that the training of apprentice scholars and the pursuit of research—as these activities are presently handled—result in a great deal of mindless specialization and irrelevant pedantry that ought not to be credited with intellectual respectability. There is probably not a single field of the social sciences and humanities that does not already boast a larger body of "knowledge" than could be "popularized"—and so assimilated into the cultural mainstream of our society—within the next fifty to a hundred years. Is it more "knowledge" of this surplus kind, expertly gleaned by precise techniques, that we really require? Or, in the protracted emergency in which our civilization finds itself, should our highest priority be placed on a scholar's ability to link his special knowledge or moral insight to our social needs? This, of course, is what I am proposing: that in assessing a scholar's intellectual quality, we be prepared to ask what the man's thought or the example of his actions has been worth in the defense of civilized values. Has he sought to elevate public debate in our society to a level of intellectual and moral respectability? If this is not the only question to be raised in our evaluation of a colleague, it ought at least to be one of the first.

What a contrast this would make with prevailing professional standards might be illustrated by the following point. I have worked in schools where my academic superiors have frowned upon the practice of identifying oneself by a school or department affiliation when signing a political petition, sponsoring a newspaper-advertisement appeal, appearing at a political meeting, or even writing to one's congressman. From such activity, clearly, the department or school seeks to extract no "prestige." But on the other hand, when it has frequently been suggested by academic wags that scholarly publication should be anonymous or at least that the authorship of an article, book, or review should carry no departmental identification, such proposals are invariably treated as frivolous—though it is unclear how such anonymity would interfere with the "disinterested search for truth."

What is asked here of individual academics ought to be

demanded of the professions generally. Suppose the professions were to be evaluated by putting to them the following question: In what intellectual areas have the leading institutions of our society—and especially the government —learned to tread lightly for fear of arousing collective, critical resistance by the academic community? The answer would not be an encouraging one. Where the humanities and social sciences are concerned (and often enough the natural sciences too), the government knows that it can, whenever it needs to, get away with any kind of propagandistically useful slapdash. It confronts, in these areas, no organized and authoritatively critical public—beyond that perhaps of the more conscientious journalists. Among the academics, it will find only scattered dissenters, many of whom may only be able to reach minority audiences; and the dissenters are easily offset by the employment of "experts" who take it as their function to provide "service" on the terms laid down by those who hire them. Experts of this sleazy kind are numerous and often enough enjoy great prestige in the learned professions.

It does not take much imagination to see how vastly enriched our society's politics would be by critical service from the professions. We do not have an intellectually respectable politics in America principally because the single largest intellectual-interest group in our society—the learned professions—has opted out of politics. It has felt no professional obligation to relate the life and work of its members to the problems of justice and survival which dominate our times. It does not insist that intellect embrace a dimension of citizenship. Instead, it understands "intellect" to be primarily a means of career building in the university world—or at best, a means of heaping up collections of "knowledge" as an end in itself. But if the major institutions of our society were made aware that the things they do and the things they say were being carefully scrutinized by a public of knowledgeable and conscientious academics, if the opinions of professional thinkers and teachers became a constant and recognized part of public controversy, at the very least that controversy might be elevated to the level of a rational dialogue, instead of remaining the province of shabby slogans, cynical propaganda, and engineered consensus. One may grant that the rights and wrongs of great public issues do not always yield to simple and unequivocal solutions. But rational solutions become impossible where, as in contemporary America, policy making remains a mystery of state sealed off from a lethargic public by vested interest and esoteric expertise.

So long as our politics retains this character, there is very little that academics—whether they are humanists or scientists, specialists or generalists, scholars or technicians— have any right to be proud of. They may indeed be cultivating a luxuriant garden of knowledge and theory, and cultivating it with fastidious skill and exquisite taste. But the obscene shadows of misguided power and thermonuclear extinction brood over that garden and all the world surrounding it. And any conception of intellect that leads men to ignore that fact is ultimately futile and cowardly.

NOTES

1. Arthur M. Wilson, *Diderot: The Testing Years* (New York, Oxford University Press, 1957), p. 333.
2. From Jefferson's Education Bill of 1779. For a study of Jefferson's theories see Roy J. Honeywell, *The Educational Work of Thomas Jefferson* (New York, Russell & Russell Publishers, 1964).
3. Frederick Rudolph, *The American College and University* (New York, Vintage Books, 1965), p. 141.
4. On the literary clubs, see H. D. Sheldon, *Student Life and*

Customs (New York, D. Appleton & Co., 1901).

5. J. H. Fairchild's historical account of this period at Oberlin appears in Richard Hofstadter and Wilson Smith, eds., *American Higher Education: A Documentary History* (Chicago, University of Chicago Press, 1961), Vol. 1, pp. 419–25.

6. Quoted in Frederic Lilge, *The Abuse of Learning: The Failure of the German University* (New York, The Macmillan Company, 1948), pp. 92–93.

7. Laurence R. Veysey has done a very thorough job of describing this historic clash of educational ideals—which he describes as a three-cornered struggle between "utility," "research," and "liberal culture." See his recent study, *The Emergence of the American University* (Chicago, University of Chicago Press, 1965).

8. This project, called quaintly enough the "Institute of Cooperative Research," has been discontinued as of the fall of 1966 in the face of faculty protest. But how did it get on campus in the first place? And how much of a "victory" is it when Penn's president explains the discontinuation on the grounds that the project "is no longer needed"? See *New York Times,* August 12, 1966, p. 4; August 14, 1966, IV, 9.

9. On Project Camelot, which has been metamorphosed under pressure of criticism into the Army's Special Activities Group, see Senator William Fulbright's remarks in the *Congressional Record—Senate,* 89th Cong., 1st Sess., August 25, 1965, pp. 20905–6. For a series of critical articles covering the project, see also the *Weekly Magazine* (published by the University of California *Daily Californian,* Berkeley) for November 25, December 7, 1965; February 24, 1966. But also see W. J. Goode's letter to the *American Sociologist,* November 1966, pp. 255–57, for a defense (an unsuccessful one, I think) of the project.

10. See Gladwin Hill's report in the *New York Times,* September 15, 1963, p. 118.

11. Abraham Flexner, *Universities: American, English, German* (New York, Oxford University Press, 1930), p. 305. For an examination of the role of the academics in Germany's cultural disaster, see Frederic Lilge's *The Abuse of Learning: The Failure of the German University* (New York, The Macmillan Company, 1948). Lilge characterizes the grand tradition of scholarly "objectivity" and social neutrality as having afforded the German academics "the happiness of permanent employment and of concealing from themselves the futility of their efforts and their lives" (p. 99). For another discussion of what *Lehrfreiheit* came to mean in the German universities, see Richard Hofstadter and W. P. Metzger, *The Development*

of *Academic Freedom in the United States* (New York, Columbia University Press, 1955), pp. 388–90.

12. Logan Wilson, *The Academic Man: A Study in the Sociology of a Profession* (New York, Oxford University Press, 1942); Theodore Caplow and R. J. McGee, *The Academic Marketplace* (New York, Basic Books, 1958); Bernard Berelson, *Graduate Education in the United States* (New York, McGraw-Hill Book Co., Inc., 1960). Or to take a survey of graduate training restricted to one particular field, see Dexter Perkins and John Snell, *The Education of Historians in the United States* (New York, McGraw-Hill Book Co., Inc., 1962). It is like walking through a surrealist nightmare to read things like Berelson or Perkins-Snell. Everything is there—all the facts and figures, all the familiar platitudes and neatly balanced little proposals—everything . . . *except* a discussion of the moral responsibility of a professional man. Toward that minor item, there is not even a gesture. Well, then: where and by whom is it to be discussed?

13. *New York Times,* September 21, 1965.

14. *New York Times,* December 30, 1966.

15. Senator Fulbright, in the remarks cited above, estimates that the federal government is spending some $15 billion per year on research and development. In 1965 the Defense Department alone accounted for $6.7 billion of this sum, of which $23 million was specifically budgeted for research in the social and behavioral sciences.

16. C. Wright Mills, *The Causes of World War III* (New York, Ballantine Books, 1963), p. 145.

17. For a complaint about this situation as it affects departmental decisions in English, see Jeremiah Finch. "College English Departments and Teacher Preparation," *PMLA,* Vol. 80 (May 1965), pp. 3–7. Finch's grievance relates to the departmental slighting of conscientious teacher-trainers in favor of fat-cat publishers. Daniel Bell gives the clearest picture of how professionalism affects general education in *The Reforming of General Education* (New York, Columbia University Press, 1966). His proposed solutions all seem to be dismal compromises with the status quo.

18. David Riesman, *Constraint and Variety in American Education* (Anchor A135; Garden City, N.Y., Doubleday & Co., Inc., 1958), pp. 101–6.

19. Laurence Veysey reviews the origins of academic departmentalization, all of which seem to be administrative or careerist in character, in *The Emergence of the American University,* pp. 321–23. Frederick Rudolph speaks of departmentalization as a development "that unleased all that competitiveness, that

currying of favor, that attention to public relations, that scrambling for students, that pettiness and jealousy which in some of its manifestations made the university and the college indistinguishable from other organizations." See his *The American College and University*, pp. 399–400. And yet, ever since the founding of the University of Chicago, it has been standard procedure to begin the organization of any major school with the establishment of departments.

20. On the French *philosophes*, see Peter Gay's excellent studies, *The Party of Humanity* (New York, Alfred A. Knopf, 1964) and *The Enlightenment: An Interpretation* (New York, Alfred A. Knopf, 1966).

21. "General Report of the Committee on Academic Freedom and Academic Tenure," *Bulletin of the AAUP*, December 1915, pp. 26, 32.

22. See Hofstadter and Metzger, *The Development of Academic Freedom in the United States*, pp. 495–504, for the story of the AAUP during World War I.

23. The Council finally came down pretty much in favor of limiting itself to the job of talking up issues and finished by producing a journal: the *Correspondent*. The journal was a good one; but alas! there are a great many good journals on the scene and another one was not what was most needed.

24. Though the examples are not wholly hypothetical. The scholarly topics mentioned all come from recent numbers of learned journals—and are typical of their contents. The activities of the instructors are the sort of things several academic acquaintances of mine have undertaken—but never with any academic reward.

THE SCANDAL OF

LITERARY SCHOLARSHIP

✑ Louis Kampf

OF THE DEATH OF ACADEMIC LITERARY
study as a serious enterprise, few seem to be aware.
Yet in spite of appearances to the contrary, it is a
fact. Well, almost: for the illusion of life lingers. As one
looks at the body, it wriggles and twitches with a nervous-
ness which simulates voluntary action. A closer examination reveals an army of vermin in frantic deployment;
creatures scurrying about and multiplying with lewd
abandon; all feeding on the corpse while the whole grows
uncontrollably.

Matthew Arnold's once cogent argument for the useful-
ness of academies comes to mind, now burdened with the
pathos of its irrelevance. An English academy, Arnold suggested, might set a standard of intelligence and significance
for literature and scholarship; as supreme arbiter, it would
put a wholesome check on the indiscriminate expressions
of critical caprice. Alas, rather than manning the dikes,

our academies have released a flood of literary solvent (one cannot call it criticism) which promises to dissolve whatever standards we have managed to retain. The latest batch of volumes in Twayne's English Authors Series (volumes 36 through 39: I suppose there is no upper bound to the number) includes one on Henry Seton Merriman. Now I trust that Twayne is not pulling our scholarly legs. I, for one, have never heard of Merriman, and I refuse to think of myself as an ignoramus. But I seem to be missing the point: as long as Mr. Merriman provides an occasion for the exercise of the critical faculty, neither his reality nor the application of a standard of significance appears to be of much relevance.

In what spirit is one to react? How many literary academics, I wonder, are trying to keep their sanity by hiding behind a mask of irony? how many by arming themselves with a corrosive cynicism? There is always the possibility of total withdrawal. But that is surely to defeat the possibilities of intellect at the source. For an exhilarating moment, the combative good humor of Alexander Pope taking on Grub Street comes to mind. But what are the combined efforts of a few pathetic eighteenth-century hacks as against the relentless mass production of one high-powered English department? The enemy has grown; furthermore, he is different; nor is any of us much like Alexander Pope.

Never mind. Most literary academics, in any case, are happy enough to pretend that their scholarly productions matter, that their duties carry some social weight. And of course they do! But not quite in the way most academics imagine.

Given the oppressive lack of intelligence characteristic of so much literary scholarship, it is difficult to work up much concern for its fate in the academy. Leafing through *Literary History & Literary Criticism: Acta of the Ninth Congress of the International Federation for Modern Languages & Literature* (New York, New York University Press, 1965)—a task whose performance nothing less than a Calvinistic adherence to duty could command—can result only in an overwhelming desire to throw every towel in sight into the nearest chairman's office, to simply give up. Here are dozens of papers, and commentaries on those papers, read at a gathering of the world's most famous literary scholars; nearly all the important names are to be found in the volume's table of contents; yet there is almost nothing worth reading—never mind arguing with—in its many pages.

We all take special delight in collecting and rehearsing scholarly horrors, and there is little point in repeating them here. The matter is hardly news. Yet we keep attaining more exquisite levels of absurdity. As the books, journals, and reviews multiply, their subjects naturally become more imaginatively narrowed and specialized. In the latest issue of *College English* I notice an announcement of a new *Henry James Journal*. I trust that this is only a beginning, for at this very moment surely an assistant professor fretting about his tenure is eagerly planning a split into early and late James. And why stop there? Perhaps James will manage to survive this glut of attention as he survived his earlier neglect—although I have my doubts. At least there is the consolation that the dissection did not take place during the course of his life. Some of our contemporaries have proved to be less fortunate.

Unhappily, these excrescences emitted by the corpse cannot be dumped aside as an irrelevance. They pile up in all places, stifling the desperate gasps of any living voice;

they corrupt the language, sully our scholarly ideals, and thus give our critical vocabulary a hollow and meaningless ring. Early in the game, any graduate student learns that the literary academic's master task is the surveillance of other academics' articles. The most memorable paper I have ever heard delivered in a graduate seminar was returned to its author with the admonition that he include a survey of the relevant scholarship, if he wished to have his work published. The moral was clear: the scholar's responsibility is not to the literary work, not to history, not to his culture or to (God forbid) life, but to other scholarship.

Still, one must care. Higher education is, in a most concrete way, at the center of our lives. If nothing else, it assigns us our place in the social hierarchy; beyond this, it creates possibilities, whether these are for a measure of intellectual self-fulfillment or the planning of nuclear annihilation. The academic origins of the student sit-ins are of exemplary significance: at least some students, if not their teachers, grasped the opportunities, and responsibilities, created by scholarship and intellect.

Our difficulties do not stem from the alleged conflict of teaching and research: this is simply another red herring dropped into an already messy barrel. Was Veblen a more effective teacher in the classroom or at his desk? Would anyone really prefer Edmund Wilson to spend more time conducting seminars? The issue is not one of dedication to our teaching, of the amount of time and effort we expend on it, but of *what* we teach, and to *what end.* Is literature really a proper field for professional study? Is it a field at all? a skill? Are there any general laws literary scholarship is attempting to discover? It is difficult to see how a graduate student's career would differ measurably if he were encouraged to devote himself to teaching. Would his fundamental intellectual concerns undergo a transformation? His time would still be spent in training other potential scholars; in putting undergraduates through mechanical drills in literary explication; and in further stuffing his own head with dead facts. His goal for scholarly education would still involve some parody of the professional demand that the student "know his field." Now every graduate student in literature preparing for his examinations does learn one thing—that no one quite knows the meaning of this mysterious phrase.

Concerning the graduate student's sense of his "field," of his academic purpose, a moral tale is in order. Not too many years ago, filled with the expectations of my recent arrival at a prominent Eastern university, I attended the semester's first meeting of its Graduate English Club. The speaker, an eminent and elderly scholar, drawing on the wisdom of his years, was to advise the young on the perplexities of a career—on their way of life. His words were an invitation to opportunism: be nice; do not get involved in politics; write only short and solid articles at first; throw modest parties; avoid intellectual aggressiveness—do all these things dutifully and the blessings of tenure await you as a well-earned reward. Perhaps naively, I awaited the students' angry retorts. There were many questions about the relative comforts of Western, Southern, and Eastern universities, on the advisability of inviting the chairman to dinner, on the prestige of various journals, even on the career value of curriculum planning, but none about literature, ideas, or one's mission as an academic. The occasion has become my recurrent nightmare; there are times, indeed, when I find it difficult to believe in its reality. But it happened. And it was, no doubt, typical.

It was the stifling seriousness of the students' questions—

enough to make anyone's lyric impulse wilt—which I found, finally, most dispiriting. It was a seriousness devoid of any intellectual concern; worse, it masked an almost total lack of interest in how intellect affects the quality of a society; all thought was turned to reflections on one's career, to the proper performance of the initiation rites prescribed by the profession. My initial reaction of incoherent anger, of hate for the merchants of this sellout, has since been tempered—perhaps redirected. The graduate students had, in truth, nothing to sell. Looking at similar groups today the feeling I find most appropriate is regret. Regret, since the pressures of the educational system, from grammar school onward, have limited the students' sense of their own possibilities; have, in fact, taught them not to take their own role—the use of their intellect—seriously. Any prospective academic knows that literature is of interest only as it offers an opportunity for personal display, only as it becomes the means to a career.

The singular quality of Modern Language Association (MLA) conventions, their capacity for spiritual corrosion, is difficult to convey. There is the terror of the unsystematic and unpredictable movements of crowds, the impersonal name tags, and the hundreds of papers to which no one listens. Yet one's fright stems from a misconception, from the perverse assumption that the MLA is concerned with intellect, that it is anything but a society devoted to trade. There is business to be done, future meetings to be arranged, new sections to be formed, and the chief commodity—bodies—to be evaluated, bought, and sold.

While working my way through the crush in the lobby at last year's convention, I felt suddenly overcome (well, almost) by the thought of Vietnam. Instead of my fellow academics, I kept seeing the specters of Vietnamese villagers being burned by napalm. Did anyone at the various section meetings care? Did any of the scholars delivering papers conceive of their work in terms of the issue? Was their humanity at all related to their technical skills? I became obsessed with the following fantasy: if all 15,000 (10,000? 20,000? who knows?) professors and graduate students attending the meeting, outraged by the slaughter in Vietnam, decided to storm the White House . . .

None of them did, of course. It would not have accorded with their enlightened self-interest. The health of the profession, the superabundance of respectable jobs, and the academy's general affluence all depend on the Cold War and its occasional hot outbursts. The buffoonery at the MLA convention is the visible sign of a competitive spirit, of an acquisitiveness, which is ready to cut throats; further, it pictures not only private feelings, but the structure of a society which has learned to exploit its men of learning. Capitalism's relentless rationalization depends on the organization of its bureaucracy. Bureaucrats must be trained at an ever increasing rate as the economy expands and rationalization becomes more complex. To maintain our social equilibrium this must be accomplished without apparent violation of received traditions, without injury being done to cherished ideologies. For the sake of order the culture must be kept intact. We need more technologists and experts, and to perform their assigned tasks they must be convinced that they are serving the interests of Western Civilization and Freedom. And so they must all study their Shakespeare. It is the chief task of literary academics to assure fledgling bureaucrats that those strange lines from *Hamlet* have something to do (mysteriously) with the functions they are to serve.

To avoid collapse, America must expand. This economic imperative has become part of the national creed; it is an ideology so deeply embedded that it affects almost every aspect of our lives. Surely it has shaped the objectives of literary studies in the academy. If English departments are to keep their place in the national consensus, they must perpetuate the myth of liberal education; if they are to expand with the rest of the economy, they must convince those in power that our future functionaries need literary training—whether the objective be to improve their job efficiency, to beautify their souls, or to better fight communism. Inspiring this swelling mass of functionaries with the beauties of poetry requires yet other functionaries: doctors of English. As our overseas markets expand, so do our English departments; the more Vietnams, the more endowed chairs. For the young whose temperaments incline them toward culture rather than technology the academic hierarchy has become a new place for "making it," both economically and socially. The professional goals they strive to achieve have become an internalization of the New Frontier; they are an organic component of the expansionist ideology we refer to as the Great Society.

In the quickening process of enlarging itself the literary academy absorbs all new cultural phenomena and finds the appropriate organizational slot for all poetic eruptions. The MLA has taken some of literature's more playful children to its bosom. But in enfolding them it has rationalized—and thus neutralized—the danger of their play. They too have become commodities: the more outrageous their games, the higher their price on the market.

Almost with regret one recalls the dismal past when the academic study of literature consisted of editing texts, hunting down sources, and compiling bibliographies. At least the split between scholarly pedantries and the honest concern for literature was clear; one knew the identity of the enemy, the difference between critical thought and pseudoscientific expertise. The profession's very attempts— be it the History of Ideas or the New Criticism—to divert scholarship from its positivist pretensions, from its obsession with mechanical tasks, have themselves become petrified into empty techniques. The History of Ideas developed into another version of source hunting. Similarly, the New Criticism, which began as an attempt to force a critical confrontation between reader and poem, has (inevitably, one feels) become a method for avoiding thought about the poem altogether: the student is so busy tallying examples of irony, paradox, tension, and so forth, that he can barely fathom the meaning of the words. Not so many years ago the mention of Brooks and Warren could make a solid scholar's hair stand on end; today *Understanding Poetry* is an enshrined, even an old-fashioned, text.

There is no apparent limit to the academy's capacity for institutionalizing, not merely innovations, but the most intemperate onslaughts against the Establishment. By now someone must surely be teaching a graduate seminar on Ken Kesey, perhaps in the form of a psychedelic be-in. Lest some backward English department falter in absorbing the latest cultural events, the MLA will lend both material and moral support by organizing the appropriate discussion sections, by publishing official journals and newsletters, and by assuring us of the national, even transcendent, importance of the task.

The MLA's power lies in its strong stomach, in its capacity to digest almost everything, thus giving it institutional sanction. It can do so because the professional standards it allegedly maintains do not exist: there is no basis on which to exclude anything. Clearly the MLA, rather than being a professional organization, is a trade association; its natural drift is toward the councils of the Chamber of Commerce, where it will best serve the social and economic aspirations of its own membership.

At the least, one should be impressed by the sheer volume of the literary academy's activity. Here surely is a sign of robust health. But it is just this bustle which confuses, which leads one to ask just what the objectives of the profession are. Are we doing anything more than gathering facts and making random comments upon them? What philosophical end do we have in mind? what truth? The scandal of literary scholarship is its lack of philosophy, its blissful ignorance of ideas. The National Endowment for the Humanities' largest award this year was made for the establishment of "a computer-stored bibliography in American studies." Even in a field where knowledge is cumulative this would be a laughable piece of hackwork; in literature it defeats even one's capacity for the cynical snicker.

This "mad-dog empiricism" (so named by the philosopher Jerrold Katz) is most clearly revealed in the objective the academy most commonly sets for literary history: the reduction of historical narrative to an inventory of facts emptied of explanatory hypotheses. Now historical explanation, by demanding that we formulate ideas about the past, links us to the dead and brings their work into our lives. But such philosophical (or simply human) concerns seem to serve no professional end. To provide scholars with time-saving machinery, to prepare students for examinations—these solid objectives are best served by some version of data processing. Literary history deprived of ideas and judgments is the servant of the status quo; it is immobile, for dead facts create no dialogue; and since it refuses to speak to us it deprives us of continuity—that is, of the possibility for rational development. In refusing to explain the historical roots of current literature we relinquish the possibility of criticizing our own performance; since this leaves us with no grounds for action, we capitulate in the face of meaningless events.

And herein lies the academy's most ironic failure: although it demands that we pour out an unending stream of literary critiques, there is to be found very little real criticism. There are the exercises in New and Aristotelian Criticism; until recently Myth Criticism kept the journals well supplied; and currently Northrop Frye's neat categories seem to be driving hundreds to their typewriters. But these methods are being used like pieces of machinery; they are gimmicks; they provide one more way of avoiding critical thought. Like the literary Marxism now being imported from France, it is criticism without real social relevance, with its teeth removed.

The function of poetry, Matthew Arnold once said, is to criticize life. Surely criticism should do no less. If we follow Arnold's counsel we shall begin by allowing the classics to judge our present experience; in turn, by arguing with them in self-defense we shall make judgments upon them. What does this have to do with our criticism? or with the way we teach our classes? We explicate, we analyze structures, we examine genres—but we ask no questions about a work's role in anyone's life. Our methods create the mere illusion of critical procedure for they are harmless; they affect no one.

Our humanity dictates that we make choices. To retain this prerogative we need the help of criticism. If the academy is to be concerned with the performance of criticism's task, if it is to confront students with the full force of our best ideas, it will have to do so as part of a communal effort. Departments of literature will have to look on themselves as members of an *intellectual* community, as part of a front dedicated to the human ends of poetry—to men's desire for the true, the good, and the beautiful. Their critical function will be to expose the enemies of literature with the light of reason and to destroy them with the passion of moral concern. Attendance at most any academic literary event will show how far removed these ideals are from actuality. During the discussion following a lecture it is most important to display one's erudition; genteel banter is wanted rather than criticism; and to argue constitutes a bad breach of manners. Ordinarily, there is nothing much to argue about in any case.

Professors of literature seem to have little sense of identity as literary intellectuals. Consequently, we relate to each other not as members of an intellectual community but as fellow bureaucrats. Worse, we are not joined to students in terms of our common work nor do they follow us as intellectual disciples. They are our trainees and, at best, we become their paternalistic protectors, helping them to get fellowships and jobs. Woe to the student who takes an idea, rather than his career, seriously; he should know that self-interest is the oil which greases the wheels of a competitive system.

The end of the academic pursuit is advancement in one's office. All communal, educational, and intellectual objectives are subsidiary to the need for individual achievement. Consequently, professors of literature often display an almost pathological fear of criticism: rather than being taken as an intellectual challenge, it is taken as a threat to one's career. This fear reflects, furthermore, a vague suspicion that there is little justification for perpetuating our academic field. No one really wants the boat rocked. Thus our curricular changes are rarely more than rearrangements of old staples, new ways of slicing a crumbling cake; their objective is, more often than not, to turn out more Ph.D.'s with greater dispatch.

More fundamentally, the fear of criticism is one aspect of the literary academy's natural conservatism. It pictures itself as the preserver of tradition, the repository of values; its ready acceptance of the past allows it to painlessly absorb the present. The slavish adherence to traditions which have hardened into ideological masks allows us to ignore our students' most basic questions: Why is literature a good? why is its study required? To most scholars the challenge is, in any case, irrelevant: they dutifully perform their bureaucratic task like any other; it is one way of making a living. The college president's lofty, and oft repeated, speech about the social importance of the humanities, the spiritual values of literature, is simply icing on the cake: it gets swallowed with everything else.

Yet these pieties need to be challenged. What relevance has the physicist's love of Marcel Proust to his work on missiles? If the love were real, he would, I assume, stop working on them. We are the inheritors of an educational ideal intended for the training of elites. The notion of a well-rounded education assumes that the study of humane letters prepares those who are to rule or administer (somehow) for their intended tasks. This ideological relic—it has no relation to any reality I know—allows us the comfortable pretense that the functionaries we train receive an education which makes them whole, humane, and enlightened. Even graduate students in Industrial Management are exposed to Melville. And how can the man who loves *Moby Dick* be a capitalist hyena?

If the critique of academic literary studies is to be

rigorous it must be based on a thorough analysis of the university's functions. What role, we must ask, does higher education play in America's social and economic system? To my knowledge, no such analysis exists. Without it we are reduced to making unsystematic criticisms of curricula and educational techniques. The move beyond such trivia requires a determination of how developments in the academy relate to developments in society, what relevance educational ideology has to social fact. At that point, perhaps, we shall be clear on what forces have lulled us into the quiet acceptance of intellectual and moral treason. Of how this analysis should proceed, I am uncertain. But surely it must begin with the recognition that the university is a servant of the economy, that its institutional function is to contribute to the technological triumphs of capitalism. In this process departments of literature are as deeply involved as departments of industrial management.

Given the lack of both a proper critical analysis and an intellectual community, the choice of strategies for opposing the system becomes highly problematic. Those wishing to effect the needed radical change will have to organize themselves into a vanguard. Effectiveness will depend on their union of purpose, on their capacity to transcend—not necessarily give up—capricious privacies. For the literary intellectual, individualism being a major dogma of his creed, this involves the most difficult of commitments. Yet we must all begin to understand that a totally self-centered individualism is not necessarily a sign of heroism or nobility; it may, in fact, serve as a mask for the competitive depredations of capitalism. The narcissistic obsession of modern literature for the self, the critical cant concerning the tragic isolation of the individual—these are notions which tie our hands and keep us from the communion necessary for meaningful action.

Another illusion of individualism is a belief in the efficacy of the charismatic teacher. One cannot be a great teacher in an evil system. To dazzle students with the brilliance of one's performance and do no more is to submit to the status quo; excelling independently, without a concerted program for change, diminishes the possible impact of one's efforts; indeed, those concerned primarily with the fulfillment of their egos guarantee the inconsequence of their ideas. Academic intellectuals have yet to learn that their independence is limited by their place in the social and economic hierarchy. They do not, as Matthew Arnold has misleadingly taught them, transcend the class system nor do they reconcile oppositions by expressing their "best selves." The very nature of the university demands that they play economic and social roles. Many have chosen to be inconspicuous members of the middle class; some have climbed to the upper reaches of the technocratic elite. Yet are we not, after all, wage earners? intellectual workers? In perverting the use of literature has the academy not alienated us from our work? In spite of our affluence are we not exploited? To understand this much is to prepare oneself for opposition. If he is to be true to his literary calling, to the honest demands of his work, the critic's function in the university will be the rather unacademic one of courting conflict.

How will the commitment to struggle affect the scholar's dedication to independent scholarship? This notion, the idea of objectivity itself, is never an absolute; the pressures of the historical moment invariably shape its meaning. For a scholarly contributor to Diderot's *Encyclopedia* independent scholarship was a freeing notion, a challenge to the authorities and, therefore, an instrument for social change. But there may be circumstances under which the notion becomes an excuse for accepting the status quo, a means for justifying our own empty response to the demands of literature, or an instrument for hiding our social fears. Today the idea of independent scholarship is a mask for the commercial activities of the academic bureaucracy; it permits us to bow, in good conscience, to the impersonal demands of the office. If literary scholarship is to have a meaning, if it is to contribute to enlightenment and have an effect, it must be committed to an end. Of such a commitment we are all afraid, lest we lose our precious independence. Yet who in the academy is really intellectually independent? How many manage to see around the blinders of official ideologies? Who has the strength to be truly objective? Indeed, the energies of our passionate commitment may be necessary for creating the possibility of objectivity and free thought.

Commitment to what? Surely not to imprinting a static literary tradition on the minds of victims trapped in a classroom, nor to instilling in them a servile admiration for the glories of the past. Our devotion to criticism demands a willingness to destroy received dogmas, to rid ourselves of the deadening burden of history: such antihumanist activity may be the going price for a study of literature which affects life. Dangerous as it is, we may have to accept some student's honest feeling that, for example, Milton's use of pastoral in "Lycidas" is a foolish irrelevance. To appeal to the tradition of pastoral for the poem's justification is merely to lull the student into a bland acceptance of authority; it will hardly lead him to reflections on the meaning of death. Again, it may be necessary to illustrate that the quiet honesty of "Tintern

Abbey" hides a lie about the morality of nature; that our passive acceptance of the poem's seductive authority may keep us from seeing ourselves, the world and, indeed, "Tintern Abbey" as they really are.

Having accustomed ourselves to the critical task of questioning—even destroying—a part of the past, having broken our chains, just how do we make the study of literature meaningful to our lives? how is it to affect the world? If we cannot turn literary visions into reality, we must at least see them as expressions of profound personal and social needs. Lest its remaining traces of life be destroyed, the study of literature must not become a haven for refugees from the pressures of the moment. There is, for example, an urgent need to explore the demands which democratization makes on the very concept of a literary culture. What poetic visions are to speak to this situation? We must propose answers and make choices if literature is to be more than a minor diversion and its appreciation more than an exercise in archaeology. The study of literature must begin with an exploration of our social needs.

This imperative was a point of departure for the great critics of the nineteenth century, their destination being the reformation of culture itself. They at least knew that humane critical standards and a disinterested love of beauty could exist only in a fitting social context—a context the critic might have to create. The moral seems clear: for my students to react fully to *The Dunciad*—to feel the cultural tragedy implicit in the victory of Grub Street and the goddess Dulness—it may be more important for them to consult Marx's work on the effects of capitalism than Aubrey Williams' useful study of the poem's literary context; the former will channel their aesthetic perceptions into social understanding and (perhaps) action; the latter, into literary criticism.

But here we have crossed the unofficial bounds of academic scholarship. A department of English has its functions, a committed intellectual has his: how is the latter to work as an activist while performing his academic task? Are the two not subversive of each other? Yet there appear to be possibilities, however faint, of working outward from the academic setting. I say this with no great confidence: clearly it might be a convenient rationalization for my own situation, for my own fears. I find it frightening to consider that the staggering concentration of intellect at the universities, the large degree of academic freedom we have attained, and the seemingly boundless resources placed in our hands—that all these should be irrelevant to the best ideas and most beautiful visions expressed by our literature. This may indeed be the case. Perhaps all significant intellectual agitation will have to originate outside the academy. But those on the inside must surely make the attempt.

Literature as an instrument of agitation: the idea seems fatuous, even old-fashioned; it sounds too much like a manifesto from the old *Masses*. In any case, there must be easier ways to agitate. Again: Why teach literature at all? Only this time imagine the question asked by a student radical. My answer: Because you and I are concerned with freedom. Vague? Obviously. But my (and others') intuition about this is so strong that it needs to be elaborated.

I can see few better ways of exploring the idea of human freedom than in contemplating the fate of a literary work. No two people, no two epochs or civilizations, have ever made the same use of a poem. Yet its meanings (its sensuous and intellectual qualities) persist. It demands that we react to a specific text—yet somehow in our own way. Shaping its meaning to our own desires we help make its fate; doing so, we not only explore the limits of free thought but learn how to make conscious use of the past. In this realm, at least, we are not the slaves of raw facts, uncontrollable events, or immutable logic, but stand in equal partnership with the creations of other men. The literary scholar's far from trivial task is to act as broker in the partnership. For this the academy may be an amenable setting.

The panorama of literature lies in the scholar's full view. It is more than a collection of words framed by the limits of his visual perception: it is history. And history is full of beautiful subversive possibilities. Their exploitation demands daring, intellectual rigor, and ultimately commitment to the possibilities of freedom. By its very nature, in spite of our academic merchants, literature is not a commodity, but the sign of a creative act which expresses personal, social, and historical needs. As such it constantly undermines the status quo.

That the schools regard the teaching of literature as a necessity points to society's feelings of guilt: literary visions are a constant reminder of its failures. Academics must exploit these feelings, they must keep touching the raw nerve. Our probes may not sunder humanity's chains, they may not directly transform our national life, nor will they stop the butchery in Vietnam. Yet they remind our students of human possibilities, of the reality of feelings, of both horror and beauty. The raw nerve we touch is, finally, our own. The pain is a fitting reminder of the scholar's need to be human, of the need to transform not only his students but himself. Here at least is a beginning.

KEYNES

WITHOUT GADFLIES

∽ Sumner M. Rosen

ECONOMISTS HAVE NEVER EXACTLY BEEN
wildcats or outcasts, but neither have they ever been as
domesticated as they are today. The number of economists
has probably never been larger nor have they ever found
their services as welcome—and as well paid—in so many
institutions of society as is now the case.

This highly agreeable state of affairs holds true for the
work of both academic and nonacademic economists. For if
it was once true that university economists carried on a
species of scholastic discourse which had little in common
with the work of practical men of affairs in the United
States Treasury, the Federal Reserve System, or the import-
export firms, this separation is no longer true. Beginning
with the New Deal and more so still during World War II,
economists in increasing numbers found themselves advis-
ing or working full time in federal agencies. The Employment Act of 1946 formalized the permanent import-

ance of economic analysis in public affairs; since that time
there has been a continuing interchange of academic and
governmental duties on the part of large numbers of professional economists. Business firms and labor unions, as
well as nonprofit agencies, have employed more and more
professional economists, until at last the Kennedy years
were the high-water mark in the reliance of government on
academic economists. Today there are few men teaching
economics who have not served, or will not serve, a stint in
government, business, or subsidized research on practical
questions at home or abroad. The nature of economics and
of the work of economists as it is treated in these pages
applies, with all the strengths and weaknesses which that
application implies, inside as well as out of the universities. Almost nowhere—except for such strongholds of conservative tradition as the University of Chicago—are there
intellectual centers where a creative and reflective minority can serve as the conscience or gadfly to the profession as
a whole. A justified inference from this analysis is that such
centers are badly needed, but there are as yet no signs of
their being provided. Nor are they likely to be until more
economists begin to state their own dissatisfactions with
the state of the art they practice, and to call for higher
standards of relevance, independence, and creativity.

One clue to the current state of American economics can
be gained through a perusal of a volume issued in 1966
marking—celebrating, rather—the "Twentieth Anniversary of the Employment Act of 1946."[1] The anniversary
took the form of a symposium under the sponsorship of the
Joint Economic Committee. A distinguished list of speakers addressed a distinguished audience, which also heard
messages from three living presidents, under whom that
famous statute has been administered. Those who came

were celebrating not an anniversary but a victory, the triumph of the "new economics." All who had served as chairmen of the Council of Economic Advisers, established in the law, took part as speakers or panelists. Among them was Walter Heller, Mr. Kennedy's economic chief of staff, who deserves much of the credit for managing the widespread acceptance of Keynesian ideas which may mark the most significant permanent achievement of the Kennedy years. In his luncheon address, Mr. Heller remarked:

> In commenting on the so-called policy revolution of the past 5 years, I have sometimes said that the Nation has simply pressed into public service the economics taught in its classrooms for 20 years and accepted as orthodox by 80 to 90 percent of its economists.

Except for remarks of characteristic bite and dissent by Leon Keyserling (not, strictly speaking, an economist) there were virtually no quarrels with the substance of this comment by any speaker, despite the low growth rates and high unemployment of the Kennedy years. The event was a celebration of a revolution well fought and finally secured, a revolution in the thinking of a nation and in the willingness of its leaders to act in accord with the new doctrines.

The Employment Act is a monument both to the effectiveness of the change in thinking which Keynes initiated, and to the deep and widely felt fear that the end of World War II might well bring back the conditions of the 1930s unless safeguards were adopted. Even so, the policy directives in the law were, in the words of Congressman George Outland, "much emasculated."

What had been conceived of as a full-employment bill, "the most constructive single piece of legislation in the history of this Nation" in the words of Congressman

Wright Patman, underwent a long process of modification
and compromise. The result, hardly digestible as a piece of
prose, much less policy, reads:

DECLARATION OF POLICY

The Congress hereby declares that it is the continuing
policy and responsibility of the Federal Government to
use all practicable means consistent with its needs and
obligations and other essential considerations of national
policy, with the assistance and cooperation of industry,
agriculture, labor, and State and local governments, to
coordinate and utilize all its plans, functions, and resources for the purpose of creating and maintaining, in a
manner calculated to foster and promote free competitive enterprise and the general welfare, conditions under
which there will be afforded useful employment opportunities, including self-employment, for those able, willing, and seeking to work, and to promote maximum
employment, production, and purchasing power. (Public
Law 304, 79th Congress)

What, one is tempted to ask, was the cheering about?

Economists have spent the past thirty years bringing to
fruition what we might call, to use Lawrence Klein's
phrase, the "Keynesian Revolution." The process has three
important aspects. One is that the revolution turned out to
be substantially less extensive than its enthusiasts claim.
Unemployment had not been solved; steady growth in response to the right fiscal and monetary stimuli had not
been achieved; inflation has remained a periodic threat. A
second is that the revolution preempted nearly all the professional energies available and dominated the development of economic studies—and of economists—throughout
most of this period. A third aspect is that its apparent
triumph, however important—and it *is* important—has
tended to cultivate among economists and their public a
complacency about the adequacy of our arsenal of policies

for dealing with economic problems. But urgent problems exist about which Keynes and Keynesianism have little to tell us. The result is a disturbing vacuum.

More perhaps than that of any other of the great economists, Keynes's work had direct and important meaning for policy and policy makers. This, more than the depth or originality of his analysis, explains the continuing degree of controversy about it. Keynes argued forcefully that the successful preservation of capitalism requires that the state intervene in the economy. The major purpose of this intervention is to secure or maintain a level of activity adequate to assure a high level of employment. Since this will not happen automatically, the state must act deliberately to make it happen.

Most economists accepted Keynes's conclusions quickly. This in itself was a new phenomenon in a field where authority has always yielded only slowly to new ideas. One reason was the deep and almost complete degree of frustration which economists had experienced in attempting to deal with the depression of the 1930s. It was an unprecedented catastrophe, wholly inconsistent, in its depth and duration, with anything in the accepted arsenal of ideas. Another reason was the essential moderation of Keynes's viewpoint. Keynes was a capitalist, and his theory was designed to restore and preserve the vigor of capitalism. He cherished its major institutions and mechanisms: prices, profits, consumer choice, free markets. He prescribed intervention as the necessary price to pay for this preservation, and economists—never a radical group—were saved the necessity of coming to grips with more radical solutions. A final reason for the success of Keynesianism was its novelty and freshness, after many decades of aridity and intellectual decay. Economists responded eagerly and gratefully to this offer of rescue, rejuvenation, and restoration to the contemporary world and its issues. The most distinguished of today's economists, Paul A. Samuelson, has described his response and that of his contemporaries as like "the unexpected virulence of a disease first attacking and then decimating an isolated tribe of South Sea Islanders." Keynes was the prophet come to save his people from that worst of afflictions: irrelevance. And he provided not a nostrum or a simple set of slogans, but an intellectual system worthy of study, ready to challenge the old system on its own ground.

With zeal, the disciples set out to complete Keynes's work. This undertaking had three aspects. The first was to bring order out of the suggestive, fragmentary, and unfinished character of much of the *General Theory*. Men like Hicks, Harrod, Meade, and Kaldor in England undertook this work, soon joined by many Americans, preeminently Alvin Hansen, Seymour Harris, and their colleagues and students. In virtually any issue of any of the important economic journals, as well as in many books on economics published each year, this work still goes on. These men and others have devoted much of their lives to the elaboration, completion, and in some cases, the correction of the original Keynesian insights. Other things have been built on to the essentially short-run Keynesian analysis, one of the most important being the integration of the original short-run analysis of the full-employment problem with an analysis of the balance between investment and the growth of the labor force required to assure full employment over long periods of time. This work, plus the elaboration of the key elements of the Keynesian analysis—consumption, savings, investment, interest, money, employment—and their interaction, has been the mainstream of economic analysis throughout most of the thirty years since the *General Theory* appeared. The work has been well done and has made us all Keynesians.

The second task was to bring the message to a wider public. This task fell, as it happened, primarily to one man. In this way, the first edition of Samuelson's *Economics: An Introductory Analysis* (1948) created a stir comparable to that of the *General Theory*. It represented as drastic and refreshing a departure from the textbooks of the previous generations as did the work of Keynes, the exposition of whose work forms its heart. It was in addition brash, irreverent, lively, and contemporary. It has now gone through seven editions, sold over two million copies in the United States, plus many more in translation abroad, and continues to dominate the textbook market in introductory courses in economics. Virtually every college graduate who has taken a course in economics in the past twenty years has come under the influence of this book and its imitators.

Among the ideas which this book articulated were that a rate of inflation of 5 percent a year "need not cause too great concern," that monetary measures are relatively ineffective in influencing the level of total spending, and that "a positive fiscal policy" is both possible and necessary to avoid cyclical swings and to help secure "a progressive, high-employment economy free from excessive inflation or deflation." Taxes are evaluated, not by their alleged effects on incentives to work, but by their progressiveness, including their redistributive effects, and the "burden" of the public debt is shown to lie more in its effects on income distribution than in any deleterious result of simply continuing to grow; in fact; Samuelson argues that a growing national debt, if required to maintain steady high employment, is perfectly acceptable and very convenient for the monetary managers. Virtually nothing is said in defense of profits and the traditional "incentives" of a free-enterprise economy.

If one recalls the orthodox ideas on which previous generations had been raised, this is a catalogue of heresies. Their acceptance has by no means been instantaneous or universal. Successive editions have hedged on some of the more unqualified of these statements, and more importantly, later editions (like the third edition of 1955) introduced the concept of a "neoclassical synthesis," bringing together the Keynesian and classical systems of analysis. Keynes and the classics were merged, a mainstream of thought mapped, and continuity achieved. In the process, a good deal of the boldness, originality, and activism of the early Keynesians has been modified or abandoned altogether.

There remained a third task: to bring Keynesian ideas to the center of effective policy making. The early impact of these ideas outside.of the academy was not great. This was largely because of their novelty, and because the urgency of the problems out of which they had arisen began to abate and, before long, to disappear completely. It was difficult at first even to imagine what might be involved in the deliberate use of state instruments to influence the overall behavior of the economy. The techniques needed to measure and define the need were lacking and had to be constructed. The skepticism, conservatism, and ignorance of important men would not yield readily to the complex and radical proposals of an intellectual, and a foreigner to boot. All this would take time. Even as these ideas were beginning to make their impact, however, the economy began to respond to the preparations for war and support of the allies. A pragmatic proof of the effects of government expenditures on the level of economic activity furnished the first demonstration that Keynes was right. As American entry into World War II grew near, the burden of depressed conditions began to be lifted. Within a few years, the entire picture had been transformed; full and overfull employment came, maximum production was the major goal, economic techniques were required not for stimulus but mainly to suppress inflationary pressures and ration scarce commodities and resources.

In 1941, the final report of the Temporary National Economic Committee was submitted. This was a different kind of intellectual investment, stemming from earlier traditional distrust of monopolies and of "bigness." TNEC was virtually its last serious effort. A major impact of the depression was to revitalize this tradition and to bring new attention to the structural features of modern American capitalism. From the time of Veblen, Ripley, and Commons, some economists had directed their attention to the key institutions which emerged in the late nineteenth century as dominating elements in economic life, primarily the investment banks and the large industrial corporations. The depression was widely interpreted as a failure of the business system. It became increasingly widespread doctrine that something fundamental had gone awry with the workings of that system, that a serious reconstruction of its structural elements was required.

TNEC conducted the only serious and broad-scale study of the structure of the economy and its defects that has ever been made. A distinguished committee, composed of senators, congressmen, and laymen, TNEC was charged by President Roosevelt to make a searching analysis of the economy. Many economists wrote monographs for the

TNEC, some of them still the best studies of their kind. Others, like Arthur R. Burns, were stimulated to research and writing. Responding to the insights of Piero Sraffa, Edward Chamberlin and Joan Robinson broke new ground in the analysis of more realistic models of competitive behavior than those which assumed no imperfections, selling costs, or irrationalities on the part of buyers. These books were major efforts to integrate a more realistic view of market behavior with conventional economic theory. But they were not successful in focusing economic thought in any serious study of structural problems and their consequences. Chamberlin and Robinson did not really deal with these questions, while Burns, Corwin, Edwards, and others who wrote were not ready to extend this analysis, or to undertake the proselytizing effort needed to give their work visibility and momentum. As for TNEC, it was a victim of changing times and concerns. By 1941, when the final report was ready, Americans had lost interest. Wholly new problems had arisen, the old ones were rapidly vanishing, and the only crusade to follow was that against the Axis powers. The one significant piece of legislation which TNEC produced was the 1950 amendment to the Clayton Act, closing a thirty-six-year-old loophole. This "Celler-Kefauver" amendment forbids mergers which reduce competition consummated by the direct acquisition of assets; the original law was confined to the acquisition of stock. This law has been used effectively in some important cases, but it has operated less to undo past acts of merger than to prevent proposed or prospective mergers. Moreover, it came very late in the day; the concentrated structure of American industry was the dominant fact when the TNEC began its inquiry, and remains the dominant fact today. Credit for passage of the Celler-Kefauver amendment belongs to the persistence and skill of a handful of crusading public servants and economists who gathered around the Kefauver antimonopoly subcommittee and worked closely with it from positions in the Federal Trade Commission and the Antitrust Division of the Department of Justice. They were few and so were their victories. Since Kefauver's death, the small band has dwindled even further; we are unlikely to see any sequel to the investigation of the drug industry which the subcommittee conducted in 1959–1960. But even here the legislative results focused primarily on industrial *practices;* no alterations in the *structure* of the industry and the concentration of market power growing out of that structure were seriously proposed.

TNEC left a scholarly legacy, but little else. The inquiries which it began have not been continued; more important, the assumption underlying the work of the Commission—that the structure of industry required a searching look and whatever alterations that look made necessary—has been abandoned by economists, almost without exception. That is one reason why, when latter-day radicals raised the "power structure" to the status of a keynote in the litany of the movements for racial justice and peace, the economists could offer no guidance or insight to give the slogan flesh, and to direct the attention of political activists to the central targets for any meaningful reform of the economic system. Antitrust is the closest we come in the United States to an ideology of economic power, but it has little meaning or relevance to those who suffer most from the use and abuse of concentrated economic power in the hands of large corporations, whether as consumers, workers, or citizens.

One of the few groups of economists whose work still

derives from a concern with important issues of public policy are those who specialize in employment and labor-market matters. Theirs is a somewhat different tradition, more engaged and problem-oriented in its very origins. The study of labor problems had its serious beginnings with Professor Frank Commons and his associates at the University of Wisconsin. It was rooted in Commons' commitment to the close study of economic institutions as the key to understanding. It grew during periods of struggle, often intense and dramatic, between employers and unions seeking recognition, status, and effectiveness. In the hands of Commons and his successors, the study of labor economics has remained responsive to the realities of labor-management relations. These scholars have followed closely and on the whole accurately the phases which characterize the evolution of the labor movement and the present pattern of industrial relations. Some have sought to write more generalized studies,[2] but these efforts have remained reasonably close to the reality they sought to describe. In this they follow the example of such earlier writers as Selig Perlman, Robert Hoxie, and Frank Tannenbaum.

These studies avoid both the aridity and the unreality of the theoretical economists, and the sweeping inferences of many Continental writers for whom labor problems have traditionally offered a basis for speculation on the larger issues of class and ideology. They have an American pragmatism at their root. But they also reflect another tradition which has grown stronger in the past two decades. This is the view that speculation on large questions is not simply dangerous but unseemly as well. The view that a scholar may in good conscience grind a political or ideological ax is anathema to most American intellectuals. It may be overstating the case to argue that we all serve what Louis Hartz calls the "liberal tradition," but the work of most scholars who study labor-management relations is influenced by certain unstated premises which are consistent with Hartz's brilliantly stated thesis. These might be articulated this way:

1. Conflict is never about basic principles and is, therefore, never irreconcilable.

2. Pragmatic compromise without total dedication to an ideological program is characteristically American; therefore,

3. Those institutions which have achieved permanence and success in the United States have done so because they understood and adapted to these conditions. The American labor movement, and the system of settling industrial conflict which it has helped to create, exemplify these characteristics; in the American setting, they are positive virtues.

It is no accident that Daniel Bell, who has announced "the end of ideology," has worked for many years in the industrial-relations area and served as labor editor of *Fortune* magazine. Seymour Martin Lipset, a central molder of the anti-ideology school, has a similar background; his study of the International Typographical Union[3] served as a laboratory for the development of many of the ideas which flow from the writings of these and other men. For them, values—democracy, participation, autonomy, choice—must be defined in terms of the institutional social structure in which men find themselves. Relativism is the keynote; the scholar's job is to explicate the structures in order to clarify their effects on the people who inhabit them. This is important work, and these men have done it well. But it is devoid of normative standards.

It summons the scholar to no issue. He observes, comments, reflects, but he does not take part or take sides. He remains strictly outside politics. I do not mean party or electoral politics, at which many scholars play with enthusiasm. I mean *issue* politics, in which deep vested interests collide or in which serious questions of social justice are at stake.

Labor economists have helped to deal with important policy questions. When high levels of unemployment began to appear and to persist in the face of high levels of economic activity, from 1956 onward, serious efforts were made to clarify the causes. The result was the celebrated "structural-aggregate" controversy. One school led by economists close to the White House, whose spokesman was Walter Heller, argued that unemployment required more Keynesian treatment in the form of measures to stimulate business investment and raise the level of consumer spending. The structuralists, a minority though an able one, argued that the labor market has imperfections so deeply rooted as to require direct and special treatment without which no amount of aggregate demand stimulus can be expected to reduce unemployment sufficiently or quickly enough. The depreciation and tax-credit provisions of the Kennedy administration, and the 1964 tax cut, represent a policy victory for the majority. Such legislative measures as the Area Redevelopment Act of 1961, the Manpower Development and Training Act of 1962, the Appalachia and Regional Development Act of 1965, and the Economic Opportunity Act of 1964 were structuralist measures, though only the first reflects any serious prior work by economists.

Keynesian remedies are consistent with a wide range of political and ideological positions; the same is true of structural ones. It is a mistake to assume, as many conservatives do, that Keynesians inevitably advocate larger public deficits, higher levels of public spending, and social welfare measures. The stereotype no longer fits, if it ever did. This is in part sophistication, in part a retreat on the part of the Keynesians from the identification with these measures which was attributed to them during the depression, when unemployment was the problem and stagnation a specter which seemed to face a mature American economy. The most deliberate application of Keynesian measures to the economy, which occurred in the 1962–1966 period, involved no significant new measures of public spending. The only really important area of nonmilitary public spending which has been greatly expanded since World War II has been highway construction, hardly a piece of social innovation. Instead economic stimulation has taken the form of tax cuts, stimuli to business investment, and manipulation of interest rates. What Robert Lekachman has recently called "commercial Keynesianism" has, like the tamed and domesticated versions of Freud which dominate psychoanalysis, come to mean all that we do now mean by Keynesian remedies. Perhaps the most ironic aspect of this trend has been the Heller proposal to dispose of prospective surpluses in federal revenues by sharing them with state governments. This proposal, made in the name of reinvigorating the states, would strengthen some of the most socially regressive tendencies in American political life. In effect, it is an abdication of any federal responsibility for creating and legitimatizing new areas of public expenditure. Even economists of the center, like John Kenneth Galbraith, reject these proposals and their implications. Yet Heller and his colleagues are the men who presided over and managed so well the conversion of Keynesian doctrine into one which almost every segment of opinion, including many of the most important business groups, finds acceptable, desirable, even indispensable.

As for the structural approach, it too fits a variety of political philosophies. The ranking Republican member of the Joint Economic Committee, Congressman Thomas B. Curtis of Missouri, has long argued that because structural imperfections explain much of our unemployment problem, we need no expansion of federal spending to solve it. Monetary and banking men, particularly those close to the Federal Reserve System, argue structural theories in order to justify their anti-inflationary bias against expansionist measures. Aggregative proponents accuse the structuralists of strengthening the case against increasing the level of demand. But those who see structural problems as important also include people who seek much higher levels of activity and expenditure in raising literacy, improving the mobility of workers, strengthening the effectiveness of the United States Employment Service, mounting effective campaigns against racial discrimination in employment, vastly improving the quality of academic and vocational education, helping to bring more economic activity into "depressed areas," etc. It is unfortunately true that, outside of the spokesmen for the AFL-CIO and a handful of others, few of these people are professional economists. But those few deserve recognition.

When one reviews the list of problems just mentioned, one is struck by the extent to which they were brought to public attention not by economists but by journalists, politicians, and sociologists, among others. The attack on depressed areas was largely organized and directed by a coalition led by the Textile Workers Union, whose leadership was alarmed by the effect on their traditional base in New England of the large-scale migration of the industry in the 1940s and 1950s. Poverty came to the fore as a result of the famous book *The Other America* (1962), by Michael Harrington—socialist and journalist—and public discussion was dominated thereafter by such writers as Dwight Macdonald, Mollie Orshansky of the Social Security Administration, Oscar Lewis, Paul Jacobs, and others. Economists have contributed virtually nothing of importance to the formation of public opinion or public policy on poverty. When the profession finally got around to discussing it at their annual meeting in 1965, little was said to indicate any urgency or to bring any special insight to bear. Galbraith's famous book *The Affluent Society* (1958), perhaps the most influential since Keynes, treats poverty as the unfinished business of a rich society, requiring only attention and some easily prescribed remedies, especially the education of the children of the poor. The tone is complacent, the treatment routine. Four years later, Harrington's book appeared and the entire tone of the discussion changed, though the facts were the same.

The structural school deserve credit for their concern with these problems, but they did little to develop the implications of this concern in ways which would effectively change public opinion, alter political priorities, or even pose an effective intellectual challenge to their professional colleagues. The best study of the problem of unemployment which has yet appeared[4] makes a scholarly and persuasive case that structural unemployment is a fundamental fact and that its victims are clearly identifiable groups in the society, including farm workers, unskilled laborers, young people, old workers, women, and particularly Negroes. Where these categories overlap, serious and persistent unemployment exists regardless of the level of overall demand. But every single one of these groups has found its principal spokesmen coming almost entirely from outside the ranks of the professional economists.[5] The development of public policy and—even more important—the discussion and critique of those policies which have been adopted in recent years in these problem areas have not benefitted perceptibly from the attention of the economists. Others have borne the burden in an era of unprecedented change in economic life. In the one case where economists have been appealed to—the case of automation—they have tended to deprecate the issue without furnishing the kind of hard evidence which would make this attitude credible, particularly to working men and women. It is one thing—and worth doing—to point out that the real world is complicated; it is another to seem to argue, as many economists do, that automation is so much like previous technological factors that it is not likely to alter long-term trends in growth or employment. Perhaps this is so, but the evidence is far from persuasive. Arguments which try to mollify the fears which automation arouses are, to say the least, premature.

Most of the other major issues of our time, some of them newly emerging and others familiar from the past, have not attracted the attention of many economists. The crises which this society and others are likely to face in future decades involve such forces as the impact of science, the nature and dominance of media of information, population pressures, urbanization, and—perhaps most important of all—the long-term relationship between "haves" and "have-nots," both within the society and in the world at large. On most of these, the economists have little to say, or when they speak, nothing of real significance or intellectual distinction.

These issues do not here require elaborate description.

Some are squarely within the presumed competence of the economist; others are more peripheral. In the first group fall those questions which directly affect economic welfare and relationships. A brief listing will indicate how these have fared at the hands of the professionals.

1. *Economic development.* Problems of the "emerging nations" and their economic future have generated a large volume of economic studies, and a substantial group of professional economists taking this as their major concern. This is one of the larger groups in the National Science Foundation listing, but numbers less than one thousand, 7 percent of the total. After some twenty or more years of intensive work, some of it excellent, we still lack a theoretical framework comparable to those which exist in such well-trod areas as monetary theory, price theory, international trade, or aggregative economics. In fact, the key components of such a theory have yet to be agreed upon; some writers stress capital accumulation and the mobilization of savings, others the creation of entrepreneurial elites, still others the central role of planning. What passes in the United States as the leading candidate for an overall framework is Walt W. Rostow's *Stages of Economic Growth* (1961), a mélange of historical and statistical generalizations of doubtful validity and of little use to serious students or practitioners dealing with hard questions. The most important theoretical contributions have been the work of men outside the United States or outside the central tradition, like Paul Baran, Gunnar Myrdal, and Raul Prebisch. What the work of these men has in common, something almost wholly lacking in the bulk of serious American work, is the central role which they assign to the industrialized nations in determining the future of the underdeveloped majority of nations. Whether from Bar-

an's Marxist perspective, Myrdal's melancholy pessimism, or Prebisch's salty and direct challenge from his position as a leading Latin American economist and spokesman, these writers assign a major share of historical responsibility for the sharp and perilous division of the world's economic units to the dominance of the Western European powers and the United States. They argue, correctly and persuasively in this writer's view, that the handful of rich countries, the United States foremost among them, will by their actions determine the possibility of ending that division short of a cataclysmic upheaval. This is putting the major responsibility where it belongs.

Most American writers, by contrast, tend to stress the importance of actions required in the developing economy, from political reform to the creation of effective capital markets. Few deal seriously with the larger issues of altering the domestic balance of power in those areas where it is concentrated in the hands of landholding or commercial oligarchies, and almost all have either ignored or denied the central role of the forces on which this handful of outsiders have focused. One result has been that American public opinion has hardly been touched with any deepening of its sense of responsibility for the future of the underdeveloped world, and American policy has scarcely altered from the improvised beginnings of the early days of foreign aid.

2. *Wealth and income.* Except for Robert J. Lampman's pioneering studies,[6] economists have scarcely concerned themselves with the question of wealth and its ownership, particularly from any broad perspective related to considerations of social welfare. Studies of income distribution have been more frequent, but tend to concentrate on one of two questions, that of "relative shares"—

i.e., the share of income going to "labor," "ownership," "agriculture," etc.—or that of the share of income going to the top 1 or 5 percent of income receivers. The prevailing view tends to echo that of Simon Kuznets, who has studied the latter question most carefully,[7] and is expressed by Galbraith:

> . . . there has been a modest reduction in the proportion of disposable income going to those in the very highest income brackets and a very large increase in the proportion accruing to people in the middle and lower brackets.[8]

This widely celebrated "income revolution" of the period since World War I has been effectively challenged and demolished, not by economists but by a historian[9] and a statistician of the Bureau of the Census.[10] These works have not received a fraction of the attention paid to less important but less disturbing works.

Similarly, the first effective treatment of the income tax system from the point of view of its equity to different population groups, classes, and categories of income was by Philip M. Stern in his *Great Treasury Raid* (1964). A fairly rich and lively vein of economic discussion of tax policy has generally neglected welfare and equity concerns in favor of concentration on the "disincentive" effects of sharply progressive rates, the relationship of the rate structure of stabilization policies, and the effects of taxes on the efficient allocation of resources. Economists generally support the principles of progressiveness and of equal treatment, but except for such notorious loopholes as the depletion allowance, have not scrutinized the prevailing tax system from the point of view of this criterion with anything like the depth or rigor required.

If we turn to such questions as the economic effects—costs, benefits, and policy requirements—in areas such as resource conservation, urban growth, the role of advertising and of mass media in affecting economic attitudes as well as economic behavior, and the effect of the dramatic expansion of research and development on economic growth, economists have little to teach us so far. On the question of population growth and its meaning, the vein is somewhat richer, but here too the major work is done by demographers.

3. *Arms and the economy.* We can conclude this survey with the most important abdication of any by the economists. This is a failure which applies across the board; the theoreticians, the institutionalists, and the aggregative economists alike have virtually ignored the most important single force in the American economy of the past twenty-five years, war and preparation for war.

Economists have sometimes been willing to discuss the question of the economy's ability to deal with the consequences of important cutbacks in military spending, but the discussion has acquired no structure or continuity, engendered no schools or positions to be debated. The level of attention has been episodic, and the intensity of involvement tepid at best. Those economists who have taken the trouble to deal with the question have, in most instances, been content to write an article for the press, or to grant an interview. These normally follow a standard pattern: the economy is sound, arms spending is a small proportion of the gross national product, appropriate stabilizing measures are available to meet any likely degree of arms reduction. Most of these writers treat arms spending as an unwelcome burden, the ending of which would free resources for constructive purposes. A few scholars have gone deeper, primarily in studying regional impacts and assessing the structural problems which arms reduction would impose. Only a handful have sought seriously to deal with the major issues which disarmament would raise.[11] Most of this discussion has taken place outside of the mainstream of economics, and only a handful of professional economists have been involved. The discussion has had virtually no impact. The Joint Economic Committee has never held hearings on the question, and the official agencies of the United States government have issued reports only reluctantly, and in response to pressures emanating from the peace movement and international agencies. This is astonishing on its face. Despite disclaimers and apologetics, the essence of the situation is as Robert Heilbroner describes it:

> . . . a central aspect of our growth experience of the past two decades is one which few spokesmen for the future candidly discuss. This is the fact that our great boom did not begin until the onset of World War II, and that its continuance since then has consistently been tied to a military rather than to a purely civilian economic demand.[12]

Unlike economists, business firms and the periodicals which serve them—*Fortune, Business Week,* the *Wall Street Journal*—pay assiduous attention to defense spending. Its vital role in economic life is acknowledged by high government officials, when they are asked, though they do singularly little on their own initiative to give this sector the attention it deserves. The chairman of the Council of Economic Advisers, Gardner Ackley, told a *Wall Street Journal* reporter on October 19, 1966, that "almost to the hour" one could date the rapid rise in GNP to the press conference on June 28, 1965, when President Johnson announced a doubling of draft calls and the imminent despatch of 50,000 American soldiers to Vietnam. He went on to say: "If the war hadn't speeded up last year, I expect we would have been looking around for further measures to stimulate the economy." But a perusal of the report of the cabinet-level committee which Mr. Ackley chaired in 1964–1965 on the need for government planning to cope with arms reductions was characterized by a high degree of confidence, bordering on complacency.[13]

This neglect would seem to fly in the face of facts of enormous magnitude, and to denote almost complete lack of responsibility. But the scholars and teachers are not consciously evading or avoiding a duty which they know in their hearts must be faced. Rather, they are conforming to a point of view about the economy and about their own role and responsibility which they find both bearable and honorable. It is part of a more general view of scholarship which effectively molds all but a handful of men, and casts that handful into the role of peripheral figures, cranks, or monomaniacs. This is at root an ahistorical, a technical or mechanical, a nonpolitical view of what the economy is and how it works. It is seen as a system with stable structural characteristics, operating within parameters which will not change. The major elements in it—consumers, banks, business firms, labor unions, farmers, government agencies—are treated as stable subsystems, to be studied so that they can be more effectively managed and their strengths and attitudes more accurately predicted. Virtually all debates among economists about economic policy are disagreement about the meaning of this kind of analysis. Most of the participants, however, agree that, given accurate studies and predictions, the policy tools available to government are more than adequate, in strength and sophistication, to deal with any problems that may rise.

This approach totally neglects what seems to one observer to be the major role of arms spending in shaping the economy and the society throughout the past twenty-five years. These effects include the role of arms spending in the degree of industrial concentration, its effects on the supply and use of scientific and engineering talent, its effects on the location of economic activity—e.g., in the growth of California, with all that implies about the pattern of our national politics—its shaping of patterns of educational investment and activity, its stimulation of a close partnership between the major contractors and the Department of Defense—the well-known but little understood "military-industrial complex," and, perhaps the most important to intellectuals, its success in blunting the interest of economics in probing the roots and basic structural characteristics of our economic system. Nothing succeeds like success, and the economy has been successful enough to suggest that basic questions are no longer as relevant as they seemed to be in the postdepression years. It has been a comforting and comfortable time.

The arms economy has been the major Keynesian instrument of our times. But its use has been cloaked as "national interest," its effects have been largely unexamined, its international consequences largely deleterious and destabilizing, its importance making for uncritical acceptance and dependence by large segments of the society, its long-run effects hardly glanced at. The arms economy has done much more than distort the use of scarce creative scientific and engineering talent, as Seymour Melman[14] and others have correctly charged. It has forced us to neglect a whole range of urgent social priorities, the consequences of which threaten the fabric of our society. A backlog of needs for schools, housing, urban facilities, clean air and water, transportation, hospitals, and a long list of other essentials cry out for attention and fail to get it. In 1966 it was necessary once more for the President to say "wait" to these and other claims long overdue, with Vietnam as the excuse. The arms economy is the major obstacle to any meaningful use of public funds for these needs, and no other funds can begin to do the job. This is the central fact; from it stem important consequences.

One is that those sectors of society whose rights, dignity, and opportunity are blocked or stunted by these social defects have a direct and vital stake in the future of the arms economy. While it preempts national energies and federal funds, their claims will not be met. Another is that those who claim to see deeper and to know more—the economists—have failed the most important test: that of relevance to major issues. A third is that our international position, dependent in the long run on our contribution to the eradication of backwardness and social injustice, cannot fundamentally improve while our international policies are shaped and dominated by our military position. Nowhere in the world has the United States or the industrial nations as a whole altered the balance of forces between growth and stagnation, poverty and hope, except where we have literally lifted a military ally with massive infusions of economic support, as in Taiwan and South Korea. Economists who correctly call for far larger American contributions to the cause of economic growth and development have not yet learned that their call must be accompanied by a far deeper concern with our military preoccupations and priorities. There are choices to be made, and economists are specialists in analyzing choices. But they have failed to perceive this one, let alone deal with it.

Long ago, economists opted for a separation of their studies from fundamentals. In so doing they adopted a prevailing American view that the fundamentals are not in question. The older fashion of joining economic and political concerns into political economy passed from the scene. Economists found new roles, some of them exciting and useful, but there were no new departures to be made. Even the major intellectual figures of the recent past—Schumpeter, Keynes, Kuznets, Hansen, Commons, Mitchell—did not cultivate or stimulate a fresh look at fundamentals,[15] and their students and disciples have seldom strayed from well-worn paths of inquiry. The major innovations of recent years have been in quantitative methods, highly useful for problem-oriented research and for practical use. Here men like Leontief and Samuelson have led the way toward what may be called scientism.

The long-cherished wish of the economists to function on a level of precision and complexity comparable to that of the chemists, physicists, and biologists now seems to have been achieved in the hands of these men. But the physicists and the others deal with fundamental questions at the heart of their field of knowledge; the mathematical economists and econometricians, by contrast, function at two other extremes—that of systematic abstraction in the one case and of data manipulation in the other.

Economists have historically worked on a foundation consisting of the central issues of their era and the central values of the writer. Adam Smith valued liberty, Ricardo productivity and progress, Marx the elimination of exploitation, Keynes the achievement of full employment.

These provided the normative tests by which they judged the economic systems about which they wrote (or dreamed), and on them they built their recommended solutions. Even when writing abstractly, economists imply, presuppose, a system and a set of values by which they judge and invite judgment. The economic ideologies derive from these roots.

The stress on scientism is itself a kind of ideology; it suggests that the central values of the economic tradition in the West—free markets, efficiency, growth—are sufficiently valid for our time to require no further serious scrutiny. Rather, they are the accepted base on which to build more effective techniques for achieving them.

There are, of course, areas of inquiry where quantitative methods are necessary and appropriate; these tend to be those areas where the fundamentals are well established and where quantity has always been the essence of the question. Examples include monetary theory and international trade.

In these areas, Keynes's additions have been assimilated, but in a "revisionist" adjustment to accommodate the American institutional structure and distribution of power. We have had enormous increases in the quantity and quality of economic information, and much of this has involved the invention of new kinds of economic measuring devices. And as noted earlier, the students of industrial relations—many of whom are only formally economists—have been diligent in studying and analyzing conflict, though they have been singularly unwilling to apply their rich insight to the field of international relations, where it might save us all.

One is left with the disappointing, indeed depressing, conclusion that economists have largely failed to meet their obligations to the society of which they are a part. Instead they have found a place—or places—in that society at a price, the sacrifice of independence and of dedication to relevance.

Long ago and in other places, this was not true. "Rightly or wrongly, economists have always dealt with policy. From Adam Smith to J. M. Keynes, each of the masters has addressed himself to the issues of his time."[16] A series of forces have combined over the past twenty-five years to change this by concealing from view the existence of major issues which require attention. It is a sobering but inescapable conclusion that until this sense of crisis returns, the economists will not respond to the challenges of our society and our world. The tragic possibility is that when this happens, there may not be time to think, and without thought, action cannot save us.

NOTES

1. Joint Economic Committee, 89th Cong. 2nd Sess., February 23, 1966.
2. Recent examples include John T. Dunlop, *Industrial Relations Systems* (New York, Holt, Rinehart & Winston, 1959); Richard A. Lester, *As Unions Mature* (Princeton, Princeton University Press, 1958); and Clark Kerr, John T. Dunlop, Frederick Harbison, and Charles A. Myers, *Industrialism and Industrial Man* (Cambridge, Harvard University Press, 1960).
3. Seymour Martin Lipset, Martin Trow, and James Coleman, *Union Democracy* (New York, The Free Press, 1956).
4. Eleanor G. Gilpatrick, *Structural Unemployment and Aggregate Demand* (Baltimore, Johns Hopkins Press, 1966).
5. For an exception see Gary S. Becker, *The Economics of Discrimination* (Chicago, University of Chicago Press, 1957).
6. *Changes in the Share of Wealth Held by Top Wealth-Holders, 1922–1956*, National Bureau of Economic Research, Occasional Paper No. 71 (New York, 1960), and *The Share of Top*

Wealth-Holders in National Wealth, 1922–1956 (Princeton, Princeton University Press, 1962).

7. *Shares of Upper Income Groups in Income and Savings,* National Bureau of Economic Research, Occasional Paper No. 35 (New York, 1950).

8. *The Affluent Society* (Boston, Houghton Mifflin Company, 1958), p. 85.

9. Gabriel Kolko, *Wealth and Power in America* (New York, Frederick A. Praeger, Publishers, 1962; rev. ed. 1964).

10. Herman Miller, *Rich Man, Poor Man* (New York, Thomas Y. Crowell Company, 1964).

11. An example of the first category is Seymour Harris, "Can We Prosper Without Arms?" *New York Times Magazine,* November 8, 1959, pp. 20 ff. The second category includes articles such as "Measuring the Impact of Regional Defense-Space Expenditures," by Richard S. Peterson and Charles M. Tiebout, *Review of Economics and Statistics,* Vol. 47, No. 4 (November 1964), pp. 421–28. The major contribution to the third category is Emile Benoit and Kenneth E. Boulding, eds., *Disarmament and the Economy* (New York, Harper & Row, Publishers, 1963).

12. *The Future as History* (New York, Harper & Row, Publishers, 1960), p. 133.

13. "Report of the Committee on the Economic Impact of Defense and Disarmament." See my discussion of this report in "The New Orthodoxy on Disarmament Economics," *Correspondent,* Winter 1965, pp. 61–69.

14. *Our Depleted Society* (New York, Holt, Rinehart & Winston, 1965).

15. "No doubt there were differences in the ideologies of Alvin Hansen and Henry Simons. I doubt that they would impress a Marxist or Buddhist." Donald J. Dewey on "Changing Standards of Economic Performance," *American Economic Review,* May 1961, p. 7.

16. Clair Wilcox, "From Economic Theory to Public Policy," *ibid.,* p. 28.

HISTORICAL

PAST AND EXISTENTIAL

PRESENT

∽ Staughton Lynd

A PROFESSION, ACCORDING TO *WEBSTER'S New International Dictionary,* is an "open declaration" or "public avowal" as well as "the occupation, if not purely commercial, mechanical, agricultural, or the like, to which one devotes oneself." The word itself suggests that a profession is not just something a person does but something he believes in doing.

"Why history?" therefore, seems to me an altogether fitting and proper question. Those who profess a religious faith recognize that their profession becomes dead unless it is renewed by frequent rediscovery of its reason for being. Accordingly, the religious "professor" may quest from a first to a second, from a second to a third profession of religious faith during a lifetime's experience of ultimate things. The man committed to a craft should ask no less of himself. He should frequently inquire what task it was that he chose this particular set of tools to perform, and be prepared to change tools if the task's requirements have come to seem different to him.

I decided to become a historian when I was twenty-nine, after I had "taken" (an odd word) no more than two or three semesters of history as an undergraduate. But during a checkered and prolonged adolescence in the course of which I did graduate work in city planning, served as a noncombatant conscientious objector in the United States Army, milked cows and made children's toys in a utopian community, and organized site tenants on New York's Lower East Side, I carried about with me two books on history: *The Historian's Craft* by Marc Bloch and *The Idea of History* by R. G. Collingwood. I liked these books. Bloch's appealed to me because he wrote it as a member of the French Resistance, without the aid of books and papers, shortly before his death at the hands of the Nazis, and because he conveyed a sense of history as a craft: something which had its own tools, which demanded (so to speak) a feel for cloth and leather before one could do it well, a discipline to which a man might apprentice himself. History as described by Bloch appeared to be controlled by the opaque, objective events with which it was concerned, and thus to be less prone to arbitrary manipulation and subjective whim than other social science disciplines.

The Idea of History was attractive for the opposite reason. It demythologized the aura surrounding the historical profession, by insisting that in the last analysis all that a man's mind could know of the past was the minds of other men, so that "history" in fact amounted to rethinking a portion of what human beings had thought before. "Progress," then, was defined by Collingwood as action proceeding from thought which had experienced the best of previous thought before deciding how to act. Taken together, the two books seemed to me the embodiment of intellectual elegance; the intellectual activity they analyzed appeared solid, and serviceable to that striving toward a better world which mattered very much to me.

When I "went into" history I began with Charles Beard's interpretation of the United States Constitution. I think now that there were two reasons for this choice, again somewhat in tension with each other.

At the time I explained my choice of subject matter on the ground that Beard's was the most important attempt to date at an economic interpretation of American history, and that I was enough of a Marxist to find this a logical point of departure. If that *was* the reason why I began my work as a historian by seeking a local microcosm in which to test the thesis of Beard's *Economic Interpretation of the Constitution of the United States,* I have mixed feelings about it now. On one hand it still makes sense to me that, like any other scientist, the historian should formulate hypotheses and test them against a restricted range of data, such as what happened in a limited area, or in one man's life. On the other hand I am now more conscious that I selected a range of data which I could be pretty certain would substantiate a thesis I hoped was true. I studied opposition to the Constitution in Dutchess County, New York, because Dutchess County had a history of landlord-tenant conflict very likely to be connected with how groups aligned themselves for or against ratification of the Constitution. The bias involved in my selection of Dutchess County did not necessarily invalidate my findings, but it raised a serious question as to their generalizability. I believe this is how bias characteristically operates in the work of other historians, too: not in deliberate mishandling of evidence, but in selection of research design.

The second reason I began with Beard became clear to me only gradually. Beard's work dealt with the American Revolution and its overall meaning. Implicitly, and to a certain extent explicitly, Beard asked the question, "Were the Founding Fathers activated by abstract ideas and a devotion to public welfare, or were they also motivated by personal economic interests?" If the latter alternative was overstated, might it not still be true (as Beard sometimes more sophisticatedly put it) that their view of public welfare was conditioned by the experience of a governing class in which individual Fathers participated by virtue of their birth and/or wealth? These questions were important to me because, as one considerably alienated from America's present, I wanted to know if there were men in the American past in whom I could believe.

This is not the kind of feeling historians are supposed to have. Not only did I have it, however; as time went on it increasingly seemed to me more honest to confront my feeling squarely for what it was, rather than pursue it in the guise of research about, say, the curious discrepancy between the portraits of the Revolutionary artisan in the books of Carl Becker and Charles Beard.

After graduate school I taught for three years in a Negro women's college in Atlanta, Georgia. Historians are not supposed to be influenced by their personal experiences, but I was, profoundly. Here were students with a greater stake than I, not just in entertaining an interpretation, but in *knowing* whether the signers of the Declaration were idealists who failed to carry out their full program, or hypocritical racists who killed Indians and bred Negroes while declaring that all men are equal. No doubt both answers were "too simple" and the truth was a more complicated third thing. But what *was* the truth? I did not know because I had not taken that question with sufficient seriousness to let it guide my own research. Incredibly, my research, like that of Beard, Becker, and other Progressive historians, had tacitly assumed that white artisans and tenant farmers were the most exploited Americans of the late eighteenth century, overlooking the one fifth of the nation which was in chains.

For my Negro students it was almost as important to know the true character of their collective past as to be at ease with their personal histories. One brilliant girl described to me the moment when, looking at the photographs in a collection of slave narratives, she realized, "These were my forefathers." After I conventionally began a survey course in American history with the Pilgrims, another excellent student, who had the courage to expose her personal past by inviting my family to her sharecropper father's home at Christmas, was also brave enough to ask me, "Why do you teach about your ancestors and not mine?" Next year I began the course with the slave ships, only to hear from a third student, "You are teaching me a special history rather than treating me like everybody else." Willy-nilly I was functioning as therapist in addition to historian; in reporting the past I turned it, whether I wished to or not, into a medium for the discovery of personal identity.

At issue was not whether history, like a lump of dough, can be made into any shape one pleases. The point was rather that if history, like a mountain, can be viewed from many different standpoints all equally "objective," perhaps it makes sense to approach it from the direction that has most personal meaning to the observer.

Meantime, I was beginning to chafe at the role of observer, no matter how defined. Teaching in the midst of the civil rights movement brought home the aphorism (here slightly rephrased) of Marx's *Theses on Feuerbach:* "The historians have interpreted the world; the thing, however, is to change it."

Thus I arrived at a conception of history which has much in common with that of the eighteenth century. Just as Jefferson found virtues to emulate in Plutarch and mistakes to be avoided in the story of republican Rome's decline, so I would have the young person of our own time (supposing history to interest him at all) encounter Jefferson (or Malcolm X) with the question, "What can I learn about how to live?"

In the nineteenth century this approach to history came to be condemned as moralistic. History, Ranke and his followers maintained, was not a lamp of experience to light the path ahead but a simple record of "how it really happened." Professional historians accepted Ranke's attitude as the definition of objectivity.

But as Carl Becker demonstrated in his *Declaration of Independence,* the creed of *"wie es eigentlich gewesen"* presupposed a belief that history "just as it happened" and "the existing social order" were "the progressive realization of God's purpose." The Rankean historian had no need to moralize because what history had achieved already was satisfactory to him. In Becker's paraphrase: "History is God's work, which we must submit to, but which we may seek to understand in order that we may submit to it intelligently." This was "objectivity" only in the sense that it made man an object of history rather than a maker of it.

It would oversimplify, of course, to suggest that radicals draw lessons from history whereas conservatives are content to narrate it. Among the lessons drawn from history by the Founding Fathers were that economic equality was impossible in a populous society, that democracy was weakened by the growth of commerce, and that, since power followed property, it would be chimerical to attempt to destroy chattel slavery by political means. These were conservative lessons inasmuch as they inclined the leaders of the Revolution to live with inequities they might otherwise have protested.

Moreover, the most influential Rankean of the nineteenth century was none other than Karl Marx. He too, like Hegel and Ranke, believed that ethical goals need not be imposed on history since they were imminent in it. He too, despite a youthful emphasis on man as historical creator, believed that "freedom is the recognition of necessity."

Accordingly, for someone like myself who was more and more committed to the thesis that the professor of history should also be a historical protagonist, a complex confrontation with Marxist economic determinism was inevitable. I do not pretend to be on the other side of this problem, certainly one of the major intellectual challenges of our time. But I have a few tentative conclusions.

Two recent neo-Marxist statements on the problem of historical determinism and man's freedom to choose are *What Is History?* by E. H. Carr and *In Search of a Method* by Jean-Paul Sartre. Let us attempt to close in on our problem by following the logic of these two authors.

Carr has been much influenced by Collingwood, whom

he describes as "the only British thinker in the present century who has made a serious contribution to the philosophy of history." Carr's book includes such Collingwood-like observations as the following:

> The nineteenth century was, for the intellectuals of Western Europe, a comfortable period exuding confidence and optimism. The facts were on the whole satisfactory; and the inclination to ask and answer awkward questions about them was correspondingly weak. Ranke piously believed that divine providence would take care of the meaning of history if he took care of the facts. . . .[1]

And again:

> The nineteenth-century fetishism of facts was completed and justified by a fetishism of documents. . . . But . . . no document can tell us more than what the author of the document thought—what he thought had happened, what he thought ought to happen or would happen, or perhaps only what he wanted others to think he thought, or even only what he himself thought he thought.[2]

Nevertheless, Carr finds his way back from these iconoclasms not only to a rather conventional view of the historian's craft but also to an orthodox Rankean-Marxist position that ethical judgments of historical events are irrelevant because the events themselves are determined. He does so by means of a most unsatisfactory argument. In the present moment, Carr appears to concede, real choice exists and ethical criteria are therefore pertinent. However, once an event has occurred it should be considered inevitably determined, and one who fails so to consider it must be suspected of wishing it had happened otherwise. As Carr puts the matter:

> . . . plenty of people, who have suffered directly or vicariously from the results of the Bolshevik victory, or still fear its remoter consequences, desire to register their protest against it; and this takes the form, when they read

history, of letting their imagination run riot on all the
more agreeable things that might have happened, and of
being indignant with the historian who goes on quietly
with his job of explaining what did happen and why
their agreeable wish-dreams remain unfulfilled. The
trouble about contemporary history is that people remember *the time when all the options were still open*
[my italics], and find it difficult to adopt the attitude of
the historian, for whom they have been closed by the *fait
accompli*.[3]

With this comment Carr seeks to dispose of what he calls
the "red herring" problem of historical inevitability. But
if in fact I have the freedom to act one way or another,
how can I turn around and assert, the moment after I have
acted, that I had to act the way I did? To borrow for a
moment Carr's own *ad hominem* approach, I am inclined
to think that his position is that of the perennial observer,
who has never devoted his energies to making his "wish-
dreams" real. It cannot be a resting place for someone
called to *making* history as well as writing it.

Sartre's argument, if I understand it correctly, is similar.
Beginning with the assertion that the abstract and sche-
matic character of twentieth-century Marxism made
necessary the creation of existentialism if real human experience were to be grasped in its concreteness, Sartre
nevertheless concludes that as a richer Marxism, faithful to
Marx's own complexity, develops, existentialism will
wither away.

The logic of a Carr or a Sartre appears to me to disin-
tegrate in the face of the twentieth-century practice of revolutionary Marxists themselves. Every successful Marxist
revolutionary has made his bid for power in defiance of
what passed in his day for the "laws of historical development." The Russian Mensheviks were right in contending
that decades of industrial development were necessary be-

fore the Russian proletariat would be large enough to make such a revolution as Marx predicted; but Lenin led the Russian Revolution regardless. The supremacy of will power and endurance—the so-called subjective factor—to all environmental obstacles was so obviously the key factor in the Chinese Revolution that it has become the defining characteristic of "the thought of Mao Tse-tung." And would anyone seriously argue that Fidel Castro's defiant handful in a fishing boat was the inevitable outcome of inexorable historical forces?

The conception of historical causation by Marx (or at least by the later Marx) followed closely Adam Smith's model of the working of the capitalist market. Like the *laissez-faire* entrepreneur, the actor in the Marxist historical drama could not correctly anticipate the outcome of his actions, for that outcome was the unplanned resultant of each actor's false anticipations. But the act of revolution is precisely the ability to take purposeful action with confidence that intended consequences can be achieved. The revolutionary transforms not only an oppressive society but the laws of development of that oppressive society. Despite his invocation of man's future passage from the realm of necessity to the realm of freedom, Marx, I think it is fair to say, assigned this transition to the period after a revolutionary seizure of power, and hence did not fully appreciate the fact that any revolution—at least as it appears to those who take part in it—requires a decision by individual human beings to begin to determine their own destinies at whatever cost.

"At least as it appears to those who take part in it": here is the heart of the matter. I have been trying to show that professional historians, whether Marxist or non-Marxist, tend to view history from the sidelines, to give too little weight to that ethical dimension which is critical only for the man who must make decisions, to regard as historically determined what is merely historically past, and in sum, to do violence to the sense of reality of the historical actor in the present moment. I hope I will not be misunderstood as believing that there are no "historical forces," that historical causation does not exist, that anyone can do anything he wants in history at any time. The point, rather, is that whereas to Marx or Sartre human energy and striving are, as it were, *at the service* of impersonal historical forces, for the man trying to make history such forces are merely matters he must *take into account* in attempting to achieve his self-determined goals. The psychotherapist Viktor Frankl, who himself lived through the concentration camps, reminds us that in that most oppressive of situations men still retained a significant ability to decide what would happen to them. To say the same thing in another way, men can be beasts or brothers at any level of technological development.

How would the work of the historian be different, if man's existential freedom to choose became the historian's point of departure?

The following are some provisional answers.

1. Historians ordinarily assume that history can better be written about events at some distance in the past than about present happenings. No doubt this generalization holds good for certain kinds of events, such as diplomatic events, the sources for which tend to be kept secret until after the passage of many years. But does it apply, for example, to the history of the common man? I think not. Anyone wishing to write the history of the post-World War II civil rights movement could undoubtedly write it better now than five years from now, and better five years

from now than a quarter-century hence. The reason is that the "primary sources" for these events are, by and large, neither written nor secret, but are the memories of individual living persons which will become less accurate and accessible as time goes on.

History in the form of chronicling of the present tends to be considered mere journalism, a debasement of what proper history should be, because the passage of time is assumed to give "perspective." Without wholly discounting this argument, it nevertheless seems to me to depend too much on the assumption that there is a single causal pattern underlying events—a skeleton beneath the living tissue—which will appear stark and clear in retrospective view.

The historian's first duty, I believe, is the sensitive chronicling in depth of the important events of his own lifetime.

2. Whether in writing about the recent or the distant past, the historian suggests to the protagonist of the present new alternatives for action. Much as, with or without the help of therapists, all of us occasionally look back to our individual pasts to find strength for new beginnings, so with or without the help of historians Americans who wish to change their present society have used the past as a source for forgotten alternatives. The past serves us as a means toward that "frequent recurrence to fundamental principles" which the Virginia Bill of Rights advised.

The difference between this use of history and that which follows from a traditional emphasis on causation may be illustrated with reference to the war in Vietnam. The entire American intellectual community has devoted itself, to an extent which must be without precedent, to becoming amateur historians of this conflict. Nevertheless, after all the books and teach-ins the simple question of "Why Vietnam?" remains almost as obscure as in February 1965. An economic explanation of American policy is difficult to demonstrate because American investment in Southeast Asia is relatively slight; but no other coherent hypothesis appears to have been offered. As to the motivation of "the other side," no doubt documents presently unavailable would help somewhat. Yet, to whatever extent Wilfred Burchett is right in his ascription of the origins of the present war to a series of spontaneous local outbreaks in 1957–1959, one suspects that the participants themselves might be hard put to it to provide a definitive causal analysis of the interaction of local grievances, National Liberation Front leadership, and encouragement from Hanoi.

Does this mean that the historian has nothing to offer in Vietnam? or even, in view of the misuse of the Munich analogy by the American government, that a solution might more readily be found if the habit of historical argument could be proscribed? I think not. Where the historian could be helpful, in my opinion, is not by deeper but still inconclusive research into the past, but by projecting alternative scenarios for the future. Considerable experience is available as to the behavior of revolutionary nationalist movements under varying environmental pressures. Without presuming to predict the future, historians might help American policy makers to be more flexible and imaginative by, so to speak, prophesying a variety of outcomes to the present bloodbath. (Howard Zinn's *Vietnam: The Logic of Withdrawal* exemplifies the use of history I have in mind.)

Thus a second, presently unfamiliar task for the historian would be the projection of alternative futures on the basis of the richness of our past experience.

I can delineate the tasks I am recommending to historians more sharply by exemplifying their opposites. Here again, I draw negative examples from radical historians so as to make it clear that the distinctions I propose are not those whereby radicals have traditionally defined themselves.

Some time ago a student of my acquaintance, a member of Students for a Democratic Society, asked me whether I thought he should do graduate work in history. I said I did not know and suggested that John write to several of the young radical historians. He did so, mentioning in his letter to each that I had told him there were others in the field of American history who were much more optimistic than I about "carving out a radical approach to the field that does not get lost in the usual hair-splitting and inconclusiveness to which the profession is prone."

One of John's answers was from a brilliant young scholar whose particular interest is the history of the inarticulate, as in the work of Albert Soboul, George Rudé, and E. P. Thompson abroad. His letter began:

> I think we know about as much about the role of the common man in American history as we would know about Watts if the McCone Commission were our only source. . . . History has been written by elitists who assumed that when the common man acted he did so for irrational reasons, or because he was manipulated in some way. Much of the excitement of the field to me is that all kinds of good things might have happened that we don't know anything about because of the distortions of history as it has been written.

My own quarrel with this argument is not with its contention that history has been distorted but with its hope that the truth can be restored. Let the reader consider any

popular movement of our own day in which he has participated. For instance, take the Mississippi Summer Project
of 1964. Half a dozen good books have already been written about it, one a collection of letters by student volun-
teers, a second narrating in detail a single volunteer's experience, a third in large part composed of documentary
appendices. In addition, the event was exhaustively cov-
ered by press and television. But do any of us who took
part in that adventure seriously imagine that anything
more than fragments of it will ever be set down in com-
municable form? Less than three years after the event, who
now knows where the idea for a Freedom Democratic party
came from or what really happened at the Democratic
party convention at Atlantic City? Considerations such as
these regarding the inevitable inadequacies of contemporary chronicling suggest skepticism about the possibility of
recovering "the history" of popular movements in the
past. A few handbills, perhaps some police records, notices
of meetings from contemporary newspapers, the gossip of
upper-class letter writers, very likely fragmentary tax and
election records: is it not scraps like this that we rely on to
reconstruct what happened? And is material like this not
infinitely less adequate than the documentary record that
is already so inadequate in the case of more recent movements? I know from experience the temptation to fill in
the gaps with personal "wish-dreams," and to present the
result with a spurious air of finality.

John received a second letter from another outstanding
young radical scholar, who said in part:

> I probably disagree with Lynd as to what we can do.
> Politically, neither love nor violence will help us much,
> because we are beyond politics in the sense that this is a
> functionally totalitarian country with a liberal rhetoric,

and reason and exemplary Christian behavior will not alter the politics of those in power. [But] in purely intellectual terms, radicals have much to do and it seems to me that they can define and analyze the nature of the beast we confront on a much higher level of sophistication and precision than we have up to now.

Is this not quibbling while Rome burns? Can it satisfactorily define the scholar's task to be able to say "I told you so" amid the ruins? Should we be content with measuring the dimensions of our prison instead of chipping, however inadequately, against the bars?

What, then, should be the historian's craft and the idea of history?

I have made the assumption that what distinguishes the historian from other social scientists is not that he writes about the past but that he considers things in process of development. "History" and "sociology" are not concerned with different objects; they are different ways of looking at the same object. Hence the historian need not be embarrassed if he concerns himself more with the present and future than with the past.

I have also made the assumption that the historian's business with the future is not to predict but to envision, to say (as Howard Zinn has put it) not what *will* be but what *can* be. The past is ransacked, not for its own sake, but as a source of alternative models of what the future might become.

Implicit in my discussion has been a third idea, that "writing history" does not necessarily involve "being a historian": in other words, that chronicling and envisioning are functions which might be as well or better done by many persons in part of their time than on a full-time basis by a professional few. He who *acts* as well as watches may acquire kinds of knowledge unavailable to him who watches only. (That the converse is also true is, of course, a commonplace.)

To these fundamental delimitations of the historian's role I should like to add two major qualifications.

Human beings, at least those born into Judaeo-Christian cultures, appear to need to formulate a collective past. Presumably it will always be mainly the job of the historian to respond to this need responsibly, that is, in a way that does not do violence either to the facts of the past or to the human beings of the present. Despite the alleged antihistoricism of the New Left, the need for a collective past is felt with particular keenness today by young people. Many rebellious young Americans have profoundly mixed feelings when they confront our country's history. On the one hand, they feel shame and distrust toward Founding Fathers who tolerated slavery, exterminated Indians, and in all their proceedings were disturbingly insensitive to values and life styles other than their own. On the other hand, there is a diffuse sense that the rhetoric of the Revolution and the Civil War spoke then and speaks now to hopes widespread among mankind. Thus in November 1965 Carl Oglesby, then president of Students for a Democratic Society, asked an antiwar demonstration gathered at the Washington Monument what Thomas Jefferson or Thomas Paine would say to President Johnson and McGeorge Bundy about the war in Vietnam. And in August 1966, when the House Un-American Activities Committee subpoenaed antiwar activists, the head of the Free University of New York issued a statement invoking the Green Mountain Boys, and the chairman of the Berkeley Vietnam Day Committee appeared in the hearing chamber in the uniform of an officer of George Washington's army.

The professor of history is among other things the custodian of such memories and dreams.

My second qualification is that in a macrocosmic sense I believe Marxism is correct in its understanding of where humanity has been and is going. Think of it as a backdrop to the stage on which historical protagonists play their self-determined parts. It is nonetheless an essential element in the drama. The historian who does not grasp the fact that mankind, whatever else it is doing, is making an agonized transition from societies based on private property to societies which are not, is in my view out of touch with what is happening in the second half of the twentieth century. I hasten to add that these new societies may not be more humane than those they replace. Still, the interesting question of our time will appear to future historians as that one—namely, Is a humane socialism possible? —rather than that which presently preoccupies the American psyche, Will capitalism or socialism prevail? And from where I stand, this is ground for hope.

NOTES

1. E. H. Carr, *What Is History?* (New York, Alfred A. Knopf, 1962), p. 20.
2. *Ibid.*, pp. 15–16.
3. *Ibid.*, pp. 127–28.

THE NEW

AMERICAN MANDARINS

∽ Marshall Windmiller

"I THINK IT IS NOTEWORTHY," SENATOR
Thomas Dodd of Connecticut told the Senate on October
22, 1965, "that of the 10,000 political scientists teaching in
American universities, only 65 were listed as sponsors of
the National Teach-in Committee, and the great majority
of these were completely unknown juniors."

Dodd then proceeded to read into the *Congressional
Record* a letter sent to the *New York Journal-American* by
a group of academicians who identified themselves as
"scholars and specialists most of whom have devoted much
of their adult lives to study and work in Southeast Asian
affairs." "Included in our number," they said, "are most of
this Nation's small nucleus of specialists on Vietnam." The
letter was an attack on the "distortions of fact and the
emotional allegations of a small but vociferous group of
fellow university teachers" who had signed advertisements
and petitions protesting President Johnson's policies in
Vietnam. "We must first observe," they said, "that those
who have signed advertisements and petitions represent a

(110)

very small proportion of all university professors. Further, the petition signers include disproportionally fewer scholars in the fields of government, international relations, and Asian studies."[1]

A similar point was made by Rodger Swearingen, Professor of International Relations at the University of Southern California, in an article published in the *National Observer* (September 19, 1966) and widely distributed by the United States Information Agency. Analyzing the signatures on two protest advertisements which had appeared in the *New York Times,* Swearingen concluded: "1. That the signers of these two ads constitute an extremely small percentage of the academic community and should not be regarded as a representative cross section. 2. That the overwhelming majority of these critics are from fields or specialties where no training, experience, knowledge or perspective on foreign policy, communism, or Vietnam is either required or assumed. . . . 3. That the recognized U.S. scholars on foreign policy, the Soviet Union, Communist China, Southeast Asia, communism, and American security problems at the major U.S. centers are conspicuously absent from the roster of critics."

My own observations and those of others who have been active in the teach-in movement around the country confirm the conclusions of Professor Swearingen and Senator Dodd: only a few political scientists and international relations and area specialists have taken a public position in opposition to Vietnam policy. A small but distingushed minority has spoken out, but in general, the academic specialists whom one would expect to be best informed on the problem have either remained silent or have supported the administration.[2]

Senator Dodd, Rodger Swearingen, and the *Journal-American* letter signers explain this phenomenon by suggesting that expert knowledge leads to support of the Johnson policies, and that criticism is essentially a function of ignorance. Max Lerner has said flatly:

> I have taken no poll but I have traveled on many campuses . . . and I find the scholars close to Asian studies support the President because they know what would happen in Asia if America were to withdraw. The men in the political studies also . . . support him because they know something about the ways of Communist expansionism. The men in the military studies support him because they know this is a minor war compared to what we would have to wage if it failed. . . . If I am right, then my guess is that there is an inverse relation between militancy or hostility to the President's policy and closeness to the subject matter.[3]

Since there are many learned books and articles on Vietnam by qualified experts who are critical of the Johnson policies in Vietnam, it is not feasible to argue that expert knowledge leads to support of the administration.[4] What then is the explanation for the general scarcity of specialists in the protest movement? Why is there so little dissent among the experts who presumably are best qualified to understand the Vietnam war, its consequences, and its dangers?

One explanation derives from the relationship of the subject matter to the professional interests of the specialist. When a mathematician, for example, takes a controversial position on a matter of foreign policy, he does not put his professional reputation on the line. His colleagues may disagree with him, but they will not look upon his political views as affecting his competence as a mathematician. But this is clearly not the case with a political scientist or an area specialist. When he comes out against a government policy he runs the risk of being regarded as incompetent, not only by other members of the profession who happen to support the policy but also by those who believe that professional objectivity requires that the scholar remain aloof, uncommitted, and impartial. The political scientist clearly risks his career when he takes a stand on a political matter, while other academicians get a relatively free ride.

But there is more to it than that. In recent years the political scientists and the international relations specialists have not only avoided taking open stands on policy issues; they have also changed the nature of their discipline to such an extent that even the analysis of policy alternatives is regarded as less and less appropriate to the scholarly enterprise.

It was not always that way. The man who is generally regarded as the father of American political science is John William Burgess, who founded the Department of Political Science at Columbia in 1880. Burgess got into the field as a result of his experience as a Union soldier in the Civil War. He was appalled by the slaughter, and took a vow on the battlefield to devote his life from then on to a search for knowledge that would put an end to war. Burgess wrote that what he intended at Columbia "was to establish an institution of pacifist propaganda, genuine, not sham, based upon a correct knowledge of what nature and reason required."[5]

Today the spirit of John William Burgess is hardly to be found in any political science department in the country. Neither pacifism nor propaganda is respectable. Instead the main preoccupation of the profession is in transforming the study of politics into a science. Value judgments are regarded as unprofessional. Value-oriented concern about policy is looked upon as a relic of the prescientific age. Thus the political theorist Stanley Hoffman writes that "the creation of departments of government in this country has frequently come from a desire for reform and therapy; political science grew largely out of a curative urge and an engineering itch—but it outgrew them too."[6] And J. David Singer, referring to history and international relations, says that "each discipline seems destined to pass through a number of states from the normative and the intuitively descriptive to the operational and scientific." He also says that international relations is "a field of study too important to be dealt with in the same artistic and intuitive fashion as literature, religion, or art."[7]

Thus reform, therapy, the curative urge, the engineering itch, norms, and intuition are all curiosities of a by-gone age, like silent movies and beaded fringe. They have been outgrown, and science is taking their place.

With science come gadgets. A characteristic of the most advanced physical sciences is the development of elaborate apparatus for observation and measurement. Mathematics and statistics are also key tools. Thus the behavioral scientist Heinz Eulau argues that "the susceptibility of problems in political science, as in other disciplines, is always conditioned by the state and development of research technology." "I do not want to labor it," he adds testily, "but I find a peculiar line of reasoning in a rather unreasonable resistance to the kind of research training which, I think, a political science deserving of its name requires. If we have to learn calculus and probability theory, content analysis, factor analysis and what not, questionnaire construction and computer work, so the reasoning goes, we might as well drop politics and take up physics. Few would admit to being too stupid to study mathematics or statistics as a requisite for theoretical and empirical work in political science."[8]

I do not mean to suggest that this preoccupation with science has produced nothing of value, or that among those

who are working to construct a science of politics there is
no one who takes stands on values and policies. Neither
would I suggest that all of the reformers, therapists, and
engineers with the curative urge have been banished from
the profession. But I would argue that they and their concerns have been relegated to the background as the profession has "outgrown" them.

A recent study of the American Political Science Association reveals contradictory attitudes on these questions
among the members. A random sample was asked a series
of questions about matters presumed to be of pressing concern to the profession, such as the status of behavioral science, the use of technical gadgets, and the study of policy
questions. The investigators found a remarkable unwillingness to take a stand. "To a rather surprising degree,"
they concluded, "American political scientists do not take
a position on these issues; on the other hand, they seem
not to be very firmly committed on the positions they do
take."[9] One question relating to public policy issues
seemed to be an exception to this, however. The following
statement elicited these responses:

> By and large, political scientists do not devote enough
> attention to contemporary public policy matters.

Strongly agree	7.7
Agree	26.9
Can't say	9.7
Disagree	47.3
Strongly disagree	8.4

These data suggest that a majority of the political scientists
believe that the profession still devotes enough, if not too
much, attention to these matters. Uncertain on other matters, they seem pretty convinced about this, despite their

general aloofness from the Vietnam debate and other issues raised by the Johnson foreign policy.

Another cause of the failure of professional students of international politics to dissent from American policy is the decline, which began during the 1950s, of the school of political thought known variously as the "idealist" or "utopian" school. These were the thinkers and statesmen who had argued for the establishment of international security organizations like the League of Nations and the United Nations, and through such organizations had sought to institutionalize on a worldwide basis a set of moral and legal principles.

It is one of the ironies of history that the two men most responsible for discrediting this school of thought are now among the leading dissenters against United States policy in Vietnam, George F. Kennan and Hans J. Morgenthau. From positions of considerable influence inside or on the periphery of the Truman administration, these men began an attack on "legalism-moralism" and "utopianism" which has profoundly influenced the academy for over fifteen years. *In American Diplomacy 1900-1950,* published in 1951, Kennan wrote:

> . . . I see the most serious fault of our past policy formulation to lie in something that I might call the legalistic-moralistic approach to international problems. This approach runs like a red skein through our foreign policy of the last fifty years. It has in it something of the old emphasis on arbitration treaties, something of the Hague Conferences and schemes for universal disarmament, something of the more ambitious American concepts of the role of international law, something of the League of Nations and the United Nations, something of the Kellogg Pact, something of the idea of a universal "Article 51" pact, something of the belief in World Law and World Government. But it is none of these, entirely. Let me try to describe it.

It is the belief that it should be possible to suppress the chaotic and dangerous aspirations of governments in the international field by the acceptance of some system of legal rules and restraints. . . .

But there is a greater deficiency still that I should like to mention before I close. That is the inevitable association of legalistic ideas with moralistic ones: the carrying-over into the affairs of states of the concepts of right and wrong, the assumption that state behavior is a fit subject for moral judgment.[10]

And in *Realities of American Foreign Policy,* Kennan wrote in 1954:

. . . when we return to the relations between governments, I think we are entitled to say that international life would be quieter and more comfortable, that there would be less of misunderstanding, and that it would be easier to clear away such conflicts as do arise, if there were less of sentimentality, less eagerness to be morally impressive, a greater willingness to admit that we Americans, like everyone else, are only people. . . .[11]

Neither Kennan nor Morgenthau argued that morality was unimportant or that statesmen could abandon ethical judgments altogether.[12] But the consequence of their attack on the idealists was that the professional students of international relations became preoccupied with the concepts that were central to *realpolitik,* namely power and national interest. It became unfashionable and even naive to emphasize morality, legality, and the interests of mankind. Academic research turned away from the task of finding out how to save the world to the task of how to preserve and enhance the power and national interests of the United States. There was, as Kennan had desired, "less eagerness to be morally impressive," and the ground was prepared for a Herman Kahn to say about the war in Vietnam:

On the whole, people in this country are not used to doing dirty tricks and playing rough. It doesn't come naturally to most of us, and it isn't pleasant. But, in this kind of war, one's standards are almost automatically going to be lower than in a normal set-piece battle. And I believe even Lincoln put some thousands of people in jail and suspended habeas corpus during the Civil War.

I don't want to be on the side of saying, "Let's be rough." I'm on the other side, typically. But, in this kind of war, you must either drop your standards or get out.[13]

It was during the period of the debate over legalism-moralism that another idea began to develop. It was the notion that the formulation of foreign policy ought to be professionalized by isolating it from the pressures of public opinion and turning it over to a properly trained elite. Here again there is irony, for two of the proponents of this notion, George Kennan and Walter Lippman, have lately been appealing to public opinion in the hope of bringing pressure to change American policy in Southeast Asia.

The elitism that has always been present among specialists in foreign affairs has been greatly strengthened by the widespread awareness of the growing complexity of world affairs. Diplomacy now requires expert knowledge in difficult subjects like nuclear testing and development economics. How can the general public be expected to understand these complicated issues? the elitists ask. How can the ordinary man appraise the nature of the threat posed by China when information about China's nuclear capability and our own capacity to respond must be kept secret? Is it not a matter for experts to decide whether a preventive war against China is the best way to serve the national interest of the United States?

One of the most frank of the elitists is Ithiel de Sola Pool, a political scientist at the Massachusetts Institute of

Technology. He minces no words in an article published
in the journal of the International Studies Association:

> The social sciences can be described as the new hu-
> manities of the Twentieth Century. They have the same
> relationship to the training of mandarins of the Twen-
> tieth Century that the humanities have always had to the
> training of mandarins in the past. In the past when one
> wanted to educate a prince, or policy-maker, or civil
> servant to cope with his job, one taught him Latin,
> philosophy, history, literature—most of which had very
> little obvious relationship to what he was going to do.
> Yet in some way, these disciplines were supposed to
> enable him better to understand human affairs. This
> training worked to a considerable degree. Today, by
> means of the social sciences we are able to give him an
> even better tool for understanding the world around
> him. The day of philosophy, literature, etc., is not over.
> They have their value. But there are a great many things
> we have learned better to understand by psychology, by
> sociology, by systems analysis, by political science. Such
> knowledge is important to the mandarins of the future
> for it is by knowledge that men of power are humanized
> and civilized. They need a way of perceiving the conse-
> quences of what they do if the actions are not to be
> brutal, stupid, bureaucratic but rather intelligent and
> humane. The only hope for humane government in the
> future is through the extensive use of the social sciences
> by government.[14]

It is not surprising that a would-be teacher of American
mandarins should have an attachment for secret organizations, for the persistence of the democratic ideal makes it
difficult to try to sell mandarinism openly. "The CIA,"
writes Pool, "as its name implies, should be the central
social research organization to enable the Federal government to understand the societies and cultures of the
world. The fact that it uses as little social science as it does
is deplorable. We should be demanding that the CIA use
us more."[15]

Among the academic specialists in world affairs, then, there has been on the one hand a trend toward an "objective" science from which values allegedly have been expunged, and on the other hand a movement toward the development of a mandarin elite of social scientists who would train the princes and determine the direction of public policy. The fact is that this mandarin elite of political scientists have *not* produced a "value-free" discipline. Rather they have become the intellectual defenders of a particular value, or what they treat as a value, namely power. They have come to esteem power for its own sake, and have relegated the traditional values of the academy to positions of secondary importance. They have transformed a means into an end. They have become the computerized disciples of Niccolò Machiavelli.

If the academy values truth, then it must surely abhor deception, for deception is the enemy of truth. The extent to which the academy is involved in deception must then be an indicator of the strength of its dedication to truth. And in the field of international relations the involvement is extensive.

Much of this is due to the close relationship that the international relations specialists have had with those intelligence agencies where deception is a valued tool. This relationship was established during World War II when the Office of Strategic Services (OSS) scoured the universities for area specialists who might help them cope with the problems of intelligence-gathering in remote, little-known areas of the world. The result is vividly described by John Gange, President of the International Studies Association in 1965. "The Office of Strategic Services," says Gange, ". . . was like a big university faculty in many respects—

sometimes, staff meetings were just like faculty meetings. Other scholars served in many other government agencies concerned with foreign affairs."[16]

This situation, so easy to excuse during a war begun with a sneak attack on United States soil, has continued to the present day. The close relationship between the academy and the CIA was described by Admiral William F. Raborn when he was director of that agency:

> . . . in actual numbers we could easily staff the faculty of a university with our experts. In a way, we do. Many of those who leave us join the faculties of universities and colleges. Some of our personnel take leave of absence to teach and renew their contacts in the academic world. I suppose this is only fair; our energetic recruiting effort not only looks for the best young graduate students we can find, but also picks up a few professors from time to time.[17]

The State Department also has its intelligence agency, the Bureau of Intelligence and Research, and the academic ties to it may be even more extensive than those to the CIA. William J. Crockett, Deputy Under-Secretary for Administration, said in June 1966:

> The colleges and universities provide us with a rich body of information about many subjects, countries, and people through special research studies prepared for many clients and purposes. For example, the United States Government is spending $30 million this year on foreign affairs studies in American universities.
>
> Here in the Department, in our Office of External Research, we have on file information on more than 5,000 foreign affairs studies now underway in American universities. Our foreign affairs documentation center lends out to State Department officers and to officers of other agencies 400 unpublished academic papers each month. The Department receives each month over 200 new academic papers.[18]

Perhaps the most dramatic example of the connection between the intelligence community and the academy came to light in February 1967, when the press revealed that the executive director, Evron M. Kirkpatrick, and the treasurer, Max Kampelman, of the American Political Science Association, were also president and vice-president respectively of a CIA-funded research organization called Operations and Policy Research, Inc. The executive director is an appointed official, paid full time; the treasurer is elected annually and receives no pay.

The disclosure of CIA connections produced an immediate uproar. Twelve members of the Department of Political Science at the University of Hawaii circulated a letter throughout the profession. Concerned about the damage to the image of American political scientists abroad, they said that "two individuals took it upon themselves to endanger an entire profession, by playing roles which, if discovered, could only further undermine overseas confidence in American political science." They demanded the immediate resignation of Kirkpatrick and Kampelman.

Three days after the original story broke in the press, the president of the Association, Robert Dahl, appointed a committee of four past APSA presidents to investigate. They reported on March 30: "The American Political Science Association has received no funds directly from any intelligence agency of the government, nor has it carried on any activities for any intelligence agency of government." What about indirect funds? The report said: "The Association has received no funds indirectly from any intelligence agency of government, with one possible exception. The Asia Foundation stated on March 21, 1967, that it had been the recipient of money from foundations named as conduits for CIA funds. The APSA has received grants from the Asia Foundation. . . ." Possible exception indeed! The Asia Foundation was originally started as the Committee for a Free Asia, Inc., and has always been a CIA front well known to Asian specialists.

The committee concluded by acknowledging, "on behalf of the membership of our organization, the great services which both Kirkpatrick and Kampelman have rendered to the American Political Science Association." The APSA executive committee went a step further. "We wish to record," they said, "our recognition of the dedication and services of these two men to the Association in the past and our full confidence in the value of their future services."

All of this was communicated to the APSA membership in a letter from the executive committee dated April 20, 1967. It was not a very informative letter. Not only did it leave many questions unanswered about Operations and Policy Research, Inc. and how Kirkpatrick and Kampelman spent its CIA money, but it also tried to create the impression that the only important question at issue was whether the Association itself had been turned into a CIA front.

It is, of course, conceivable that political scientists who are accustomed to analyzing the world with computers and punched cards might fail to perceive that extraordinary power could be wielded by a full-time bureaucrat who had CIA monies to distribute to other political scientists. It is also possible that the APSA executive committee forgot that Kirkpatrick came to them after long service in the intelligence community, where he was undoubtedly familiar with techniques of organizational manipulation. But it is more likely that the leaders of the organization sought to shape the attitudes of the members by limiting the amount of information they received. The elitists within the APSA were dealing with their own members just as the political scientists would deal with the general public. At any rate, the executive committee manifested no real concern about the danger to the integrity of their organization from the intelligence connections of two of their officers.

I would like to relate a personal experience which I believe is relevant in this context. Just prior to the APSA's annual meeting in Washington in September 1965, the Association allowed the Department of State to circularize its membership with an invitation to come a day early to receive a special, top-level, background briefing on Vietnam, the Dominican Republic, and the United Nations. There was nothing on the Association's own program to balance what was clearly an effort to sell President Johnson's foreign policy to the membership. Ultimately about seven hundred political scientists went to the State Department auditorium and heard Walt W. Rostow, William Bundy, and others.

When I received the invitation, I urged the Inter-University Committee for Debate on Foreign Policy to organize a complementary briefing to present some facts which I felt sure the State Department would not adequately cover. They agreed, I was put in charge, and I approached Kirkpatrick's office to arrange for a room in the convention hotel. I was told that we could not have such a room because the Association would, in that case, have to give a room to the State Department which was at the moment, they said, pressuring them for time on the official program. I was given no cooperation, and was forced to schedule our briefing in another hotel, where it was not well attended. Of four speakers who had agreed to speak, two were newspaper correspondents based in Washington. Just before the program, one was ordered by his paper not to appear, and the other simply didn't show up. He explained later that he was sent on assignment suddenly. Meanwhile, the APSA gave in to State Department pressure and called a full-scale meeting to hear Secretary of State Dean Rusk. The speech Rusk gave was the one in which he paid tribute to the "gallant" intelligence agents who were serving their country by fighting "a tough struggle going on in the back alleys all over the world."

The ties between the government and the academy, then, are many and subtle. I do not want to suggest that all of them are necessarily bad or corrupting. Neither would I argue that the government should not be allowed to recruit its personnel from the universities or draw on the knowledge that is developed there. I am suggesting, however, that the line which separates the government from the academy is becoming blurred, and that specialists in international affairs are not only failing to distinguish between the aims of the government and the aims of the academy, but are also allowing themselves to be made over into instruments of the state.

Not all of this involves deliberate deception. But when scholars accept secret contracts, go on secret missions, ask questions abroad in behalf of intelligence agencies, refuse to discuss the purposes for which the government funded their research, then that is both deception and subversion of the academic tradition. Unfortunately, these are common practices in the fields of political science and international relations.

More subtle, but equally damaging to the academy, is the willingness of specialists to lend themselves to particular policy aims of government without questioning those aims. The best example concerns the scandal surrounding

"Project Camelot," a research project set up by the Department of the Army to find out how to detect revolutions in their early stages and put them down before they get out of hand.

It should not require a Ph.D. from MIT to be able to see that to serve Project Camelot was to take a value-laden political position and to become an accomplice to counter-revolution. Yet many academic specialists were eager to participate and were outraged when the project was ultimately canceled after its true purposes had been exposed in Chile. While there was some general discussion about how Camelot damaged the profession, about the only thing the political scientists did was appoint an ad hoc committee on professional ethics.[19] The problem then, as many specialists see it, is not whether the policies of the American government are worthy of support, but how they can get government money for research without bad publicity that will compromise them abroad.

All of this is clearly related to the trend in the academy away from teaching and toward research. Teaching undergraduate courses in political science and international relations is a low-prestige assignment in the profession. The greatest status comes from devoting full time to research. Supervising graduate students is acceptable because it is stimulating, and because the instructor can profit from the student's research. But the idea of educating citizens for their role in a democracy has little appeal to most political scientists, largely because democracy itself has lost its appeal to many of them.

It is in large measure the failure of the international relations professionals, both to educate the undergraduates and to face up to moral questions raised by American foreign policy, that has given rise to the teach-ins and various extramural "experimental" and "freedom" colleges. Because professionals would not fill an obvious need, amateurs and academicians from other disciplines have moved in. The result has not always been scholarly or disciplined, and sometimes the teach-ins have superficially seemed more akin to a circus than to the meetings of learned societies. This quality of the May 1965 teach-in at Berkeley prompted Robert Scalapino, the leading academic defender of President Johnson's Vietnam policies, to issue the following statement:

> The May 21 meeting on the Berkeley campus is symbolic of the new anti-intellectualism that is gaining strength today. A few individuals, most of whom would not dream of treating their own disciplines in this cavalier fashion, have sponsored a rigged meeting in which various ideologies and entertainers are going to enlighten us on Vietnam. Only a handful of the performers have ever been to Vietnam, or made any serious study of its problems. . . . They urged us to appear with ratios of up to 8 to 1 against us. . . . Can we be blamed if we did not want to lend our names and reputations to that effort? This travesty should be repudiated by all true scholars irrespective of their views on Vietnam. It can only damage the reputation of Berkeley as an institution of higher learning.[20]

This criticism is fairly typical of much that has been leveled against the teach-ins by the political science establishment. The teach-ins are bad, they say, because not all of the participants are experts, because the speakers have not been to Vietnam, because the opponents of the administration outnumber the supporters, and because the meetings do not observe the decorum customary at academic meetings.

Many political scientists refuse to recognize that the

teach-ins came into being as a result of the failure of the experts to confront the moral issues of American foreign policy in the classroom. The hostility that these experts sometimes encounter when they do participate in teach-ins is frequently due to their attempts to patronize their audiences with absurd assertions like the suggestion that one cannot evaluate the Vietnam war without having been there personally. As for the problem of supporters of the administration being outnumbered, there are good reasons for that. Qualified speakers who are willing to defend the Johnson policy in a fair debate are extremely rare, as program arrangers all over the country will testify. Nevertheless, many teach-in organizers have gone out of their way to see that the administration point of view is expressed, only to meet with a response like that of Professor Scalapino. It is no wonder, then, that Staughton Lynd of the Yale history faculty would reply to the Berkeley political scientist with some emotion:

> You say that no self-respecting intellectual would attend this meeting. The entire educational world looks back now on those few professors who protested what was happening in Nazi Germany with gratitude. And I predict that some day the entire academic community of this country will look back on the few professors who have publicly protested our Vietnam policy and say, "They kept the spirit of truth alive."[21]

While the professionals may never thank the teach-in professors for keeping "the spirit of truth alive," a lot of young people will have learned from the teach-ins a great deal, not only about Vietnam, but also about elitism and the distribution of power in America.

It is one thing to explain, as I have tried to do in this essay, why so many political scientists and international relations specialists actively or passively support the counterrevolutionary thrust of United States foreign policy as manifested in Vietnam and the Dominican Republic, and why they have failed to confront the moral issues posed by American power. It is more difficult to propose reforms. Hard questions must be answered. For example, how can expensive social science research be financed, if not by the government? Private foundations (those that are still genuinely private) cannot handle it all. Isn't intelligencegathering a necessary function of government and don't we want ours to have good information based on the best research? Should academics do research for the government only when they agree with its policies? But if they do this, aren't they politicizing scholarship beyond any claim to impartiality?

These questions can be answered properly only within the context of an analysis of American political institutions. In my opinion these institutions, particularly the Congress and the parties, need a fundamental overhauling which it is outside the scope of this essay to describe. Thus I cannot make detailed proposals, but can only suggest some general guidelines for the international relations specialists that might be considered during the immediate period of crisis in the academy.

First, we must get military and intelligence research off the campuses and into specialized institutions like the RAND Corporation. If scholars want to work for the military-industrial complex they should not do it in the academy. Under no circumstances should secret research be done on the campuses, nor should the academy be used as a cover for intelligence work abroad.

Second, we must press for legislation that will finance research and teaching that is independent of the intelligence and military services. The International Education Act passed, but not funded, by the Congress in 1966 is a step in the right direction. It will be administered by the Secretary of Health, Education and Welfare, not the State or Defense Department. We should insist that adequate funds be made available for the loyal academic opposition. Establishment supporters who criticize the teach-ins as lacking in balance thereby assert that balance is theoretically possible. Unless they propose to enforce a mandarin orthodoxy, they should make every effort to achieve a balanced academy by seeing to it that the opponents of a predominantly military and· counterrevolutionary foreign policy have the wherewithal to pursue their scholarly studies.

Third, we must re-examine our value assumptions and theories of government. What values should our foreign policy be designed to defend? What do we mean by "democracy," "pluralism," and "representative government," and can we protect them when we support authoritarian regimes abroad? How can this country justify its consumption of a disproportionally large share of the world's wealth, and if it can't be justified, what should we do about it?

Fourth, we must dedicate more of our resources in money and talent to the art of teaching. We must combat anti-intellectualism by making learning relevant, stimulating, and valuable. We must give as much attention to the dissemination of knowledge as we do to its acquisition, and we must carry our teaching off the campus in order to help close the gap between specialized knowledge and public opinion. We must work to improve the quality of the discussion of international affairs in the mass media of communication.

I make these suggestions, not for the mandarins of the American Political Science Association who will surely ignore them, but for the young people just entering the profession. The teach-ins have given many of them some insight into what the academy might become, and it will be up to them to forge it into an instrument that can make power the servant of truth.

N O T E S

1. "Academic Support for our Vietnam Policy," *Congressional Record*—Senate, 89th Cong., 1st Sess., November 15, 1965, p. A6644.
2. Among the academic political scientists, experts on international law, and Asian area specialists who have taken public positions in opposition to President Johnson's policies in Vietnam are the following well-known individuals: Robert Dahl, Sterling Professor of Political Science, Yale; John H. Herz, Professor of International Relations, City University of New York; Stanley Hoffmann, Professor of International Law, Harvard; George M. Kahin, Director of Southeast Asia Area Studies, Cornell; Daniel Lev, Center for Southeast Asia Studies, University of California, Berkeley; Stanley Millet, Professor of Government, Briarcliff College; Hans Morgenthau, Director, Center for the Study of American Foreign and Military Policy, University of Chicago; Franz Schurmann, Director, Center for Chinese Studies, University of California, Berkeley; Mary C. Wright, Professor of Chinese History, Yale; Quincy Wright, Professor of International Law, University of Chicago.
3. U.S. Senate, Committee on the Judiciary, Subcommittee to Investigate the Administration of the Internal Security Act and Other Internal Security Laws, 89th Cong., 1st Sess., *The Anti-Vietnam Agitation and the Teach-in Movement*, 1965, Committee Print, p. viii.
4. To mention only three: George M. Kahin and John W. Lewis, *The United States in Vietnam*, (New York, Dial Press, 1967). Don R. Larson and Arthur Larson, *Vietnam and Beyond* (Durham, N.C., Duke University Press, 1965). Franz Schurmann, Peter Dale Scott, and Reginald Zelnik, *The Politics*

of Escalation in Vietnam (New York, Fawcett World Library, 1966).

5. "Political Science Dinner," Columbia University Quarterly, Vol. 22 (December 1930), p. 382.

6. Stanley Hoffmann, ed., Contemporary Theory in International Relations (Englewood Cliffs, N.J., Prentice-Hall, Inc., 1960), p. 10.

7. J. David Singer, ed., Human Behavior and International Politics (Chicago, Rand McNally & Co., 1965), pp. 1–2.

8. Heinz Eulau, "Segments of Political Science Most Susceptible to Behavioristic Treatment," in James C. Charlesworth, ed. The Limits of Behavioralism in Political Science (Philadelphia, American Academy of Political and Social Science, 1962), p. 41.

9. Albert Somit and Joseph Tanenhaus, American Political Science, A Profile of a Discipline (New York, Atherton Press, 1964), pp. 13–18.

10. George F. Kennan, American Diplomacy 1900–1950 (Chicago, University of Chicago Press, 1951), pp. 95, 100.

11. George F. Kennan, Realities of American Foreign Policy Princeton, Princeton University Press, 1954), p. 50.

12. Morgenthau wrote: "The contest between utopianism and realism is not tantamount to a contest between principle and expediency, morality and immorality, although some spokesmen for the former would like to have it that way. The contest is rather between one type of political morality and another type of political morality, one taking as its standard universal moral principles abstractly formulated, the other weighing these principles against the moral requirements of concrete political action, their relative merit to be decided by a prudent evaluation of the political consequences to which they are likely to lead." Hans J. Morgenthau, "Another 'Great Debate': The National Interest of the United States," American Political Science Review, Vol. 46 (December 1952), p. 988.

13. "Thoughts on How to Fight the War in Vietnam," interview with Herman Kahn, War/Peace Report, Vol. 5 (July 1965), p. 10. It should be noted that Mr. Kahn does not favor getting out.

14. Ithiel de Sola Pool, "The Necessity for Social Scientists Doing Research for Governments," Background, Vol. 10 (August 1966), p. 111. An interesting description of the mandarin system in China can be found in Franz H. Michael and George E. Taylor, The Far East in the Modern World (New York, Holt, Rinehart & Winston, 1956), pp. 23, 28: "Chinese society in imperial times was dominated by an upper class of educated men, the scholar-gentry, the so-called shen-shih. . . . The members of the scholar-gentry held a monopoly

of official positions; no one outside this group could be appointed. Office-holding was a source of authority and wealth, but at any one time only a small proportion of the gentry was in office. The bulk of the gentry carried out, on a quasi-official basis, the management of local affairs. . . .

"Membership in the scholar-gentry depended on educational qualifications. . . . During the last centuries of imperial China the government established an examination system by which it set up formal standards for educational achievements. Successful candidates in the examination were granted academic degrees which entitled them to the privileges of membership in the scholar-gentry. The scholar-gentry were thus a certified educated group. . . .

"Descriptions of the Chinese examination system have often put considerable emphasis on the fact that any intelligent farm boy could be admitted to the examination and therefore had a chance to rise to the highest position in the land. In practice the selection was limited because success in the examinations depended on an expensive and lengthy education to which the candidate had to dedicate all his time from early youth. While examinations were public, education was private, and only those with means could provide teachers and books for their sons. . . .

"There was . . . a marginal group of would-be gentry composed of aspiring scholars and of candidates for the examinations. This group of non-certified scholars shared some of the functions—such as teaching—and even some of the prestige of the scholar-gentry. But they shone only in reflected glory; they spent their lives in the scramble for degrees because it was only by acquiring degrees that they could enjoy the full status and great advantages of the scholar-gentry."

15. Ithiel de Sola Pool, *op. cit.,* p. 114. Political studies at MIT have been heavily financed by and involved with the CIA. Pool also helped form the Simulmatics Corporation designed to facilitate the manipulation of electorates by means of computerized analyses of voting behavior. The Simulmatics analysis allegedly helped the Kennedy family decide how to treat the religious issue in 1960. See Thomas B. Morgan, "The People-Machine," *Harper's,* Vol. 222 (January 1961), pp. 53–57.

16. John Gange, "The New Intelligence Requirements: Introduction," *Background,* Vol. 9 (November 1965), p. 117.

17. "What's 'CIA'?" interview with Admiral William F. Raborn, *U.S. News and World Report,* July 18, 1966, p. 80.

18. William J. Crockett, "Two-Way Communication with the Educational Community," *Department of State Bulletin,* Vol. 55 (July 18, 1966), pp. 73–74.

19. It was scheduled to report in September 1967 "on criteria to be applied to the professional activities of political scientists." *American Political Science Review,* Vol. 60 (December 1966), p. 1079. For some discussion of the issues raised by Project Camelot, see *Background,* Vol. 10 (August 1966), and U.S. House of Representatives, Committee on Foreign Affairs, Subcommittee on International Organizations and Movements, 89th Cong., 1st Sess., Report No. 4, *Behavioral Sciences and the National Security,* 1965, Committee Print.

20. U.S. Senate, Committee on the Judiciary, Subcommittee to Investigate the Administration of the Internal Security Act . . . , *op. cit.,* p. 25.

21. Norman Mailer et al., *We Accuse* (Berkeley, Calif., Diablo Press, 1965), pp. 153–54.

WORLD

REVOLUTION AND THE

SCIENCE OF MAN

∾ Kathleen Gough

> *You, who are so liberal and so humane, who*
> *have such an exaggerated adoration of culture*
> *that it verges on affectation, you pretend to for-*
> *get that you own colonies and that in them men*
> *are massacred in your name.*

> —Jean-Paul Sartre, Preface to *The Wretched*
> *of the Earth* by Frantz Fanon[1]

SINCE EARLY 1965, UNITED STATES MILI-
tary forces have been responsible for exterminating large
numbers of people in Vietnam. Both the political circumstances of the Vietnam war and the peculiar weapons used
in it make clear that this has been no conflict between
nations of comparable strength. It has been an attempt
by a great industrial power to impose a native tyranny on a
small, preindustrial nation in defiance of international law.

By January 1967 about a quarter of a million children had been killed and over a million burned or otherwise maimed for life.[2]

A naive observer might have expected that anthropologists, among whom respect for human life, tolerance of cultural differences, and equal regard for races are axiomatic, would have risen to condemn this slaughter collectively and uncompromisingly. This did not happen. Many anthropologists have signed public protests, and some have taken part in teach-ins. One or two anthropologists who had worked in Vietnam added their voices and wrote up their research,[3] and at least one visited Saigon independently and interviewed American intelligence agents. Significantly, this study was published in liberal and left-wing journals,[4] not in the *American Anthropologist*. It was not until November 1966 that the American Anthropological Association, at its annual business meeting, passed a resolution that condemned "the use of napalm, chemical defoliants, harmful gases, bombing, the torture and killing of political prisoners and prisoners of war, and the intentional or deliberate policies of genocide or forced transportation of populations." It asked that "all governments" put an end to their use at once and "proceed as rapidly as possible to a peaceful settlement of the war in Vietnam."

The Vietnam resolution had, however, a history that illustrates some of the conflicts and strained loyalties among anthropologists. It came from a small number of socialists and left-wing liberals whose views cannot be called representative of the Association at large. Its introduction was opposed by the president-elect and by a majority of the executive board. The chairman felt obliged to judge the resolution "political," and hence out of order, since the Association's stated purpose is "to advance the science of anthropology and to further the professional interests of American anthropologists."[5] A hubbub ensued at the conference in which the resolution was salvaged when one member suddenly proclaimed, "Genocide is not in the professional interests of anthropologists!" This allowed the proponent to cite previous "political" resolutions passed by the anthropologists on such subjects as racial equality, nuclear weapons, and the lives and welfare of aboriginal peoples. A motion to overrule the chair then passed by a narrow margin. Amendments were next introduced that removed an allegation that the United States was infringing international law by using forbidden weapons, and transferred responsibility for the war from the United States government to "all governments." The amended resolution was passed by a large majority, some of whom later said it was the strongest, and others the weakest, that they could hope for. The proceedings showed that under pressure, most anthropologists are willing to put their profession on record as opposed to mass slaughter. But most are evidently unwilling to condemn their own government.

Why this ethical ambiguity among anthropologists, and why their doubts whether the life or death of a Southeast Asian people has anything to do with them, in their professional capacity, at all?

One answer is that there have been too many massacres in the past thirty years for anthropologists, as a profession, to take positions on each of them. If anthropologists discussed and lobbied against every atrocity, they would have no time for research and would not be anthropologists. This is a serious argument, as anyone knows who has tried to carry on his own particular work side by side with action against the war in Vietnam.

Even so, anthropologists do afford time for relatively trivial pursuits. Each of their annual conferences presents several hundred highly specialized papers; and their business meetings are filled with tedious discussions of budget problems and of the numbers of words and pages their journals devote to various kinds of book reviews. Some of this time, surely, could be set aside to discuss issues of national and international significance, instead of having these issues crammed into the last ten minutes of the business meeting and the first ten minutes of the cocktail hour. Anthropological journals are full of articles on such very limited subjects as, for example, prescriptive marriage systems, kinship terms, or the Tzental words for "firewood." Such topics are of course legitimate, even fascinating, in their own right or as illustrations of new research methods. However, they bypass the most crucial problems of world society. Cumulatively, they also evade a central question: Who is to evaluate and suggest guidelines for human society, if not those who study it? It is as though the more we study the world's cultures, the less capable we feel of making judgments as citizens; certainly, the less able to speak or act collectively on the basis of our knowledge.

This partial paralysis results, I think, from the way in which, over time, the social settings of anthropologists have affected their research problems, theories, and conceptions of social responsibility.

The roots of modern anthropology can be traced back to the humanist visions of such writers of the Enlightenment as Rousseau and Montesquieu in France, Lord Monboddo in England, and Adam Ferguson in Scotland. These thinkers and others who followed them in the early nineteenth century were concerned to develop a complete science of man which they assumed would automatically result in the enhancement of mankind's welfare and the expansion of human freedom, knowledge, and power. It was a grand vision, and one we have not entirely lost sight of. As a modern empirical science, however, anthropology came into its own in the last decades of the nineteenth and the early twentieth century. The period was one in which the Western nations were making their final push to bring the preindustrial and preliterate peoples of virtually the entire earth under their political and economic control. Thus modern anthropology, as a university discipline, is a child of Western capitalist imperialism.

Before World War II, fieldwork was almost all done in societies under the domination of the government of the anthropologist's own country; occasionally, under that of a friendly Western power. In the Old World the imperial powers were clearly recognizable and predominantly European. The world of most American anthropologists was, of course, different from that of Europeans, for the primitive peoples chiefly studied by Americans were conquered Indian groups who had been placed on reservations. Nevertheless, there were essential similarities, and in some respects it is justifiable to regard the American Indians, like the Negroes, as colonial people living under varying forms of Western imperialism. In the course of their field studies anthropologists worked out customary relationships with both the conquered peoples they studied and their own imperial governments. Living in close contact with "the natives," anthropologists tended to adopt liberal attitudes toward them and to uphold their interests against the encroachments of their conquerors. At the same time, anthropologists were usually white men, higher in rank than those whom they studied, virtually immune to attack or judgment by their informants, and protected by imperial law. Of necessity, they accepted the imperial framework as given.

Since World War II, a new situation has come about. Today some 2.3 billion people live in "underdeveloped" countries, that is to say, countries outside Europe, North America, Australia, New Zealand, and Japan, that were formerly colonies or spheres of influence of industrial capitalist powers.[6] About 773 million out of these 2.3 billion, or one third, have, through revolution, passed out of the orbit of capitalist imperialism into the Communist states of China, North Korea, North Vietnam, Mongolia, and Cuba. Because of the Cold War, they have also almost passed out of the purview of American anthropologists, although a few Europeans like Jan Myrdal and Isabel and David Crook have made recent studies. On the other hand, another 49 million, or 2 percent of the total, remain in colonies or former colonies under white governments. Most of these governments are European or of recent European origin, but American capital and influence have penetrated them deeply since World War II. The largest of these colonial states, containing 39 million people, are in southern Africa. Three of them (South Africa, South-West Africa, and Rhodesia) have lost or severed their connection with the mother country. In general, southern African colonial governments are now so repressive that it is difficult for foreign anthropologists to work in these colonies.

Between these extremes live some 1.5 billion people, or 65 percent of the total, in nations that are politically at least nominally independent yet are still within the orbit of Western power and influence. Outside the American

Indian reservations, this is the world in which most anthropological studies are made today.

In order to grasp the situation in which most anthropologists carry on their professional work, let us briefly survey the political geography of their world.

About 22 percent, or at least 511 million of the 1.5 billion people who inhabit underdeveloped societies remaining outside either Communist or more-or-less classical colonial control, live in what we may call "client states." The largest of these states (those with populations of over 5 million) are Colombia, Argentina, Peru, Brazil, Ecuador, Chile, Venezuela, the Philippines, South Vietnam, South Korea, Thailand, Taiwan, Malaysia, the Republic of the Congo, Nigeria, Iran, Saudi Arabia, Cameroon, and Turkey. These are nations with indigenous governments which are, however, so constrained by Western military and economic aid, trade, or private investments that they have little autonomy. Many of their governments would collapse if Western aid were withdrawn.

About 318 million people, or 14 percent of the underdeveloped world, live in nations whose governments are beholden to the United States; most of the rest, to Britain or France. Most of the United States-sponsored client states lie in Latin America, the traditional preserve of United States capital, or on the borders of the Communist world, where the United States has established satellite regimes in an effort to prevent the spread of Communism.

Client states are more difficult to identify than old-style colonies, for modern neo-imperialism varies in intensity. It is hard to determine the point at which the government of an underdeveloped nation has surrendered its ability to decide the main directions of its country's policy. My list of client states is therefore tentative. If, as many would, we add Mexico and Pakistan to the list of United States client states, this brings the population of client states to 657 million, or 28 percent of the underdeveloped world. United States client states (as distinct from actual colonies) then contain 464 million, or 20 percent of the underdeveloped world.

There remain some 873 million people, or 37 percent of the total, in nations usually regarded as relatively independent and politically neutral. The larger nations in this category (those with populations of over 5 million) are Burma, Cambodia, India, Ceylon, Afghanistan, Nepal, Syria, Iraq, Yemen, the United Arab Republic, Algeria, Morocco, Kenya, Tanzania, Sudan, Ethiopia, Uganda, Ghana, and Indonesia. The governments of these nations, whether military, one-party, or multiparty, tend to contain popular nationalist leaders, while those of most of the client states tend either to have been installed by Western powers or to have arisen as a result of military coups that had Western approval. Most of these more independent nations trade with and receive aid from both Western and Communist industrial powers. Most profess to be in some sense socialist. The appeal of their governments is of multiclass, or what Peter Worsley calls a "populist," character.[7] There is a public sector of the economy and an emphasis on national planning, as well as a large private sector dominated by foreign capital.

During the 1950s many liberal social scientists and others hoped that these neutral nations would form a strong Third World that could act independently of the Communists and the Western powers. These hopes have crashed in the past few years, chiefly because of the expansion of American capital and military power, the refusal of European nations to relinquish their own economic strongholds, and the neutral nations' failure to raise the standard of living of their burgeoning populations, leading to ever greater dependence on the West.[8] In the past fifteen years, at least 227 million people in sixteen nations have, after a longer or shorter period of relative independence, moved into, or moved back into, a client relationship, usually with the United States. These nations are Guatemala, Honduras, the Dominican Republic, Guyana, Venezuela, Brazil, Argentina, Bolivia, Ecuador, Trinidad and Tobago, South Vietnam, Thailand, Laos, the Congo, Togo, and Gabon. In most of these countries the shift in orientation followed a military coup.

A further 674 million in India, Indonesia, Afghanistan, Ceylon, Kenya, and Ghana, which I have classified as "independent," have, moreover, recently moved into much closer dependence on the United States, so that their future as independent nations is very uncertain. This is especially the case in Ghana and Indonesia since the recent military coups.

If in fact all these nations are moving into client status, this leaves only 199 million, or 8 percent of the underdeveloped world, in the category of neutral nations, and brings to a total of 1.14 billion, or 48 percent of the underdeveloped world, the people who live in client or near-client states of the United States or in its colonial dependencies. We must also remember that United States capital and military power now exert a strong influence on the colonies and client states of European powers (11 percent of the total), as well as on the remaining 8 percent of "neutral" states. In these circumstances, United States power can truly be said to be entrenched with more or less firmness throughout the non-Communist underdeveloped world.

Countering this reimposition of Western power, armed revolutionary movements now exist in at least twenty countries with a total population of 266 million. These countries are Guatemala, Peru, Venezuela, Ecuador, Paraguay, Brazil, Honduras, Bolivia, Colombia, Angola, Mozambique, the Congo, Cameroon, Portuguese Guinea, Yemen, Southern Arabia, the Philippines, Thailand, Laos, and South Vietnam. About 501 million people live in seven other countries where unarmed revolutionary movements or parties have wide support, namely India (especially the states of Bengal and Kerala), Rhodesia, South-West Africa, South Africa, Nicaragua, the Dominican Republic, and Panama. In more than one third of the underdeveloped world, therefore, revolution is a considered possibility, while in another third it has already been accomplished. Even in the remaining relatively stable colonial, client, or neutral states, a majority of the people are staying poor or growing poorer, while a small minority of rich are growing richer. Populations are increasing, discontent is widespread, and revolutionary ferment is probable within the next decade or two.[9]

This is the background against which anthropologists make their field studies today.

Fundamentally, the contemporary anthropologist's dilemma springs from the fact that much of the non-Western world is in a state of actual or potential revolution against the Western powers and against the kinds of native elites that are supported from the West. The United States government is the foremost counterrevolutionary force pitted against this revolutionary tide. It is at times aided by European governments, who also have their own counterrevolutionary interests to protect. This means that anthropologists are increasingly being caught up in struggles between the powers that fund them and many of the people they are wont to study. This disrupts the whole pattern of relationships that anthropologists have built up over the past eighty years between their own governments and the non-Western objects of their studies. It also faces them with grave kinds of value problems.

Before World War II, anthropologists could console themselves with the thought that neither they nor others could do much to dismantle the existing empires. It therefore behooved the anthropologist to analyze the institutions within colonial society as a service to posterity, and to aid reforms where he could. Later, in the 1940s and 1950s, it appeared possible that many colonial societies might gain genuine political *and* economic independence by peaceful means. Today this is no longer the case. Western dominance is continuing under new guises, even expanding and hardening. At the same time, revolutionary movements exist. Events in Vietnam suggest that in at least some areas, non-Western peoples will henceforth be "controllable" from the West only through extermination, if at all. Revolution to overthrow Western dominance in the underdeveloped world increasingly presents *the* alternative to progressive deterioration under Western control.

In these conditions, the practical decisions that anthropologists must make impose value judgments on them as well. For example, in countries where revolutionary movements have arisen or where there is revolutionary ferment among peasants and urban workers, shall the Western anthropologist try to work among these people?[10] Shall he do so even if this involves disobeying or risking offense to his own government? If he is able to gain entry to revolutionary segments of the people, can an anthropologist in fact study them adequately without making political and value commitments, or will his work not then remain wooden and superficial and his problems arid? Shall he remain in the suburbs of the cities among groups who are favorable to the local regime, and at least half favorable to his own government? Shall he, as an applied anthropologist, place himself in the service of his own counterrevolutionary government abroad? Or shall he retire to the remotest hill tribes, if he can still find any, and try to avoid the conflict?

In his home university, shall an anthropologist try to teach about the questions that are shaking world society: the dynamics of latter-day neo-imperialism, for example, or the genesis of guerrilla movements and the conditions for their success? Shall he inquire into the relative efficiency for economic (and spiritual) development of the various communist, "populist," or capitalist models? Or shall he immure himself in the political economies, kinship systems, and religious institutions of preconquest and early colonial societies, or of small local communities in the remaining relatively stable parts of the world? If he sticks to the latter course, by what theoretical criteria is he to justify the limitations of his approach?

To touch on immediate problems, how shall an anthropologist, just back from India or Southeast Asia, counsel the student who comes to him with the confidence that he does not wish to be sent to burn, bomb, or shoot Asian peasants who are fighting for their national independence —or merely hiding in their villages? How for that matter shall he confront the student who, confined from birth in a jingoist and anticommunist frame of thought, is quite ready to do this work? How shall the anthropologist act when he learns that the grades he gives these same students, on the basis of their knowledge of non-Western societies, are to be used by the United States military to determine whether or not they are to be sent to destroy Vietnam?[11]

Unfortunately, many anthropologists seem ill-equipped to respond adequately to these challenges and value problems, being too parochial and specialized and sometimes, indeed, too ignorant of the general state of affairs.

In particular, over the past fifty years, in spite of unquestionably great advances in knowledge of primitive societies, I suggest that anthropology has been weak in two respects.

First, anthropologists have failed to evaluate and analyze, as a world social system and an interconnected political economy, the structure of Western imperialism and the common and variant features of its impact on the non-Western world. In the past few years this defect has been somewhat remedied by a few new studies. The early chapters of Peter Worsley's *The Third World* give an overview of Western colonial expansion, and the later ones an analysis of developments in the new nations of non-Communist Asia and of Africa. Immanuel Wallerstein's *Social Change: The Colonial Situation* (New York, John Wiley & Sons, 1966) makes a useful contribution by drawing together relevant extracts and articles by anthropologists, nationalist leaders, and others over the past twenty years. It is remarkable, however, that so few anthropologists have studied modern Western imperialism as a historical epoch and a distinctive social system.

It is true, of course, that anthropologists have made numerous studies of modern social change in preindustrial societies, especially in local communities. They have, however, usually handled them through very general concepts: "culture-contact," "acculturation," "social change," "modernization," "urbanization," "Westernization," or "the folk-urban continuum." Force, suffering, and exploitation tend to disappear in these accounts of structural processes, and the units of study are so small that it is hard to see the forest for the trees. These approaches, in the main, have produced factual accounts and limited hypotheses about the impact of industrial or preindustrial cultures in local communities, but have done little to aid understanding of the world distribution of power under imperialism or of its total system of economic relationships.[12] Until very recently there has also, of course, been a bias in the types of non-Western social units chosen for study, with primitive communities least touched by modern changes being preferred over the mines, cash-crop plantations, white settlements, bureaucracies, urban concentrations, and nationalist movements that have played such prominent roles in colonial societies.[13]

The second weakness I would point to is that in the accumulation of factual detail and of limited hypotheses, we have gradually lost sight of the initial question of the Enlightenment: How can the science of man help men to live more fully and creatively and to expand their dignity, self-direction, and freedom?

Relating this question to the methods and immediate problems of anthropology is of course difficult. Social science is not social philosophy, and tends to become bad social science when it tries to be. Nevertheless, I suggest that social science, like all science, becomes morally and socially either meaningless or harmful unless its skills and knowledge are periodically referred back to the question, "Science for what purpose and for whom?" If we cease to ask this question, we cease to seek wisdom and cease to be intellectuals in any meaningful sense of the word. With the loss of responsibility for our learning, we also cease to be fully social, and therefore human.

Moreover, values do enter anthropological research at many points, whether or not this is recognized. They enter into the selection of problems, the choice of variables, and thus the interpretation of data. I suggest that an anthropologist who is explicit about his own values is likely to frame his problems more sharply and to see more clearly the lines between values and data than one who has not examined his values.

A contrary view of the ethical neutrality of science and of its complete irrelevance to social responsibility is, however, often advanced nowadays in departments of anthropology. In fact, whether consciously or unconsciously, the "ethical neutrality" position seems to be taken up as an excuse for not espousing unpopular viewpoints or getting into controversies. Most anthropologists, for example, make no theoretical objection to applied anthropology. Yet an applied anthropologist both influences policy and also necessarily accepts, at least in part, the broad framework of policy of an administrative body—often, an imperialist government.

In sum, therefore, it must be acknowledged that anthropology has not been and cannot be ethically neutral. Rather, what seems to have happened is that in circumstances of increasing specialization, bureaucratization, and management of research by governments, anthropologists have virtually ceased to ask explicitly what the human goals of their science are. More and more reduced to the status of hired functionaries, they have tended to make productivity of facts and of mutually unrelated hypotheses their goal. The fear of being speculative and "unempirical" (a fear that may bear some relation to the less conscious fear of producing politically or socially "subversive" theories) has made much current anthropological work fragmented and dull. In abdicating the search for beneficent goals for our science, we have ceased to be its masters and have turned into its slaves.

For a speculative and questioning anthropologist in America, the networks of research and teaching within which he must work are increasingly repressive. Although part of the responsibility lies with the size, specialization, and complexity of universities, the main sources of constriction stem from the government and the military and industrial institutions, which now penetrate education so deeply. This is not surprising. The United States is the world's wealthiest and most powerful nation. It is dedicated to delaying or preventing social change throughout two thirds of the world, and anthropologists are either salaried employees of its state governments, or are funded by its federal government or by private segments of its power elite. While professors need not always actively support current policies, they may be handsomely rewarded if they do so and they are discouraged from effectively opposing them. The fact that constraints are usually unofficial and vaguely formulated, and that they operate within a rhetoric of democratic and academic freedoms, only adds to the bafflement and frustration of unconventional scholars.

University teachers seldom publicize painful professional incidents, and rumor is unreliable. To document examples of constraint I must therefore fall back on personal experiences. In October 1962, while employed as assistant professor at a small Eastern university of liberal reputation, I made a speech at a public meeting of students and faculty condemning the American blockade of

Cuba. This brought on a furious blast from the university's president in a private interview. It was followed by a false written accusation, lodged with my department, that I had said I hoped Cuban missiles would destroy American cities. Later came the news, passed to me in private by a group of senior faculty members, that regardless of my colleagues' recommendations the university president had decided not to renew my three-year contract in 1964. In 1963, after months of argument and mental turmoil, my husband and I resigned from the university.[14]

Later in 1963 I learned from various parts of the country that the Immigration and Naturalization Service was making private inquiries among my colleagues as to whether they considered me a danger to the security of the United States. (I was at that time a British immigrant of seven years' standing in the United States.) Nothing happened, so my fellow anthropologists must have been convinced of my harmlessness. In 1964 I applied for a grant from the National Science Foundation to restudy two South Indian villages after an absence of fifteen years. I wanted in particular to find out why most of the villagers had become Communist supporters. A reply by letter informed me that the Foundation was unable to finance this research. Later, I heard privately that the committee of anthropologists appointed to judge the application had approved it, but that the Department of State had vetoed it on the grounds that federally financed research into the causes of revolutionary movements was not thought desirable in India at present.

Nonetheless, in that same year, as later became known, the United States Army alloted four to six million dollars for social science research in thirty-one countries of Asia, Africa, Latin America, North America, and Europe under

Project Camelot, designed to "assess the potential for internal war in national societies,"[15] or in the words of one sociologist, "to learn how to measure revolutionary forces, and to understand the processes by which revolutions are generated."[16] The anomaly sprang, of course, not only from differences of policy between the Department of State and the Army. The researchers under Camelot were intended to discover how to prevent revolutions (a subject known as "insurgency prophylaxis"), while I, with my confessed warmth toward Castro's Cuba, might be suspected of sympathy with them. Fortunately, whereas Camelot was canceled in the midst of an international scandal in 1965, I did scrape up the dollars, partly privately and partly from an auxiliary research award from the Social Science Research Council for research of my own choosing, to carry out my work in India. On my return, the State Department's initial squeamishness did not prevent its research department from immediately writing to request a copy of the first paper I read on the research before a regional conference of anthropologists.

The profession itself, however, seemed less interested. An editor of a firm publishing books in the social sciences told me that American readers "simply would not be interested" in a book dealing with the spread of Communist ideas among Indian villagers. It was not "standard, classical anthropology" and therefore could not command a university market as assigned reading in anthropology and other courses.

These experiences may be atypical. It must be said, however, that American anthropologists in general are now showing deep uneasiness over the temptations and restraints to which their profession is increasingly exposed by the policies of government agencies. In 1965, in the wake of Project Camelot, the American Anthropological Association appointed a Committee on Research Problems and Ethics under the chairmanship of Professor Ralph L. Beals. The committee has since published a report on such matters as "access to foreign areas, governmental clearances, professional ethics, and our responsibilities toward colleagues at home and abroad, the peoples with whom we work and the sponsoring agencies."[17] In a thoughtful and illuminating discussion, the report comments on the damage already done to American anthropology abroad by the Central Intelligence Agency's alleged employment of non-anthropologists in the guise of anthropologists, and by its secret employment of some trained anthropologists who are said to have falsely represented themselves as engaged in anthropological research, in some cases for universities that in fact no longer employed them.

At the same time, genuine anthropological research is now being increasingly curtailed or circumscribed by government restrictions on foreign travel. In August 1965, following the adverse effects of Project Camelot's publicization, President Johnson wrote to the Secretary of State: "I am determined that no Government sponsorship of foreign area research should be undertaken which, in the judgment of the Secretary of State, would adversely affect United States foreign relations." In response to an inquiry from the executive board of the American Anthropological Association, Mr. Thomas L. Hughes, Director of Intelligence and Research of the State Department, stated in a letter on November 9, 1965: "It does not seem desirable to us to impose on private research projects supported by the National Science Foundation or the National Institutes of Health the review and clearance necessary for foreign affairs research funded by operating agencies [i.e., presumably, by agencies such as the United States Army or the Central Intelligence Agency—K.G.] Neither have we the desire nor the intention of including Fulbright scholarships or National Defense Education Act grants within the scope of our review possibilities."[18]

This information is, however, inconsistent with my own experience with the Department of State and the National Science Foundation in 1964, as recounted above. The report of the Anthropological Association's Committee on Research Problems and Ethics indicates, moreover, that as of January 1967, Department of State clearance *was* required of anyone going abroad under grants or contracts with the Department of Health, Education and Welfare, or with funds obtained under the terms of the National Defense Education Act, contrary to the information received from Mr. Hughes. Moreover, in "sensitive areas," notably Africa, *every* American scholar is advised to provide an itinerary, list of contacts, and list of methods of pursuing research to the American Embassy in the country and to "comply with Embassy guidance," a set of directives virtually incompatible with normal methods of conducting anthropological research.

It is true that many of the present restrictions apply only to government grants and not to those received from private foundations, and that in the present international climate it is often easier for an anthropologist to carry out his work if he can make it known that he is *not* funded by his government. Nevertheless, it is also true that by far the largest portion of research money comes today from federal agencies, so that an anthropologist who is banned from receiving such funds is severely handicapped. With the addition of these recent restrictions on foreign research to the older ban on research in Communist nations, American anthropologists have become extremely circumscribed in their possibilities for fieldwork.

Using the report of January 1967 as background, Professor Beals and other members of his committee proposed a "Statement on Problems of Anthropological Research and Ethics" for mail-vote approval by the Anthropological Association's members. In March 1967 the statement received the support of a large majority of the membership. It includes a set of guidelines for sponsoring agencies and for anthropologists. These advocate, among other things, freedom to publish research findings without censorship or interference, refusal by academic institutions to become involved in clandestine activities, readiness of anthropologists to supply information about all aspects of their research to people in their host countries, and the lifting of government restrictions on foreign research that has the approval of the researcher's professional colleagues or academic institution. Anthropologists are also warned of the dangers of receiving funds from the Department of Defense and other "mission-oriented" agencies or from private foundations which do not publish the sources of their funds, and are urged scrupulously to avoid entanglement in clandestine intelligence activities. If such guidelines are in fact respected by anthropologists, the profession will at least save itself from active complicity in police-state methods of foreign penetration and domination, and will reassert its own right of free inquiry—whether or not it proceeds to make use of this right. If the United States government acts on them, it will reverse a twenty-year trend toward restraint of free inquiry in non-Western regions and constriction of anthropology.

The future of anthropology as an independent science is thus very uncertain, especially in America. The recently revealed involvement of a large contingent of anthropologists in the Army's counterinsurgency Project Agile in Thailand gives little reason to hope that the field will soon salvage its autonomy as a humane endeavor.[19] If serious resistance to such corruption of the science is confined to a scattered minority, that minority is likely to be purged one by one and dropped into obscurity. In the universities of the West, the anthropologist's best hope may be his students. These, far outnumbering their elders, are forcing us to reexamine our subject matter, theories, and aims. As they insist on creating a space in which to think freely and to grow in dignity, they will shake the foundations of our academic institutions. With them, we may be able to help in reshaping our own society, and in so doing to find new goals for the science of man.

NOTES

1. Frantz Fanon, *The Wretched of the Earth*, tr. Constance Farrington (New York, Grove Press, 1963), p. 12.
2. William F. Pepper, "The Destruction of a Culture," *Viet Report*, November–December 1966, and "The Children of Vietnam," *Ramparts*, January 1966. Pepper estimates 60 to 70 percent of the population of South Vietnam to be children under 16. Total civilian casualties in Vietnam since 1961 are estimated at about 2.6 million.
3. See Gerald Hickey's study of a Mekong delta village, *Village in Vietnam* (New Haven, Yale University Press, 1964).
4. Marshall Sahlins, "The Destruction of Conscience in Vietnam," *Dissent*, January–February 1966, pp. 36–62. Part of this article was earlier published in the *Nation*.
5. The resolution appears in *Science*, Vol. 154, No. 3756 (December 23, 1966), p. 1525. For reports of the debate see the *New York Times*, November 20, 1966, and "Constitution and By-Laws of the American Anthropological Association," *Fellow Newsletter of the American Anthropological Association*, Vol. 7, No. 8 (1966).

6. The figures used here are from *The World Almanac and Book of Facts* (New York, 1967), and are derived from United Nations estimates.
7. Peter Worsley, *The Third World* (Chicago, University of Chicago Press, 1965), pp. 118–74.
8. For discussions of U.S. economic and military expansion in the underdeveloped countries, see Robert Wolfe, "American Imperialism and the Peace Movement," *Studies on the Left*, May–June, 1966, pp. 28–44; Paul Baran and Paul Sweezy, *Monopoly Capital* (New York, Monthly Review Press, 1966), especially pp. 178–217.
9. In his study "Hunger" *(Canadian Dimension, in press),* Professor A. G. Frank of Sir George Williams University, Montreal, uses data from the United Nations Food and Agricultural Organization to show that per capita food production has been decreasing in most of the non-Communist, non-Western nations since 1960. His statistics come from the FAO's *The State of Food and Agriculture, 1964* (Rome, 1964). Also on the growing disparity of incomes in non-Communist underdeveloped countries, see Gunnar Myrdal, *An International Economy* (New York, Harper & Row, Publishers, 1956).
10. For a rare example of such a study, see Donald L. Barnett and Karari Njama, *Mau Mau from Within* (London, MacGibbon & Kee, 1966).
11. The practice has a special irony for anthropologists. It means that they are now using their students' reception of the knowledge they themselves obtained from non-Western tribal and peasant peoples, in order to select functionaries who will go to exterminate precisely such peoples in Vietnam.

    In these circumstances, a few anthropologists have resigned their teaching appointments or have refused to grade their students. Professor Donald L. Barnett of the University of Iowa, for example, an anthropologist and father of four children, has received notice that his pay will be cut off from the day that he fails to hand in his grades. He has refused to submit to this threat, thereby endangering—or more probably, ending—his professional career in America.
12. There is, of course, a large literature on this subject, much of it influenced by Marx. Early studies, besides the classic treatments by J. A. Hobson, Lenin, and Rosa Luxemburg, include Parker T. Moon's *Imperialism and World Politics* (London, Macmillan & Co., Ltd., 1926). More recent works include Paul Baran's *Political Economy of Growth* (New York, Monthly Review Press, 1957); Frantz Fanon's *Studies in a Dying Colonialism* (New York, Monthly Review Press, 1962) and *The Wretched of the Earth* (New York, Grove Press, 1963); and

Kwame Nkrumah, *Neo-Colonialism, the Last Stage of Imperialism* (New York, International Publishers, 1966). Such works are not, however, very commonly used in departments of anthropology and seldom appear in standard bibliographies of the social sciences in America.

13. For this and other criticisms of modern anthropology see *The End of Anthropology?* a paper prepared for the Sociology and Anthropology Working Group of the sixth World Congress of Sociology, by Peter Worsley, Department of Sociology, University of Manchester. Important exceptions to this criticism in the last few years have been A. L. Epstein, *Politics in an Urban African Community* (Manchester, Manchester University Press, 1958); Michael P. Banton, *West African City: A Study of Tribal Life in Freetown* (New York, Oxford University Press, 1957); and Julian H. Steward, *The People of Puerto Rico* (Urbana, University of Illinois Press, 1956).

14. For further details, see the *Justice* (Brandeis University, Waltham, Mass.), March 26 and April 2, 1963.

15. I. L. Horowitz, "The Life and Death of Project Camelot," *Trans-Action*, Vol. 3, No. 5 (November–December 1965), p. 4.

16. William J. Goode, defending the project in the *American Sociologist*, Vol. 1, No. 5 (November 1966), p. 256.

17. *Fellow Newsletter* of the American Anthropological Association, Vol. 8, No. 1 (January 1967), p. 4.

18. *Ibid.*, p. 5.

19. The *New York Times* reports on the work of 157 anthropologists, engineers, and ordinance specialists at the Thai-American Military Research and Development Center in Bangkok. The *Times* decribes Project Agile as "the Pentagon's worldwide counter-insurgency program," concerned with methods of countering guerrilla warfare in Northeast Thailand. "The old formula for successful counterinsurgency used to be ten troops for every guerrilla," one American specialist remarked. "Now the formula is ten anthropologists for each guerrilla." (Peter Braestrup, "Researchers Aid Thai Rebel Fight," *New York Times*, March 20, 1967, City Edition, p. 11.)

THE CIVILIZATION

OF THE DIALOGUE

∽ John Wilkinson

THE PHRASE "CIVILIZATION OF THE DIA-
logue," or some variant of it, has become à la mode. But
since more often than not modish words and phrases, like
the Phoenix, prove to be names without bodies, it seems
reasonable to inquire whether this particular phrase is or is
not in the same case as the Phoenix; especially as I maintain that we are or should be living under the conditions
that the phrase denotes.

The formula "Civilization of the Dialogue" seems to
have been used first by Kierkegaard in the nineteenth century to describe the emergence of parliamentary democracy, and by Camus in the twentieth century in a somewhat different sense. But the idea is an ancient one. It is to
be found in Homer, whose heroes debated with each other
and with the Gods, and it would accurately describe the
democracy of the Athenian and other city-states, not only
as it really became on many occasions between episodes of

tyranny or oligarchy, but as it was ideally described by
Plato, Aristotle, and other less well known philosophers.
Dogmatic Christianity forced even the ideal out of exist-
ence, except as it was sporadically incarnated in dubiously
orthodox places, like the medieval University of Paris, or
the Platonic Academy at Florence, which inaugurated the
Renaissance with the aid of Greek refugees from fallen
Constantinople.

The Civilization of the Dialogue is, then, a Greek invention. Wherever it transiently appears, it is always due
to the revival of the Greek tradition. Induction would thus
lead one to identify it with democracy, which must be
considered as existing in proportion to the number of citizens able and willing to engage in dialogue. Unfortunately, reasonableness in discussion is only a necessary but
not a sufficient condition for civil harmony. The good life
can only with difficulty be lived on an insufficient diet, or
without sufficient leisure, or under a variety of other conditions. More generally, the sufficient condition for dialogue which would be equivalent to a definition cannot be
stated. In this study no more than some of the necessary
conditions are given. This logical state of affairs means that
we cannot tell with precision how to institute a dialogue;
but we often know very well when something which goes
by that name has no legitimate title to it.

There are "harder" and "softer" versions of the dialogue. The hardest would be that which would "convince
the Gods themselves." Insofar as this version implies a single Truth, from which all subsidiary truths derive, it has
rightly become suspect, even though the attempt to find a
unitary account of things remains the supreme regulative
principle of inquiry. In this way, the object of the hardest
version of dialogue has shifted from a preoccupation with,

say, the Platonic notion of the Good to a universally applicable construction of the inductive logic of the sciences. John Dewey's work is familiar to Americans; on the Continent, Chaim Perelman, in his "new rhetoric," has endeavored to revive in a modern form the ancient dialectic of argumentation, which, for all practical purposes, ceased with Quintilian.

Adam Schaff, philospher and president of the Polish Academy of Sciences, is a good example of a protagonist of a softer version. Schaff holds that it is unnecessary to agree ideologically. Dialogue, according to him, may be instituted for limited objectives: for example, the coexistence required by the emergence of nuclear weapons. Many persons have announced similar principles, but proved in the sequel unwilling or unable to agree to the conditions *sine qua non* by making any concession at all to rigid structures of thought and habit. Excluding those who are merely confused, it is clear that these people are palavering to gain time or to make propaganda. Schaff is noteworthy because of his brilliant exposition up and down the length and breadth of Europe of the principles of limited dialogue, a willingness to make the necessary concessions, and sufficient political leverage with his government to make them go along.

Even the softest version must imply at least an interaction of meaningful words (including the "invented" words of mathematics, science, and logic) with a view to rational approximation to the truth, however truth may be conceived. Many communications, such as shrugs, groans, blows (or even the subtle reply that Herodotus reports Amasis sent to his royal Egyptian master), are different codifications of what might be said with words. They can, therefore, function in dialogue. But as of now, extrasensory perceptions, sacramental observances, and so on may not so function, however valid they may or may not be in other important respects. The dialogue, if any propriety of language is to be retained at all, must refer only to what can be mediated by the *logos*. This last term refers to choice from a known set of alternatives, and corresponds remarkably well to our concept of "information." The "word" as a translation of *logos* assumes myriad forms and should of course be conceived of as a complex mental event and *not* as a puff of air or a small mountain of ink.

Special pleadings, dogmatic statements, the lies of politicians and publicists, are not dialogue, whatever other useful qualities they may occasionally possess. At the most, their propositions enter negatively into dialogue only insofar as dialogue mercilessly exposes them by testing their pretensions against evidence available to any man who takes care to examine it. It is clear that different cultures elaborate widely variant criteria of truth, rationality, and persuasive evidence; and an inability to reach *any* tentative agreement on fundamentals sometimes makes dialogue impossible even to begin, or, having begun, to continue. My own experience has been that these differences most often prove to be much less pronounced than usually imagined; even in debating issues with members of non-Western cultures we have usually reached some agreement.

Consensus, as Martin Buber has emphasized, never means the suppression of individual and cultural differences; it means, rather, that the dialogue that generated it has been able to elaborate a spectrum of alternative available beliefs or strategies, regardless of where the center of gravity within this spectrum might lie for a given person. It would be unthinkable to find any Moslem, for example, who could plausibly deny that the sun rose this morning and will almost certainly set tonight. It would be almost as unthinkable to find one who would not admit that the mean distance of the sun from the earth is very near to 93,000 miles, as soon as he had apprehended the meanings of the words being used. It would be a shade less likely, but yet very probable, that he would agree that in 45 B.C. Caesar crushed the sons of Pompey. But nearly no one at all could be brought to agree with him that the learned and pious Sheikh Abdullah could really fly, except in the biographies of him composed by his disciples.

Even those Moslems who preferred in conversation with me to affirm that the Sheikh *could* fly always readily granted that this belief was not founded in reason and therefore afforded no easily visible basis for activity with respect to the future. On the other hand, they readily asserted the belief *as a component of their own loyalty system,* of whose truth they could not expect me, or any other nonmember of the community, to be rationally persuaded. Of course, had I become a member of the community, I too would have been expected to affirm it even if I continued to disbelieve it. This state of mind is very different from that of Christians, or at least from the state of mind of those who retain a belief in miracles. I find it difficult to ascertain with exactly what kind or degree of belief Roman Catholics are expected to receive miracles; say, the belief in the levitation of saints, like that of Saint Joseph of Copertino, who was canonized partly because he was observed "by unimpeachable witnesses" to fly like a bird into nearby trees. But it is clear that Catholics cannot make the convenient distinction between affirmation and belief so useful to the devotees of the Sheikh.

This state of affairs is, of course, not completely unexpected. Except perhaps to more or less orthodox Jews and Christians. No Moslem dreams of setting up a separate system of mosques for the worship of the different sects of the community, no matter how divergent may be their theological conceptions. The Sufis and the Sunnis (comparable, perhaps, to Protestants and Roman Catholics) worship Allah side by side. It is well to recall in this connection that the "two-truth" theory (according to which the *truth of inquiry* may even totally contradict the *truth of religion*) is philosophically well established in Islam. More important, it seems that it is well established almost everywhere, except among Jews and Christians. It was the early Christians who manufactured from the Greek *hairesis,* which simply designated a school of philosophical thought, our word "heresy," a condition of soul worthy only of damnation in the next world and extirpation from this.

No educated Roman thought that the Emperor was really a god. The pinch of incense on the altar, to which the Christians took such exception, was a form of loyalty oath to the community and, beyond that, committed no one to anything at all. "Intolerance" and "fanaticism" are perhaps not too harsh words for what seems to me the sole cultural product *uniquely* associated with Judaism and Christianity, at least in the forms they have maintained until very recently. War and brutality have existed in every culture; but only in the Judaeo-Christian cultures have they been systematically exculpated and even glorified with reference to some fixed concept of orthodoxy. The ideological genocide practiced on the Amalekites by the Hebrews and on the Cathari by the Church, both in the name of God, are the prime examples of this hideous practice until the twentieth century's attempts against the Armenians and the Jews.

These considerations hold nowhere better than in respect to the development and history of communism. Marx and his followers simply secularized Christian (or better, European) culture. It is true that they junked many Western concepts, but the idea of the *one true belief* was maintained intact in their secular theology.

The point I have been attempting to make, perhaps too laboriously, is simply that the dialogue becomes impossible when it is overlaid with some concept of orthodox dogma, secular or religious. Every man has the natural right, and even the duty, to contrive himself a habitation in the difficult and different times, places, and circumstances of this world, and to make it meaningful by an appropriate ideology. But he makes life unnecessarily difficult for himself, and nearly impossible for everyone else, when he refuses in principle or in practice to engage in colloquy with those who may think differently from himself in important matters. The *tiers monde* always seem particularly incensed by the dogmatism of the claims of Christendom and its progeny, communism. Nehru is once reported to have murmured (in Cromwell's formula) to a meeting of certain uncommitted nations and intransigent Marxists: "Bethink you, by the bowels of Marx, you may be wrong!"

The motto of the dialogue is Augustine's phrase: *"Si non rogas, intellego"* (roughly, "If you don't ask me, I know"). Otherwise formulated, this most important result of Augustine's philosophy of knowledge means that dialogue must take seriously *any* allegation of fact or value put forth by anyone who is not obviously a madman or liar until it is clear that he *is* a madman or liar. And it pays to take even them seriously if we reflect how epithets like "madman" and "genius" have been so frequently interchanged in the vicissitudes of time. Facts and values lose their privileged status the moment they are challenged, no matter how true or sacred they may previously have been held to be. They may, of course, be reestablished, and it is the function of the dialogue to perform this task if it can. But more often than not, a responsible challenge leads to a reformulation that incorporates the previous eternal verities as special cases. The shift may be very slight or it may be radical.

According to one philosopher, "time makes ancient good uncouth," and according to another, it "makes more converts than reason." Even so, a "dialectic" of history is not dialogue at all, except insofar as any *force majeure* or compelling historical event is rendered symbolic. Compulsive nonsymbolic forces of many kinds act to change men's actions and minds, but they do not do so in the ordered and rational way, based on values explicitly formulated, which is the way of the dialogue.

There are, in the Western world, a small number of institutions in which something approaching a dialogue is being carried on. The British House of Lords (but not the House of Commons) is often such. In France Bertrand de Jouvenel (in his regular meetings, *Futuribles*) and Pierre Massé, along with a number of his associates in the Plan, notably Bernard Cazes, seem, from a distance, to engage in a genuine dialogue. In Holland, a group centering about Arendt Th. van Leeuwen, and in Germany the *Sozialforschungsstelle* under the sociologist Helmut Schelsky, as well as a group of Evangelical theologians associated with Heinz Kloppenburg, seem to do the same.[1]

One's judgments of foreign institutions are reached

largely at second hand. But as far as the United States is concerned, I am convinced that the dialogue is proceeding only in the Supreme Court, on the couches of *some* psychoanalysts, and at the Center for the Study of Democratic Institutions. The outward forms of the dialogue are cultivated elsewhere but the tendentious character of the institutions concerned, which receive their financial support from "mission-oriented" bodies, to use Gerard Piel's rather too urbane words, make their operations into arms of war, hot or cold, or of business enterprise for profit. However useful such ends may be, they are not the end of dialogue, which is truth and justice. And even where this tendentious character is not clearly marked, most other American attempts at dialogue are too sporadic to be useful.

Almost seven years ago the Fund for the Republic moved from New York to Santa Barbara and rechristened itself the Center for the Study of Democratic Institutions. But the change was more than one of place and name. Henceforward, instead of giving away money for studies, it was to have studies conducted *in situ* by resident staff members, aided, as occasion arose, by distinguished visitors from every discipline and nation. The nucleus of the program was and is a daily dialogue at which a study paper contributed by a staff member or a visitor undergoes a thorough examination. Many of these papers and discussions ultimately find their way into print, and many are broadcast from tape, in the framework of the Center's fundamental identification of dialogue with education. A number of important international symposia have been held and more are planned.[2] There is complete freedom of discussion, subject only to certain courtesies and procedural rules that are sometimes more subconsciously felt than consciously formulated. It is still uncertain whether the Center's program fully answers to the lifelong attempt of its president, Robert Hutchins, to establish what he has variously described as a center of independent criticism, a community of sages, and so on. But if the program of the Center is imperfect, it is nonetheless perfectible.

It is above all things difficult to institute a dialogue and even more difficult to continue it. There is nevertheless no viable alternative. The social and political crises of a world that is socially and politically fragmented but that is rapidly reaching a technological unity, in which everything is concatenated with everything else, occur with increasing frequency and amplitude. The sole alternative to letting things solve themselves through the mechanism of a crash is rational dialectical awareness of things as they are *and* as we should humanly desire them to be.

Because I argue that the dialogue is absent in the main from any observable reality in our society—with the exception of the few examples I mention above—it might be worthwhile to examine some of the loci where institutionalized dialogue should be and is frequently thought to be proceeding.

Philosophy, the supreme historical example of continuing dialogue, has been instrumental in its own downfall. To take but a single example: certain analytical "philosophers," disciples of Wittgenstein, who understand nothing of philosophy *or* Wittgenstein, have become the dominant school in many American faculties of philosophy. Their "analysis," compounded of equal doses of bad lexicography and bad behavioral psychology, has gutted philosophy by showing most of its terms to be either meaningless or of such restricted meaning as to be useless. (They might better have heeded Leibnitz' dialectic remark that philosophers are right in what they affirm and wrong in what they deny.) Perhaps I may be excused if I tell how I set a student of mine on such a successful path that at the age of thirty he has become one of the leading lights of American analytic philosophy, overthrowing my own dictum that there could be child prodigies in music and chess but that this was unthinkable in philosophy as a contradiction in terms.

Influenced perhaps by recollection of Dean Swift's Professor of Eloquence, who was able, by turning a crank, to compose scholarly works with no knowledge, I suggested to this student that I could put him in possession of an infallible recipe to make a great Analytic Philosopher of a numbskull. I suggested that he take, say, the Categories of Kant, plus the Kantian time and space, plus God, freedom, and dialectic, and look them up in the *Oxford English Dictionary.* For each he was to list the tabulated meanings with some (preferably unintelligible) connecting tissue in between. He was to discard at random certain meanings and to retain others. For example, he might discard the first two and allow the others a limited meaning. But *any* rule could operate; for example, accepting the odd meanings and rejecting the even. Or he could affect to reject them all. As of this date, this philosopher-king has published nine papers that have been extremely well received by analytic "philosophers." I little thought that my jocular suggestion would prove to be such a *pons asinorum* to success. I am grateful to record that, perhaps in deference to me, he is about to establish "dialectic," principally by reversing the reasons for which Kant rejected it.

Our own National Academy of Sciences ought, one might think, in considering some of its individual members, to represent something like a body devoted to thinking critically about the common good. What it is, in fact, is the scientific organ of the Establishment. It has the morals and manners of the DAR, "correct," no doubt, but hardly anything more. For example, at the recent celebration of NAS's first century of existence, one Academician suggested, reasonably from his point of view, that moon exploration might tell us something important—I think, about the isotopes of tin. When my colleague at the Center for the Study of Democratic Institutions, Linus Pauling, suggested that for everything of interest that might be discovered by the expenditure of such incredible sums of money one could certainly expect to find for less a thousand medical facts that would each singly add more to the happiness of the human race, he was furiously wigged by the president, a savant of little originality and, one must fear, of even less moral sensitivity, in terms that might be freely paraphrased: Do you want to spoil this nice little racket?

As the NAS illustrates, *our* science has come down hard on the politically convenient idea that it must be "value-free" in order to be "objective." The transition from discourse about fact to discourse about value has become for us, to use Jaspers' language, one of those *Grenzsituationen* where we "suffer shipwreck." Some few centuries ago it was as laudable as it was dangerous to assert scientific fact *in defiance of* the ends of some corrupt political or religious Establishment that lacked elementary attributes of humanity or justice, *reo Galilaeo.* That was moral behavior of the highest order. Today, the use of the same dodge to assert fact in order to *further* the ends of the current Establishment (which, for all the apparent democratic political changes that have occurred, probably is sequacious of the same goals as its worst predecessors) is the highest immorality a real academy could imagine. I have not read that satellites and the rest of NASA's hardware have instructed us importantly on the cosmic distribution of the isotopes of tin, and would not care if they did; but I do read that they have recently become meteorologically instrumental to the conduct of bombing raids in the Vietnamese war, not to mention the military value of the innumerable pieces of spy-in-the-sky junk circling the earth, none of which comes under the treaty interdicting the "military use of space," presumably on the basis that governments are willing by treaty to forbid only those things which they are at the moment unable to accomplish. The very highest authority warns us of those hypocrites who can interpret the sky but who cannot recognize the signs of the times.

As for the American universities, with their overspecialized faculties and untaught bodies of students, these are no longer centers of any sort of dialogue, even if we suppose that they ever were. The bottom half of them, as usually ranked, are unworthy of notice; and most of the upper moiety can scarcely be considered anything other than a proving ground for the military establishment and industry, especially the former. Nearly all the top twenty multiversities are arms factories which would have staggered the imagination of Herr Krupp or Sir Basil Zaharoff. No scheme for the destruction of the human race is wanting in their programs of "research." It is, of course, not completely excluded that social benefits emerge; but such benefits are mostly by-products, "fallout," or "spinoff," most of which the government or other funding agency did not conceive of and certainly did not mean to pay for. And even so, such "benefits" are nearly all purely quantitative, which in practice excludes quality except perhaps in the sense that a miser's gold, which is meant to be counted but not otherwise enjoyed, is a kind of attenuated value.

It is not impossible that some sort of discussion sometimes goes on in the university; but if it does, it is usually in a very desultory fashion in the local airport (which has become the true faculty club) or in the jet flight following. Since Ph.D.'s have been trained in American graduate schools to talk exclusively with their fellow specialists and to the national and international fraternity to which they owe their only fealty, apart from their source of cash, it seems unlikely that they have the vocabulary, even if they had the desire, to do more than exchange commonplaces with their colleagues in other disciplines as they wing their way to Washington and other places to give expert advice on how to put an end to the human race. Some of the monies enlarged by government handouts naturally trickle down to the professors of humanities, very few of whom are yet of much use in planning holocausts. But it must not be imagined that, *faute de mieux*, these "humanists" willingly consent to be thrown back on instructing students. The publish-or-perish regime (in addition to the obvious fact that there is something naturally repulsive in the process of teaching students whose lips move when they read) makes these second-class academics as loath to suffer contacts with students as their more highly advantaged confrères in the "hard" sciences. They prefer and indeed are forced to attempt to emulate the scientists. Often this takes the form of applying the "methods" of the more prestigious natural sciences to realms of discourse where these methods obviously cannot apply. But what can the poor humanists do when they are continually challenged to "justify" their "slots" according to the test: "What have you to contribute to General Motors?" I have not invented this quotation; it is taken verbatim from an insolent allocution of the head of a large American university to his Department of English. This latter-day Squeers should have been forthwith scourged from his Dotheboys Hall with rods. Instead, being answered with servility, he was encouraged to repeat his question to the Greek Department.

Most of these institutions have set up inexpensive and little-patronized programs in the liberal arts. It is possible that some of them are meant seriously; but the obvious intent behind most of them is to silence dissatisfied parents and rampaging legislatures whenever it becomes clear that nothing remotely describable as education is going forward.

As to the students themselves, my thesis is simple: Very few can enter into any conceivable dialogue because their vocabularies are so exiguous that the primary condition for a dialogue (as distinguished from a mere "bull session") is lacking. For many years I administered a test of general information and vocabulary to all of the students in certain philosophy courses. These students were a representative sample of the student body. I gave the test in six different American colleges and universities. More than 90 percent of the students proved, as freshmen, to have a usable, active vocabulary of about 800 words. A further 500 words would be passively understood by them in something vaguely resembling their proper meanings. Another 1,500 or so words lay in such a penumbra of understanding (or misunderstanding) that more could hardly be averred than that they remembered having heard them before. Beyond this, Stygian darkness.

It is interesting to note that there was about a 20 percent *decrease* in these numbers during the four-year passage from freshman to senior. This attrition was made good in part by an accretion of perhaps a couple of hundred specialized terms drawn from the technical jargon of the faculty in which they had "majored." English of any literary merit can be read by these students only with the aid of a kind of translation into a sort of basic English. For example, in that university where the welfare of General Motors is the criterion of excellence, "translations" of Shakespeare into just such a crude basic English are actually on sale in the university bookstore. Even the New Testament, which was written for a population not remarkable for its education and which contains only, say, a third of the number of words to be found in Shakespeare, might as well be left in the original Greek for all the ability the average "educated" American has to read it.

I discovered later that a very large proportion of these students had created a special life of a very narrow sort for themselves, presumably as a means of avoiding alienation from some human community or other. For example, they had become adepts at skiing, skin-diving, political agitation, drug taking, chess playing, or some one or other of a host of other activities. Most of these ways of life have, at least implicitly, an ethic, an aesthetic, and even a metaphysic; and it is probable that the specialized vocabulary that is almost certainly necessary to these pursuits fell through the interstices of my vocabulary testing; I am therefore unable to estimate the extent of these specialized and mutually exclusive vocabularies. But it is nonetheless clear that a dialogue about affairs transcending certain specialized modes of existence cannot be carried on with this kind of *Fachjargon*. In this respect the students much resemble their supposed mentors.

I am far from supposing that Americans are born less capable than the Athenians of carrying on dialogue. Paraphrasing Saint Matthew, one might say that they were not so much born stupid from their mothers' wombs as that they had become so for General Motors' sake. But whatever the cause, the retreat from dialogue is a retreat from reason. Even the Athenians became irrational (sometimes violently so) on occasion. Socrates, for example, found it prudent to wheel his children in a kind of costermonger's barrow into the court where he was to be tried, with a view to influencing the nonrational sentiments of the jurymen. But it is one thing to lapse occasionally from grace and quite another to be *in principle* incapable of it.

I have no objective measurements, but a very strong subjective impression, that ten years after graduation the vocabulary of these students is even smaller. This intuition is confirmed by analyses of the vocabularies used in the mass media. It would be fatuous indeed, therefore, to suppose that the great majority of Americans are in a position to deliberate about political or other issues for which they have no words. The ability to think pictorially is known to be an independent mode of thought, but it is of little value in coping with anything important, with the sole exception of the graphic and plastic arts.

American political scientists, who prove seldom to have read more of Aristotle than the *Politics* (and in rare cases, the *Ethics*), often quote with evident self-satisfaction his remarks to the effect that "Man is a political animal" and that "Politics is the architectonic science." They have even taught practicing politicians—at least those who are capable of pentasyllabic words—to quack these slogans forth, too. But Aristotle was not speaking of that modern political opportunism which is more aptly described as the "art of the possible," understanding this last phrase in the most pejorative sense to include every shabby trick to get into office and stay there, with nothing more sublime in mind than to have a preferred place at the trough. Aristotle meant by politics the difficult philosophic science and art of living, and living well, in the *polis,* a collection of villages organically and harmoniously related to its rural hinterland. Aristotle's politician (better rendered by the English "statesman") had to be a philosopher who knew rationally how to persuade those who were capable of reason of the best course to be followed in debated problems of law, ethics (for Aristotle a part of politics), religion, and even medicine. A Sophist might cajole the people into following a certain course by rhetorical tricks; but such a fellow was a mere demagogue like Alcibiades. Aristotle seems to have made a more favorable assessment than Plato of democracy. And he preferred "deliberation" and "persuasion" as terms to be opposed to "polemic." But their accounts are essentially the same.

Just how far our modern cacistocracy has strayed from the Greek ideal of politics as rational persuasion of those capable of it to the hegemony of the base and ignorant *by* the base and ignorant is suggested by the triune component parts of Greek Justice, the true end of the *polis,* which was not unlike the conception of our Founding Fathers: One must know what one is doing, one must publicly and rationally choose to do it for its own sake, and what is done should be the resultant of a settled moral state.

In Augustine's words: "Where justice has failed, what are States but great robbers?" Political dialogue is, if not dead, moribund. And as a corollary, modern states are bands of robbers.

The American republic is running on the momentum given it nearly two centuries ago by a galaxy of political virtuosos, who might have rivaled Athens. It is vain to rail against any one thing or any one group of persons as the cause of our loss of political momentum. What is perhaps most at fault is the degrading tendency of Americans to assess the worth of everything by purely quantitative yardsticks like money. We need not believe that there has been some conspiracy. It is tempting but not necessary to suppose that our oligarchs meet secretly (as some Greeks did), swearing to do everything in their power to harm the people. But the effect is the same as if they had. If democracy is the civilization of the dialogue; if, as Scott Buchanan has held, "persuasion is the life of politics"; if, as Robert M. Hutchins has written, "With an educational system that does not educate and a system of mass communications that does not communicate, we have become incapable of the discussion by which political issues are determined," then it is easy to see why a self-styled political elite *must* be a cacistocracy if there be not a single one among them (and very few among their advisers) who could bring forth a clear and distinct idea if he lived as long and wrote as much as Varro himself.

As I have already suggested, this may be due to our deficient methods of education, for very little in the way of language is necessary for a man to be in a position to "contribute to General Motors." In the technologized society, in the Republic of Engineers, numbers suffice for the purposes of quantification; and since the language of numbers, mathematics, is more and more an arcane science known to few, the rest of the population slips more and more into a position in which political thought is impossible. All the old ideas are present in the political air, but as fading and indistinct echoes.

Perhaps a better simile would be that the good coinage

of the English tongue has been debased so that a kind of inflation has set in. Alain Clément, writing in *Le Monde,* says, apropos of the Vietnamese war, that the Americans are "a nation that consumes in its public vocabulary prodigious quantities of great words like 'ideas,' 'imagination,' 'vision,' and even attaches the adjective 'creative' to insignificant and money-grubbing activities. Now they find themselves in the position of being reduced to confessing that they have no idea where they are going"—or what they are doing.

The Vietnamese war represents the final catastrophic result of substituting the manipulation of images for the political dialogue. Where images have no reference, and where any set of words and ideas is as good as any other—that is to say, where thought has ceased—we can blame no one if he votes for a presidential candidate who promises, probably sincerely, not to escalate the war in Vietnam while he is in fact being forced to do so; for a man who, the instant following a point in time when he was relatively ignorant of foreign policy, was forced to become omniscient of it, and, for lack of anything better, was delivered over to the dialectic of the military (who really have something going in the way of a lopsided and truncated dialogue) because he had none of his own.

This infernal military dialectic might be described briefly: "If we don't use power, we don't know if we have it; if we don't continue to use it, we don't know if we continue to have it." The military therefore found it necessary to escalate some war somewhere as a proving ground for their armamentarium. But the tormenting question remains: "Do we have power or do we not?" The quantitative military mentality can probably solve this problem to *their* satisfaction only by escalating right up to the use of the ultimate weapon; and the sole duty of the nominal commander-in-chief is to provide "political" support for this operation as well as he can. With a prodigious expenditure of all M. Clément's "great words," the President announces every possible position on every subject connected with the war. Contraries and even flat contradictions are successively put to the people, sometimes even in the same speech. But they are mere *ballons d'essai* launched to see which ones the Gallup poll, or something like it, will shoot down. This procedure is possible only with a people who are historical amnesiacs.

Similarly, Ambassador Goldberg, in the United Nations, follows what European journals call the "Goldberg Line." This consists in voting for any measure that is likely to win, particularly among the *tiers monde,* in complete disregard of what he said the day before or what his principals 225 miles to the south are actually doing. If poor Mr. Goldberg, like his predecessor, were not incapable of doing anything else, we could not acquit him of lying. Dr. Johnson in the shades must be meditating changing his definition of an ambassador as a man sent *abroad* to lie for his country.

Some Americans think that the whole crew of political and military instigators of the war would look more at home in the dock at Nuremberg than in the seats of power in Washington or in the executive suites of the great foundations. But this is unjust. In the quantitative society those who are supposed to control our destinies have no more real power of decision than their underlings. Only the mathematically skilled can hope to have any power, and the way things are accelerating, even they cannot be expected to have it very long. Civilly and militarily, the only answer to anything is: more of the same, which is the *reductio ad absurdum* of dialogue.

It is hardly true that the Americans are experiencing a

moral crisis over Vietnam, or will experience one. The malaise that the opponents of the war feel is due to the fact of their being unable symbolically to cope with any crisis at all. The reporter who was sent forth by *Life* to interview the "doves" told us at the Center for the Study of Democratic Institutions that most of the people he had met who were against the war were, as far as he could tell, against it on legalistic rather than moral grounds. They just could not figure out why we were fighting a war as far away from the homeland as the dimensions of this terrestrial ball permit. The decline in unemployment and the acceleration upwards of the GNP were rightly deemed to be very fugitive benefits. It is my fancy that the majority of the opponents of American involvement have come to have a strange facial resemblance to the apes Schopenhauer saw and described in the zoo who, according to him, were vainly longing (he saw it in their eyes) to be rational but had not the understanding to bring it off. Mr. Johnson must be suffering from the same malaise. Imagine being involved in a war where "victory" (or anything else) is indefinable and perhaps in a war that was lost before it began. Some people have professed to see in the current debate between the "doves" and "hawks" (especially in the Fulbright hearings) a modern replication of the Athenian debate that took place between Nicias and Alcibiades just before the disastrous Sicilian expedition. But it is not much of a compliment to compare the supposed high point of American politics with the low point of Athenian. Nor must it be supposed that many other countries are much better situated. André Philip, one of the world's most experienced negotiators on the international scene, recently bore unimpeachable witness at the Center to what all of us already knew: that politicians of the

United Nations (or anywhere else) make speeches exclusively for home consumption, and that it is only when they
leave that technicians can agree on rational solutions, for
which almost always political support, or even understanding, is lacking.

Charles Dickens wrote in a letter to John Forster from
America: ". . . I do fear that the heaviest blow ever dealt at
liberty will be dealt by this country, in the failure of its
example to the earth." He was, in 1842, referring to the
imminent War between the States, which opposed two absolutely intransigent parties. Much the same phrasing applies to the war in Vietnam. If the dialogue fails now, and
I feel that it will, the hopes of democracy must be tenuous
indeed.

NOTES

1. Robert Jungk's admirably conceived Institute for Problems of
the Future has recently been done to death by the stringency of
the Austrian budget. Slavko Sagaroff's Institute for Higher
Studies in Vienna and Nuri Eren's similarly named Institute in
Istanbul have met the same fate, not, indeed, because they had
too little money but because they had too much. These last two
were generously endowed by one of the great American foundations whose golden rain waters only the middle of the road. The
Golden Mean of the Greeks and the Romans—*aurea mediocritas*
—has achieved a very different translation.

2. At one of these Symposia, dedicated to discussion of the Technological Society, one of the world's most distinguished physical
scientists, noted for his penetrating writings on the problems
of the future, surprisingly said that he had never before talked
with representatives of the humanities, whom he thought to be
so many "flat-earthers." In this last point we believe him to
be wrong, but it does indicate the difficulty of finding a mode
of procedure and elaborating a common vocabulary that will
serve the ends of dialogue rather than promote confusion.

SOCIAL SCIENCE AND

SOCIAL CONSCIOUSNESS

The Shame of the Universities

∽ Robert Engler

A NATION WHOSE POLITICAL ORIGINS are in the age of reason, we live on the edge of violence. A people whose ideological roots are in the ethic of individual power and responsibility, we dwell in a setting of collective irresponsibility.

Internationally, the United States is on a collision course, whether through a direct confrontation bringing World War III closer, or through an endless series of counterrevolutionary actions against national liberation movements. We are never more than an incident away from a nuclear holocaust.

The United States is the world's great military power. We serve as arms merchants to much of the world. We have military agreements with more than sixty nations.

Change of the status quo through external force is not to be countenanced anywhere, White House adviser Walt Rostow tells us. And we interpret such episodes as the civil war in Vietnam in this light.[1] Secretary of State Rusk has made it clear that "no would-be aggressor should suppose that the absence of a defense treaty, congressional declaration, or U.S. military presence grants immunity to aggression."[2]

The United States is the self-anointed policeman of the Western and the Eastern world. We support corrupt ruling oligarchies whose first commitment is to order—the order of scarcity upon which their own power and privilege are based. In the holy name of anticommunism we frustrate the rising egalitarian demands for social change that might bring land, food, and political expression to the many. We also make increasingly remote the possibility that such expectations might yet be realized peaceably.

At home our resources and institutions have been recruited to support this self-image of beleaguered guardian of universal morality. Troubled congressmen admit, in the privacy of their offices, that they do not know how to stop the warfare juggernaut. Thoughtful journalists say they have never seen the military perspective so dominant in Washington. Moderate men debate whether the President is a cynical tyrant or a petulant prisoner. The peace movement has recruited an impressive number of essentially nonpolitical citizens fearful of our warring course, although lost as to alternatives. All to little avail, it would appear. In Vietnam we are face to face with ourselves and all the assumptions which shape our picture of the world. Challenged at every point, from communism as demonological conspiracy to capitalism as messianic liberation, we redouble our military efforts.

At home we live atop a social powder keg. Fundamental tensions of race, poverty, technological change, overcrowding, and alienation fester beneath the euphoric statistics of a rising gross national product and the rituals of practical politics. The familiar American theme of "getting yours" has been accelerated to "get yours now." All classes, from Negroes in Watts to oil barons in Saudi Arabia, the lean grabbing and the fat clinging, live as if there were no recognizable tomorrow. Wary public officials are haunted by the specter that a chance street-corner brush might spark an uncontrollable explosion in the urban jungle. The recurring concern of those who hold power is how to buy time and maintain privilege by cutting in the malcontents, or at least their political leaders, whether on the Lower East Side or in Latin America.

Meanwhile, absorption in our daily routines, from meaningless work and insatiable buying to frenetic recreation and rudderless politics, feeds the comforting lie that all is well—or as well as can be expected. An official alchemy, supported by all the arts and instruments of mass persuasion, perpetuates the illusion that corporate determination of productive priorities is privacy, that multinational business goliaths are just like small boys selling lemonade, that unfettered consumption of gadgetry and sex are exercises of social power, that the primacy of personal enhancement is inevitably socially beneficial, that poverty is character weakness, that organized insecurity is welfare, that addiction is deviant behavior, that boredom is freedom, that mass political impotence sustains the pluralist idyll, that paranoid hysteria is reason, that anticommunism is prodemocracy, that force is strength, that totalitarian drift is life-affirming direction, that our cumulative disabilities are cultural lags affirming the basic rightness of our course (for what system is perfect?). Institutionalized myths protect us from adding up the score, while assuring that somehow time, technology, and morality are on our side. The American way remains inviolate.

The cumulative hypocrisy has assaulted the idealism that has been described as the "growing edge" of society. A sensitive minority of young people, the natural heirs to idealism, have been angered by the pervasive corruption and injustice and by the ugliness, planned and unplanned, of a looted environment. They have been awakened, morally if not politically, by the crusades for nuclear disarmament, civil rights, economic opportunity, and peace in Vietnam. But they find themselves frustrated by their growing awareness of the integrated character of the forces that coalesce to cripple basic social change. Traditional political processes seem more traps than channels for consciousness and expression adequate to meet the perceived urgency. Revered ideologies emerge as manipulative masks for rule by irresponsible technocratic bureaucracies over a citizenry whose dominant political tone is trained passivity. Students have also to face the ever tempting alternative to the rewards for "growing up absurd"—contracting out.

The students' harshest judgment is directed, and *deserves* to be directed, not against corporation or federal bureaucracy, the CIA or FBI, captive mass media or tired trade unions, but against the structure closest to their daily lives: the educational apparatus culminating in the colleges and universities. (How long before this anger will be extended downward to the even more vulnerable and culpable high school system?)

For the university is one institution which could illuminate the historical and social context of private discontent. It offers the time and resources for the pursuit of questions and approaches which would develop an understanding of how we arrived at the present malaise. It offers a setting for challenging the premises of the present society, for appreciating what deserves to be retained, and for developing a new environment worthy of the best in man. If ever there was a need for an oasis where young people, together with an older generation, could contemplate the past, appraise the present as history, and gird themselves for tomorrow, while learning to live with intelligence, integrity, and wonder, that time is now.

But what does one find on campus? There is no one answer, given the great numbers and purposes of the modern university. But some central thrusts become uncomfortably apparent.

The university has joined the team. It has become another vested interest in a great protective society, and as such, an integral member of the chorus celebrating the American Way.

This is not to argue that there was once a golden age when higher learning was simply teacher and disciple on a log, sharing a common search for knowledge. The university has always been caught up in the going system. Its inhabitants have always had to struggle for intellectual independence against those who viewed the schools as instruments for culture-breaking the young and developing loyalty to the social order. Resistance to fuzzy-minded nincompoops and clear-thinking bigots of all persuasions has always been a minimum requirement for meaningful survival.

Once American colleges were built as cathedrals and their function was to recruit gentlemen in the service of

God. The newer public universities were designed to prepare the middle class for agrarian and mechanical arts and
for teaching. Now that we are a society of professionals,
technicians, office workers, and consumers, the new man-
date is clear: training for marketable skills and unlimited
consumption. It is not surprising that many of the newer
houses of learning are architecturally indistinguishable
from office buildings, supermarkets, and airports. These
are the refineries for white-collar America. Soon half of
our high school population will be "on stream."

No one is selling shares in education, and universities
are not listed on the stock exchanges, at least not at this
writing. But "learning" is a boom activity in capital investment, size, numbers, and prestige. The United States
has a school population of seventy million. About six million are now undergraduate or graduate students. In thirty
years the latter figure may be tripled. One estimate holds
that within a decade colleges will be founded at a rate of
one a week.

Population projections and budget requests make legis-
lators painfully aware of this trend. Corporate boards are
under pressure to aid private institutions. The corporations are also planning ahead as the American society elim-
inates traditionally defined work as its central activity.
"Leisure" and "learning" have become private investment
targets as government at all levels allocates billions for
educational services and equipment. Publishers scramble
into the lucrative textbook market (approximately one
third of all industry sales), and *they* become listed on the
market. "Textbooks," reports the chairman of Crowell
Collier & Macmillan, "may reasonably be expected to constitute the single most important classification of product
for the next ten years."[3]

Electronics and business equipment manufacturers are heavily involved in closed-circuit television, videotape, visual aids, teletypewriters, and computers. "You can have a friendly relationship with a computer that a teacher couldn't find time for," an American Telephone and Telegraph Company educational marketing specialist explains.[4]

Other corporations move to integrate the publishers into their communications and entertainment networks. RCA has taken over Random House, which had previously acquired Knopf and taken over Pantheon. CBS moves to purchase Holt, Rinehart & Winston, and also Creative Playthings (toys and educational systems) and the New York Yankees. Xerox acquires American Educational Publications from Wesleyan University, University Microfilms, and Heritage Library, and has explored buying CBS. The Raytheon Corporation swallows D. C. Heath, Litton Industries takes over the American Book Company, and International Telephone and Telegraph buys Howard W. Sams. General Electric and *Time* create the General Learning Corporation.

In appraising the role of the university it is helpful to recognize that while many are marginal enterprises struggling for status and survival, many others are vast propertied complexes. They have substantial holdings in real estate and in manufacturing and oil stocks. Yale's portfolio, for example, includes stock in American Broadcasting-Paramount Theatres. Universities have large payrolls, and behind the studied gentility are thousands upon thousands of underpaid and unorganized service employees.

The trustees are recruited largely from the business centers and from law, finance, and related areas which service the corporate world. Local colleges tend to tap local businessman; national institutions draw upon national figures.

The presidents, savagely portrayed by Thorstein Veblen as captains of erudition, are generally safe men, chosen because of a hoped-for adroitness in managing the plant, personnel, and public relations of a large-scale organization. They meet frequently with leaders from other power centers. The shuttling of executive personnel from foundations to government to educational corporations to the university is a contemporary pattern. Presidents and even deans are often found on boards of industrial and financial institutions. Grayson Kirk of Columbia, for example, has served on the board of directors of Consolidated Edison, Socony-Mobile, International Business Machines, and Nation-Wide Securities Company. The faculty newsletter of one large college in the East recently reported as a first item under a section entitled "Other scholarly activities" that its president "was elected a member of the board of trustees of the Bowery Savings Bank."

The rising tide of applications creates tremendous demand on academic resources and perspectives. Few college presidents can escape the edifice complex, a drive which makes them first-name intimates and more remote suppliants of men who can get things done, i.e. raise or appropriate money. Campuses are dotted with buildings commemorating the achievements of robber barons and the newer corporate entities. These monuments in turn provide, as Veblen noted, visible assurance to a lay public of the worthiness of the ongoing enterprise. The expanding property holdings become enclaves which serve to insulate the university from undesirable elements in the surrounding community. Columbia's growth pattern is a notorious but not exceptional example.

The American university is increasingly concerned with its "image" in dealing with legislatures, foundations, federal agencies, corporations, alumni, and the general public. Some schools maintain a larger payroll for public relations and fund raising than for professional librarians. While individual educators evidence genuine concern over the life of students, much of the current academic tempest over drugs and sex suggests more of a concern for the quality of the public relations of the institutions than for that of the private relations of the young.

Now that education is established as a prime national resource for technological superiority, dealings with the federal government become crucial. Just as offices of corporate vice-presidents in quest of political and economic favors line Connecticut Avenue, so do the universities have representatives in Washington in quest of research and development contracts and grants. The educational administrators find allies in congressmen who, just as they logroll for dams, post offices, missile bases and war contracts, now fight for more equitable regional distribution of funds. One estimate shows 40 percent of total federal educational support money concentrated in twenty-five universities. Princeton and Columbia, for example, derive over half of their total budgets from governmental sources.

Learning itself has been recruited in the service of power. Scientists and, increasingly, social scientists now march jauntily behind the banner of the benevolent warfare-welfare-corporatist state. They provide rhetoric, techniques, and manpower for enhancing and legitimizing the Great Society. Idle curiosity and its loyalty to the life of the mind remain a tattered ideal upheld by amiable humanists, stray scientists, and outraged poets.

Punishments and coercions have played a part here. Investigations and loyalty purges have left their deadening mark. One can estimate the number of teachers fired, but it is not possible to tally those not hired or promoted. And no statistic will reveal directly the number of professors and administrators who have internalized the policy of constraint for both on-campus and off-campus utterances and activities. It is also true that caution rather than daring is a major motivation leading men to enter academic pursuits.

But the seduction of the not-so-innocent scholar is made possible primarily by a highly developed reward system reflected in the academic hierarchy. Adminstrators, those who administer research (a relatively new breed), and researchers are at the apex. Graduate teaching is next on the prestige ladder. Those who can't or won't, teach undergraduates. Teaching itself has been downgraded to the level of manual labor. On many campuses the introductory course—often the critical determinant in the educational life of the student—is the ultimate in social shame for the professor and hence abandoned to the cynical clown or to the earnest and inexpensive graduate assistant.

As for the professors, they too have become operators. Not merely within their own institutions do their alert eyes search the horizon for the main chance. The more successful have learned to deal with other institutions—universities, institutes, foundations, business, government. Social scientists increasingly serve as consultants to corporations and trade associations. Columbia's Bureau of Applied Research and the University of Michigan's Institute for Social Research, for example, have provided research for many such clients. Business management is especially interested in behavioral studies relating to personnel problems. In a speech at the University of Michigan, Arjay

Miller, president of the Ford Motor Company, explained the mutual attraction:

> The corporation in a sense is a clinical laboratory where theories about human nature are put to the test of the marketplace. The social scientist and humanist have much to learn from the experience of the corporation. And the corporation has much to learn from the broader and more theoretical approach. Each will be better off if ways can be found to bring their people together in closer and more frequent working relationships.

Knowledge brings economic growth and economic growth provides the basis for more financial support for universities, Mr. Miller further explained. He thought that the growing relationships between such institutions in an interdependent world "can be smooth and constructive —or they can be abrasive and damaging." But he felt that

> the conflict between the profit motive and the acceptance of new responsibilities by business is more apparent than real. By the same token, the apparent conflict between the educational functions of the university and the acceptance of broader responsibilities is also an illusion. The specific goals of education and the broad goals of society will both be better served as the university increases its participation in the outside world.[5]

The professors are interested in income, status, the respect of their peers, and power—or access to the ears of power. Or at least to convey the illusion of the latter to themselves and their associates as they confide knowingly to their students how things "really are." Their writings, when they return from tours of duty at federal agencies, the White House, or corporate headquarters, often qualify them more as court historians and economists than as disinterested scholars. Even on campuses traditionally noted for respect for teaching and honest inquiry, those who can create revenue-producing projects and the attendant good public relations are looked upon with favor.

Grantsmanship becomes an essential academic art. Universities on the make bid heavily for faculty who can bring money and prestigious research. (Universities also take very generous overhead cuts on research grants transmitted through the institution.) Minimum teaching demands are placed upon their time and these men become recognized as leaders in their professions. These commercial talents attract graduate students who quickly learn where the rewards are, how to pursue them, and with whom. Ten campuses now annually generate one third of all the social science and humanities doctorates. Big research money, going to name universities, serves to distort research, the more richly supported areas drawing heavy attention and others being neglected.

The big men on campus become professional conference goers and givers, scurrying back and forth across the land (and sea) to one another's meetings. They meet at businessmen's bars, hotels, and resorts, scarcely distinguishable from the salesmen and second-echelon corporate executives who frequent these spots. Occasionally, they may pause in their cups to deplore the pressures on their scholarly time and to lament the passing of the lonely contemplative life.

Meanwhile, interlocking networks linking foundations, governmental agencies, and academic entrepreneurs are forged. Those who learn to play the game are inducted into the higher circles. Grants, honors, offices, appointments, review opportunities, and even mention in one another's footnotes and bibliographies, are among the plums.

What is the style and character of the knowledge being offered in the schools? Essentially marketable skills. Professors are experts who teach techniques, whether in economics, sociology, politics, or the behavioral sciences. Research is elevated as the ultimate goal. Amply footnoted platitudes elucidate the obvious. Isolated events are magnified out of all proportion to their value. Painstakingly gathered data are used to bring more clarity to subjects than may be inherent in them. Relationships not worth developing, but lending themselves to verification, are documented, while fundamental patterns of social structure remain obscured. All these findings are packaged in the most formidable and fashionable pseudoscientific language. For the quantitative approach rules. Measuring the measurable rather than asking fundamental questions of content, value, and alternative, becomes the road to a vigorous ordering of evidence. Numbers become equated with validity as statistics, computers, systems analysis, and game theory become the order of the day. Similarly, output is equated with contribution to knowledge. "The candidate [for promotion] has written seventeen articles since we last reviewed his contract, although of course I haven't read any of them"—the latter aired without a smile by a senior colleague.

Underlying the claim of scientific objectivity so cherished by the newer breed is the proud assumption of moral detachment. This attempted emulation of the physical and natural sciences confuses thoroughly the essence of science. At its best, science is a spirit, not a technique. Trusting imagination and intuition, it is speculative and creative, tentative rather than final, while deeply committed to the continued and vigorously honest search for larger understanding.

The distorted scientism so prevalent in modern social

science means that its inquiries are not guided by any sense of urgency or priority. As Robert S. Lynd concluded in *Knowledge for What?* "Research without an actively selective point of view becomes the ditty bag of an idiot, filled with bits of pebbles, straws, feathers, and other random hoardings."[6] First questions are not asked, but assumed, thus feeding the myth that the new research techniques start with no a priori assumptions. Yet modes of analysis and tools are never neutral. They shape and are shaped by their cultural contexts and their users.

In economics the employment of so-called neutral tools means that the current goals of the economic system are taken for granted. Indeed, the teaching of economics in college is often a thinly disguised dressing up of business education in a more respectable liberal-arts garb. Growth is good and the gross national product (how apt a label) is a value-free measure. That is, the manufacture of harps and napalm, cigarettes and cancer research, all are dumped onto the same scale to record the onward march of the economy—and incidentally, to justify the way we live and assess priorities.

Some economists feel that their tools are so far advanced that policy alternatives about such issues as resources, investments, and depressions boil down to technical questions of the right decision mix. Projections of present data into the future give the appearance of scholarly capacity to understand and master the broader sweep of events. What often becomes obscured is the recognition that economic choices involve values and hence are political alternatives which have to be fought for. Neat charts extending back into the past often conceal bloody battles while perpetuating the comforting illusion that technology and time will solve our problems. Gains in particular areas of social policy have accrued because people have effectively mobilized intelligence and power for them.

But economists have preferred to treat issues of power gingerly. Many still presume the competitive model to be an operative reality. They see antitrust and regulation providing the necessary checks on big business where rivals, labor, small business, and consumers somehow fail to countervail. Organized labor is viewed as a strong balancing force, and little attention is paid to the ways its genuine gains in such areas as collective bargaining have led it to be integrated into the larger industrial process. Corporations are described simply as economic institutions functioning within the frame of capitalism rather than as private governments whose economic power often spills over to become political and social power which ranges through the entire political system and across national boundaries.

Sociology was born in the promise of a larger view of the institutions and values of a society. Its practitioners sought to theorize about the total structure in relation to the daily lives of the people who experience it. Many sociologists reflected compassion for individuals and a reforming concern for the society. And there still are a minority in the field whose disciplined probing has been imaginative and purposeful. But in the hands of acquiescent researchers, sociology's focus on modern organizational society became fragmented and ahistorical. Sociologists have become involved in a buckshot variety of problems, from voting behavior to dating patterns. These are endlessly documentable. But they are generally isolated in self-contained systems and rarely defined in terms of significant relationships.

The methodologists who took over the field have tried

to build a body of facts and to sharpen their tools on such investigation, reasoning that theory would emerge only after adequate (statistical) data was accumulated. Small-scale research backed by large-scale grants is now typical. The quest for truth about trivia provides limitless full employment for a growing procession of dutiful graduate students trained in methodology but culturally deprived and innocent about social realities. It also makes possible seemingly impressive collaborative projects under senior professors—and small-scale findings.

This "abstracted empiricism," as C. Wright Mills called it, is divorced from any deep sense of social urgency and thus from sensitivity to the desperate needs of people on the fringes of an acquisitive society and the equally real torments of those who presumably have made it. The underlying premises of a society presumed to be egalitarian and mobile and functioning in a progressing harmony are accepted as central. Illustrations to the contrary, whether of slavery, racism, class structure, hard-core poverty, or political helplessness, are categorized as temporary or as deviations from the cultural norms.

Sociologists studying in such tension areas as race, poverty, violence, delinquency, and population movement have tended to emphasize the approaches of accommodation and adjustment within the factory, the ghetto, the deprived school, the welfare state. Some have become staff members and researchers for the modern welfare bureaucracies, liberal and reformist in origins and now conservative and often antihuman in function. Their clinical approach, sometimes a defense against the unanticipated and relentless grimness of what they experience, when combined with a deeply built-in class bias, helps to set them almost hopelessly apart from their clients.

Some have become the open agents of business management, directly involved in social engineering. Other sociologists find employment in the related areas of advertising and public relations. Here they work with psychologists to manipulate the irrational in order to encourage consumers and citizens to make choices which support the going system, all the while believing that they are thinking and feeling freely.

Even those whose careers are not directly with the state, the big private welfare systems, or the corporations are often conscious of the need to be sound and respectful. To cry out that something in the social structure is fundamentally wrong is to lose one's professional cool, and possibly the next grant, a consultancy, an academic reputation. Meanwhile, sociologists continue to teach the skills and grace necessary for successful living in a bureaucratic world. Or they theorize on an abstract level divorced from all reality. Few questions are asked about the alternatives to the social disciplines now operative in our industrial economy. Yet as Robert S. Lynd warned in 1939:

> . . . no culture can be realistically and effectively analyzed by those who elect to leave its central idols untouched; and, if fundamental change is required, it does no good simply to landscape the ground on which these idols stand.[7]

Political science has also devoted considerable energy to the quest for a methodology which would establish the objectivity and hence the "scientific" quality of the discipline. Perhaps the clearest accomplishment of this concern has been the essentially apolitical nature of the field and its teaching.

Paradoxically, the focus has been on proving that the American system of governance works—a very old tradition in political science indeed. The argument runs: "There are problems, yes; but these are due to new conditions and are shortcomings to be resolved by the education and administration of good men."

Students are expected to be involved in the mastery of descriptive details of the process, in learning what is supposed to be, rather than engaged in the search for what actually happens and why. Questions as to why the channels do not always seem responsive to mass needs tend to go unasked. Approaches which seek to locate effective social power are often viewed with suspicion as conspiracy theories, especially when they explore beyond the formal legal mechanism of the community. Or they are answered by the convenient doctrine of pluralism which reassures that the organized private power forces of the society balance one another so as to preclude concentrated irresponsible rule. (*"We* are pluralist; *they* are monolithic. *We* built through freedom; *they* built through controls.")

Pressure groups are examined apart from their actual social context. Their competition is seen as fitting into a larger harmonious process called "political democracy," which is held together by what has been described as "reciprocal tensions." Public opinion and communications are also areas for "realistic" discussion. But measurement studies dominate and limited attention is paid to the power of the mass media to shape opinion and to sustain the apolitical cultural belief that individual torments and triumphs are always private ones.

Thus, wise public policy is assumed to prevail, explained by a mystique not unlike Adam Smith's invisible hand. Pluralism is seen to emerge unscathed from the grinding reshaping of society by giant, technologically rooted forces. Liberal democracy remains viable enough to invite whatever reforms are needed. Thus the science of politics serves as conservative civics training for the status quo. Progress just happens—or is destined.

There is no sustained focus on how social change comes about or on political action beyond working within the present system. "Human nature" is assumed to be a constant, and little attention is paid to how particular cultures shape it. For professional political science prefers the tame questions. It offends few and serves fewer. It rarely asks what meaning can be given to political democracy in an integrated industrial environment. It is of marginal help in developing the conditions for a genuine climate of freedom and a respect for politics as a creative activity which might help solve the problems which trouble individuals and preclude community. The bulk of political science thus abdicates from responding to the crying need for a new theory of democracy.

The related field of planning has attracted increased interest as recognition of our cumulative disabilities has become inescapable. For planning involves the organization of human and physical resources in harmony with defined goals and values. But thus far the dominant versions of planning have not ventured far beyond the basic faith in the essential rightness of American political thought and the market mechanisms. Piecemeal physical planning is still the safest approach.

In many instances even the physical focus of planning remains not far removed from the burning question of how to funnel traffic in and out of shopping centers.

More militant planners do have visions of rehabilitation on a scale to match our imperatives. But there remains a profound reluctance to go beyond pleas for intelligence and administration, to move from welfare and fragmented intervention to broad-gauged social planning commensurate with the scope of modern technology. For the troublesome question remains of how a professional gains the popular political support necessary for democratic rule and for challenging the private power forces which fear such directions. Shifting from the combustion engine to the electric car and curtailing air pollution, to cite two current examples, may be desirable ways of improving our physical environment. But at their heart these are political questions, not simply technical ones, as one discovers in fights for appropriate legislation to guide both the direction and the consequences of private investment.

The social sciences have also played their part in the furthering of national policy abroad. Accepting the underlying ideological assumptions of this society, they have helped to translate them into moral absolutes of universal relevance and have thus contributed to keeping supposedly dispassionate social inquiry on a plane with religious devotion. Democracy is defined in terms of prevailing Western political arrangements, or the idealized versions of how they are supposed to work.

American economic expansion abroad is generally accepted. Little attempt is made to relate foreign policies and the domestic forces that may produce them. Kremlinologists, area specialists, and other experts have staffed our public agencies or found ready audiences at the War College, the Defense and State departments, the National Security Council, and the CIA. Books, journals, and reviews have been secretly subsidized. Americans lecturing abroad and the setting up of schools often have the quality of cultural imperialism, sharing the generally missionary intensity of the agriculturalists now bringing 4H clubs to the farmers of South Vietnam. Political scientists have thus helped to package the simplistic cold-war doctrines of anti-communism in the more acceptable wrappings of liberal reform, national security, and scholarship.

The cruder reality of the recruitment of political science is also prevalent. The Michigan State University project in Vietnam is a conspicuous but by no means unique case of a university aggressively on the make. The initial arrangements are believed to have been made between then Vice-President Richard Nixon and John Hannah, the university's head who has held many posts in national Republican administrations. Professors in political science, along with experts from Yale, UCLA, and Pittsburgh, ultimately served as covers for the CIA and supported activities which violated the Geneva Agreement. The mask was technical assistance and administrative reform, causes which the academics could readily accept. But in a setting where the larger purposes of the South Vietnamese and United States governments were to block fundamental social change and where the professors chose not to ask the larger questions, the reforms turned out to include training the secret police and generally backing counterrevolution. The university and its faculty also accepted the controls over research and publication set by the two governments with whom the contracts were drawn.[8]

Working directly with the military is also commonplace, and classified social science projects are widespread. It is reported that MIT has awarded a number of higher degrees for classified theses. One loses the capacity to distinguish between satire and reality when an applicant for a university position in political science, currently employed by the RAND Corporation, explains modestly on his vita, under the heading of publications, that many of his writings are classified and hence not available for listing or inspection.

The social quietism and eroded erudition so prevalent in academia might be written off as amusing or pathetic charades for a genteel elite. Costly, yes, but then much of the affluence of contemporary society is rooted in waste and irrelevance. But now the university directly reaches the many, not the few. The question as to the impact upon the recipients of such education produces chilling evidence.

Genuine students, admittedly a minority and often screened out by our antieducational system, come because of a curiosity. They hope to be exposed to the excitement of original and independent thought, sharing with inquiring and trained minds old insights and new directions. Their first discovery is that they have to search very hard for such oases. What they find instead is that the emphasis and rewards are upon recitation and continued dependence upon authority. Students are trained and indoctrinated as passive, powerless recipients. Truth is often equated with techniques and regarded as revealed. The main job is mastery. Thus, finality rather than doubt and wonder shapes much of the offering and climate.

For the advanced student rigid methodology and narrow specialization easily become equated with professionalism. Gaining an overview is the luxury of wishy-washy and undisciplined humanists. A veneer of "culture" may be offered to help them decorate their lives and homes with stereo sets and fashionable talk and tastes. But the message is to learn to identify with the prevailing social order and to advance within it. What Veblen called a trained incapacity provides the groundwork for a lifelong trained innocence.

Good undergraduates, when not completely turned off, are generally intellectually more open-minded and alive than all but the best of graduate students, a commentary not on graduate genes but on graduate systems. Emulating their betters, the latter's attraction to status and income often leads them to display cynical and opportunistic approaches to their studies and ultimately to their careers. Competitive zeal and junior gamesmanship and grantsmanship become their equipment for survival and success in the academic marketplace. Idealism comes to be deprecated, whether about learning or about the society. Playing it cool is the model, the professor merely reinforcing what prevails in the so-called real world outside.

Students are generally treated paternalistically, undergraduates as children and graduates as apprentices. Their involvement in the shaping of educational policy is minimal. Their rights are limited and their newspapers are frequently subject to censorship. Academic freedom, both in the classroom and beyond, is generally thought of as the prerogative of faculty. Papers, records, grades, class standings, and organizational membership lists are part of dossiers which many administrations have made available, without student consent, to other universities, corporations, Selective Service, the military, and other government agencies including the FBI and the House Un-American Activities Committee. The American Civil Liberties Union has charged that the University of Michigan's president turned over to HUAC on request sixty-five names drawn from three campus organizations critical of the Vietnam war. President Harlan H. Hatcher "told the faculty after the House committee hearings that 'the university must abide by the law . . . like HUAC or not, it is a duly constituted arm of Congress.' "[9]

University administrators have also cooperated with loyalty-security programs and have tolerated the presence of local police, FBI agents, and informants on campus.

They have continued military training programs. And they have welcomed National Defense Education Act programs even where this affiliation posed a challenge to university autonomy by defining who shall not teach and who shall not be taught. Sometimes the motive for going along as an arm of national security was eagerness to prove to the public and potential benefactors that the institution was sound and trying hard to get money. Faculties, operating with a crippled or archaic faculty government, often chose silence.

The students who maintain the spirit of curiosity and caring often do so in spite of their education. (The convention-bound professors have long since abandoned most of the problems and needs of students to professional guidance counselors and administrators. The latter, ironically, are often the only ones on campus with an overall concern about the school and higher learning.) These young people who have to go South, to the grape vineyards of California, to the urban ghetto, to underdeveloped countries, and to wherever they sense injustice and perceive a chance to identify with their times, are not only showing their own emotional and moral needs and concerns. They are also proclaiming that history has to be lived and felt and shaped. And they are asking about the relevance of the university which too often has abandoned and betrayed them from behind the ivy of tradition and objectivity. C. Wright Mills remains an authentic hero for some, not because he sought their favors or because his answers were necessarily right, but because he engaged their intelligence and passion by trying to ask the questions that mattered.

The most socially conscious students are exciting to work with. At the same time the readiness to display wholesale contempt for the past, the indiscriminate assault upon "the Establishment" (Berkeley, General Motors, and the Pentagon are all held to be the same—an understandable view from the perspective of those who feel acted upon), the outbursts of anti-intellectualism and the preference for instant experience and gut values, the attraction to direct confrontation rather than conciliation, can be frustrating. But if the student activists do ultimately turn against the best of what the world of learning might offer, this will be no tribute to the university. Nor can the society afford to lose the many middle-level students whose sights might be elevated by a faculty who showed concern for the world and for them.

A credibility gap in government is tragic, but not unprecedented. On campus it is fatal. The United States needs the perceptions and imagination of those able to cut through the powerfully manned defenses of a sick social order. It needs the reasoning power for defining with integrity the nature of the malaise. And it cries out for alternative directions which would spark the development of social consciousness and political activism among the American people. They might then support the building of a more satisfying society at home, one which would expand meaningful personal choices and the potential of reasoned political behavior, while identifying with the aspirations of mankind everywhere.

There are many decent and talented people in the academic world. But like others they need help in putting their decency into a broader context. Some of this concern can be found among poets, playwrights, novelists, journalists, politicians, and crusading lawyers. The university might do well to infuse its own ranks with the best of these creative people and with some of the students in exile. But translating skepticism and criticism into social inventiveness is the major challenge for the social scientist and the university.

The odds may be overwhelmingly against the radical reconstruction needed for a democratic society. But genuine education represents a buying of time. The university offers the ideal and the potential mechanism for a community of intelligence and conscience which might yet develop dialogue in the larger community. If the teachers and the students, theoretically the last of the unorganized and unintegrated, do not recognize the imperative, then where else can this society turn?

NOTES

1. Walt W. Rostow, address at the University of Leeds, England, February 23, 1967.
2. U.S. Senate, Committee on Armed Services, Preparedness Investigating Subcommittee, 89th Cong., 2nd Sess., testimony by Secretary of State Dean Rusk, "Worldwide Military Commitments," August 25, 1966, p. 9.
3. *New York Times*, May 3, 1967.
4. *Wall Street Journal*, February 13, 1967.
5. Arjay Miller, address at the University of Michigan, Ann Arbor, Michigan, September 15, 1966.
6. Robert S. Lynd, *Knowledge for What?* (Princeton, Princeton University Press, 1939), p. 183.
7. *Ibid.*, p. 226.
8. In a revealing commentary, the *New York Times* (April 15, 1966) carried the following dispatch: "The disclosure of the C.I.A. incident caused deep chagrin on the Michigan State campus. According to sources there, officials were concerned about threats of a special investigation by a committee of the State Legislature. They were also worried that news of the C.I.A. link would injure their operations in a dozen developing nations."
9. *New York Times*, November 14, 1966.

THE

CHEERFUL SCIENCE OF

DISMAL POLITICS

✍ Christian Bay

THOMAS CARLYLE IN 1850 REFERRED TO
academic economists as "respectable Professors of the
Dismal Science" and thus, as John Kenneth Galbraith
has observed, "gave to economics a name that it has
never quite escaped because it was never quite unde-
served." The economists of Carlyle's day were intent on
proving, as are most recognized economists and other social
scientists at most times, that there must always be privileged and underprivileged classes, and that the present
with all its suffering at the lower end of the social ladder
nevertheless constitutes the best of all possible worlds, at
least right now and in the foreseeable future.

Respectable professors of politics traditionally have had
much the same concerns. If political science has had an

easier time escaping the label "dismal," it is perhaps for two main reasons. First, it is in many ways less of a science, still, than economics was even a century ago. Economists have had handy units of measurement to work with; money happens to be quantifiable and yet not unimportant; and with the aid of mathematics economists have been able to figure out prices for almost everything. Political scientists have worked manfully to develop their own quantifiable key concepts, but it seems that they have advanced toward increasing exactness only at the expense of increasing triviality. Thus it may be said that while economists and political scientists are equally remote from the comprehension of values in social life, they differ in that political scientists don't even have price tags to work with.

Secondly, if the academic study of politics is less of an exact science, its style is also less gloomy and its image less dismal, because there are strong institutional pressures favoring a more cheerful stance. Every social order is dominated by its privileged classes, whose patriotism celebrates the status quo. While economists are busy explaining the necessity of poverty and, incidentally with increasing effectiveness, seeking to prevent recessions that hit the well-to-do as well as the poor, the central task of political science as a profession apparently is to extol the present order, criticize other existing systems, and debunk radical and utopian political thought. In America in the 1960s, the task is to praise democracy, identifying this particular concept with the existing social order by way of praising pluralism and "free enterprise" in the same breath, and to condemn communism; in fact, all *ideologies* are suspect, and the familiar end-of-ideology literature seeks to conjure them away.

A basic element in this development is the redefinition of "politics." The end of politics, Aristotle tells us, is the highest good attainable by action. For of all creatures, man alone "has any sense of good and evil, of just and unjust, and the like. . . . Justice is the bond of men in states, for the administration of justice, which is the determination of what is just, is the principle of order in political society." Politics, then, is the master science, for its aim embraces the aims of all other scientific pursuits; the study of politics is the study of how best to promote the common good of the political community.

The idealism of Socrates, of Plato, and of Aristotle is a vital part of our intellectual heritage. Innumerable philosophers and intellectuals through the ages have insisted on their right and obligation to keep alive the difference between perceptions of man as he *is* and conceptions of man as he *ought* to be, between existing social institutions and potentially more humane social institutions.

But the modern study of politics stands in stark contrast to this classic conception. Increasingly it becomes identified with the study of existing patterns of political behavior. And for this study the Aristotelian concept of politics is clearly unsuited, focusing as it does on an assumed state of tension between the actual and the ideal, or between existing realities and the optimal common good. It is, rather, formulations like that of Harold D. Lasswell that now seem more pertinent. "Politics," according to Lasswell's boldest and best-known definition, refers to "who gets what, when, how."[1] Other modern behavioralists like to add a "why" to their conception of politics, by way of relating their definitions not only to "power" but to "authority" or "legitimacy" as well. But the latter terms are invariably intended as descriptive rather than normative:

"legitimacy" is established by way of opinion surveys and "authority" by way of communication or decision-making as well as survey research. Neither term has anything to do with justice, inherent rightness, or any other normative concept.[2]

Thus, even the study of legitimacy may be just as far removed from a concern with justice or with the needs of man as is the study of power. For the exertion of power in our time relies on the manipulation of political attitudes as much as on coercion. Regardless of political or socioeconomic system, the political leaders and the strata they represent are in control of the bulk of the various media of communication and persuasion. Bayonets are not comfortable to sit on, as Napoleon is said to have remarked; and happily for the powers that be, modern technology makes it possible for almost any present-day regime to establish a comfortable position of "legitimacy," except in revolutionary situations. Hence, a consensual concern with legitimacy *in the empirical sense only* tends, by implication, to make illegitimate for political behavioralists any scientific concern with normatively conceived legitimacy— i.e., the justification of institutions in terms of human needs, justice, freedom, or whatever the conception of the common good may be.

It is not difficult to understand why this capitulation to the status quo has taken place on the part of professional students of politics. "A political science that is mistreated," writes Hans Morgenthau, "is likely to have earned that enmity because it has put its moral commitment to the truth above social convenience and ambition." But a political science that is respected, he continues, helps the powers that be by way of mollifying the conscience of society, justifying existing power relationships, etc. "The relevance of this political science does not lie primarily in the discovery of the truth about politics, but in its contribution to the stability of society."[3]

Conversely, every political philosophy which is concerned with humane ideals and their implications in logically rigorous ways is subversive of every existing order; for it is in the nature of political philosophy, as distinguished from merely linguistic or logical analysis, to contrast existing realities with more ideal alternatives. There is always a strong temptation, then, even for philosophers to adjust to the most basic demands and assumptions of the status quo, for in most societies it is rather uncomfortable to be treated as a subversive. And when political philosophers and other social scientists establish professions and take on public educational employment, the adjustment of basic philosophical assumptions to the postulates of the established order almost inevitably becomes institutionalized. That is, perspectives on the aims of politics or philosophy or social analysis become transformed from a focus on man's needs and potentialities to a focus on systems maintenance; and most individual recruits to the social science professions are spared the agonizing ethical dilemma of choosing between being true to their role as intellectuals and embarking on comfortable careers. Indeed, they are carefully trained *not* to discover this existential dilemma.

It is not only the average academic student of politics, however, who has become theoretically incapacitated for scientific concern with issues of justice or the common good. In their descriptive studies of the political behavior of the supposedly "developed" American and other Western electorates, political scientists have discovered that the public too appears unconcerned with the Public Interest. Quite correctly, they describe most voters as either apathetic or anxiety-ridden, and as rarely able to see their private and group interests in the perspective of their stake in the public interest. The rule, in short, is what I prefer to call "pseudopolitical" rather than "political" behavior.

By "political," I refer to all activity aimed at improving or protecting conditions for the satisfaction of human needs and demands in a given society according to some universalistic scheme of priorities, implicit or explicit. "Pseudopolitical," on the other hand, refers to activity that *resembles* political activity but is exclusively concerned either with alleviating personal neuroses or with promoting private or interest-group advantage, deterred by no articulate or disinterested conception of what would be just or fair to other groups. Thus, pseudopolitics is the counterfeit of politics.[4]

Now, I am in no way opposed to the study of pseudopolitical behavior. The behavioral literature of our profession is an invaluable source of facts about our political and pseudopolitical life; my plea is for more and better behavioral research. What I ask for is a more comprehensive, more humane, more truly *political* framework of theory for the study of pseudopolitical and political behavior. There should be no excuse for jumping from the fact of prevailing pseudopolitical behavior in our competitive, unjust, anxiety-ridden social order to the enormous conclusion that pseudopolitics is "normal" in a "developed society"—that, in other words, we are doomed to a *permanent* eclipse of genuine politics in the modern democratic world, and that no educational liberation from *Time, U.S. News,* and their intellectual equivalents is ever to reach more than a small minority of our electorate.

I plead, further, for the necessity of liberating our political science literature from the following prevailing assumptions: (1) that political research in America must take the present system for granted, leaving out the study of experiments directed toward radical change; (2) that this nation is "politically developed," even though its electorate behaves by and large pseudopolitically, not politically; (3) that it is either impossible or not worthwhile to develop assumptions about national goals (e.g. reduction of suffering, maximization of justice or of freedom) and to study their empirical implications; and (4) that it is either impossible or not worthwhile to develop and apply psychological models of need priorities as a basis for research into their political implications—i.e., to develop a scientific study of politics founded on the study of basic human needs, as distinct from manifest wants and demands.

One would have hoped that our own profession had maintained a Socratic commitment to the defense of genuine politics, particularly in this age of conspicuous, high-powered, systematic propagation of mindless pseudopolitics. But as we have seen, the tendency has been to conform to the powerful demands on us, much as the autonomous spirit of the university has been replaced by the more pliant stance of the "multiversity." We study expressed wants and demands, often the result of indoctrination from the outside, and are unconcerned about inner needs, or prerequisites for social and individual health. We willingly submit to the deception that our corporation-ridden pluralist order is to be called "democratic" and that our laws are to be judged as democratically enacted and therefore legitimate in more than a descriptive sense of the term. Worst of all, we continue to think of our bailiwick as the study of means-ends relationships, while conveniently claiming that ends cannot be studied "scientifically."

It will, I think, be instructive to examine the way in which one very important mainstream textbook currently influences the professional study of politics. *Comparative Politics: A Developmental Approach,*[5] by Gabriel A. Almond and G. Bingham Powell, Jr., is probably the most widely used textbook today in the field of comparative politics. Professor Almond, the book's senior author, was in 1965–1966 the president of the American Political Science Association, and for many years has been one of the most influential members of the profession. Not only is he undoubtedly the most influential name in the currently important field of comparative politics, but he has also distinguished himself as a scholar in the neighboring social sciences where he has done creative, influential work on a variety of problems. And apart from his own writings, Almond's editorship of the Studies in Political Development series, published by the Princeton University Press, is another monument to his commanding influence.[6]

Almond and Powell acknowledge that "the functional approach" acceptably describes the orientation of their book. They place themselves to this extent in the tradition of the *Federalist Papers,* but contend that their own concept of "system" is more explicit, as they have the advantage of building on modern developments in sociology, anthropology, and communications theory. And let it be stressed here that Almond's and his (present and earlier) collaborators' conceptual contributions to the analysis of political input, output, and conversion processes are most fruitful and have helped to brighten considerably the prospects for future political research. Also, the often judicious and illuminating use of survey data and other empirical materials in the context of conceptual and theoretical discussions in this literature constitutes a real contribution to sociological as well as political knowledge.

My chief objections are to the *uses* made of this knowledge, in Almond and Powell and more generally in the modern comparative politics literature. I object, not to a functional approach, but to a functional approach that has no normative reference beyond the range of data it seeks to order and make use of. The range of data is simply called "the political system." The trouble with this theoretical framework is that it has little bearing on politics as distinct from pseudopolitics; for it has little bearing on the problem of man and his needs, as distinct from, in Herbert Marcuse's phrase, the "one-dimensional man" and his manipulated propensities as consumer of political outputs and contributor of inputs.

Almond and Powell acknowledge some merit in the criticism that has been made of Almond's past work to the effect that it carried static, conservative implications. They contend that their latest book substantially modifies or complements the earlier Almond approach: "We need to take a major analytical step if we are to build political development more explicitly into our approach to the political system. We need to look at political systems as whole entities shaping and being shaped by their environments."[7] But alas, no "major steps" are likely to remedy the problem of conservatism and irrelevancy to humane politics if the *political system* is to remain inviolate as the frame of reference for functional analysis. Far too easily the problem of "system maintenance and adaptation" comes to fill the normative vacuum and becomes the main evaluative standard; indeed, should we expect political scientists who disclaim professional competence with respect to normative issues to be untouched by conventional patriotism, or unconcerned with the defense ("system maintenance and adaptation") of their country and its present institutions?

Almond and Powell's concern with the empirical problems of system maintenance and adaptation is of course legitimate and praiseworthy; these are issues to be faced up to by intelligent political inquiry anywhere. But in the absence of concern with politics in the classical sense, the imagery they evoke is rather frightening in its inescapable normative implications. For example: "For an automobile to perform efficiently on the road, parts must be lubricated, repaired, and replaced. New parts may perform stiffly; they must be broken in. In a political system the incumbents of the various roles (diplomats, military officers, tax officials) must be recruited to these roles and learn how to perform in them. New roles are created and new personnel 'broken in.' "[8]

True, the authors do not go on record as favoring bigger and better automobiles as ends in themselves, regardless of where they would take us. But in so many ways, if by implication rather than explicitly, they testify to their faith in the present pluralist American system as if *it* were an end in itself, regardless of what it does to forestall politics in the classical sense, to prevent human development, or even to destroy human lives at home and abroad. If the virtual absence of effective political dialogue and of control by public opinion on the national level has left the American "military-industrial complex" free to develop a frightful military machine, with feeble brakes and strong accelerators (or "escalators"), these are problems to which Almond and Powell's analysis pays no attention.

Indeed, their tendency is to see all firm political commitments as a developmental stage to be overcome for the good of the political system: "An ideological style emerges when the individual develops a *specific* set of political orientations, but fails to develop the open, bargaining attitudes associated with full secularization."[9] In fairness, their stress on "specific" indicates their chief concern with making a point that I consider valid: that cognitive rigidity associated with ideological politics can create irrational conflicts. My objection is to their clear assumption, in the concluding phrase, that free, entirely flexible bargaining is *and should be* the essence of "developed" politics.

Last year I had my students in a graduate seminar read Frantz Fanon's *The Wretched of the Earth*[10] alongside Almond and Powell's book. The work of Almond and Powell is far superior in its conceptual clarity and sophistication; the romantic revolutionary Fanon is more concerned with exhortation than with analysis. Yet the fact that we inhabit a world filled with desperation and explosive indignation is a manifest reality, eloquently described, perhaps exaggerated, but hardly conjured up by Fanon. Where is this reality accounted for, or even acknowledged, in the Almond-Powell scheme of analysis? It appears as "anomic interest groups"! "Political systems may be marked by a high frequency of such violent and spontaneous group formation (as in France of the Fourth Republic, Italy, and the Arab nations), or notable for its absence."[11] In less than a page the "wretched of the earth" are disposed of; the implied norm appears to be that the more the state is able to monopolize violence the better, while the state of wretchedness is at best a secondary issue. Which is perhaps a suitable value premise for those hardy professionals who wish to justify the American warfare in Vietnam; but it hardly contributes a realistic approach toward understanding the political behavior of such "anomic interest groups" (what an anemic phrase!) as, for example, South Vietnam's National Liberation Front.

In their discussion of the "capabilities of political systems" Almond and Powell quite explicitly confine the universe of their inquiry to the welfare of systems rather than people. Broadly speaking, they write, "elite responses to inputs or demands may take the form of repression, indifference, substitution, or accommodation."[12] For Almond and Powell these four responses appear to exhaust the possibilities. They will not allow that revolutionary leftist or even established communist systems occasionally may at least have *attempted* a fifth kind of response: namely, to *facilitate* the development of political demands. They write as if the four types of response listed are the only possible responses. No midwifery for just causes, no massive relief in response to the often muted longings of the hopelessly oppressed can find even the smallest niche of a category within this particular input-output scheme of analysis.

It is this point that gets to the core of my main objection to the pluralist philosophy, or perhaps I should say "stance": a concern with human needs according to priorities dictated by justice is virtually ruled out, even as a problem for empirical inquiry. The vision of political inquiry is limited to articulated demands, occasionally deplorably "anomic" and violent, but usually neatly promoted by well-behaved (and well-heeled) organizations in pursuit of legitimate private interests. Regimes have a choice of suppressing demands, ignoring them, trying to placate those interests with alternate rewards, or granting the demands—presumably depending on the strength and persistency of the interest groups involved. Granted, this may well be how American and Western governments in fact behave, and possibly communist governments too. But to suggest that this is *all* there can be to "developed" politics is to abdicate all concern with justice or *human* development as the aim of politics, and to sanction, if not sanctify, pluralist pseudopolitics forever.

It bears repetition that Almond's conceptual scheme for analyzing the processes and capabilities of pluralist political systems, including their developmental potentialities if any, is a most valuable contribution of tools for political inquiry. But what the authors fail to see is how these tools can be, and predominantly are, used for the purpose of celebrating pluralist oppression and stagnation rather than as means for seeking ways toward a politics in the service of human needs. There are myriads of possibilities for empirical study of how specific output and input processes or aspects of processes relate to conditions of human well-being; yet Almond and his collaborators and students have tended to content themselves with studying the development and maintenance of the political systems as the general dependent variable. Pressures and bargaining processes are seen as the important things for elites to be concerned with, not human waste or fulfillment; and "political development" takes the place of a concern with justice and individual freedom for the least privileged.

The implications of Almond's approach, for American domestic as well as foreign policy, show up clearly in the work of one of Almond's former collaborators, Lucian W. Pye. With respect to the general population the key elements of political development involve, Pye writes, "a change from widespread subject status to an increasing number of contributing citizens, with an increasing spread of mass participation, a greater sensitivity to the principles of equality, and a wider acceptance of universalistic laws." In the United States, more than half the citizens vote,[13] while possibly still larger numbers participate vicariously in the glories of Vietnam victories as TV viewers and as readers of *Time* and *Life,* have a great sensitivity to the right of equality under the law for General Motors Corporation and the individual worker, and firmly believe in the sanctity of universalistic laws of contract. If American political development might lead to something better some day, Pye is not about to suggest the direction; his chief concern, at least in the fuller discussion in his more recent book, *Aspects of Political Development: An Analytic Study,* is with how the more benighted, still developing countries can come to resemble the Western systems more.

On this occasion Pye reviews ten types of definitions of "political development" but ends up by seeking to establish empirically "the developmental syndrome," seeking "to isolate those characteristics of political development which seem to be most widely held and most fundamental in the general thinking about problems of political development."[14] Widely held among whom? Why, among fellow American political scientists, of course, and especially, it would seem, among those who have served on the Social Science Research Council's Committee on Comparative Politics, whose past chairmen include Almond as well as Pye. By a natural habit of citing primarily each other's work, this school of thought has produced quite an imposing consensus on the meaning of "political development."

What concerns me is that I have yet to find in this literature even a hint of the possibility that "political development" ought to be defined relative to *human* development in some sense; certainly there is no such possibility left open in Pye's work. And this is particularly remarkable in view of the fact that both Pye and Almond belong to that rare species of political scientist who are articulate and well read in dynamic psychology. The most plausible explanation is that Pye, too, has become caught up in the system, i.e., in the fashion of theorizing about political systems in functional terms, in a normative vacuum in which easy patriotism rather than a more complex and less professionally rewarding concern with humanity and justice has come to dictate the underlying value standards.

True, it is hard to do research on genuine human needs as opposed to the neater categories of expressed wants, demands, and the volumes of noise and cash displayed by pluralist interest groups. But needs as distinct from conscious wants do exist, as every clinical psychologist and psychiatrist can testify, and as delinquency experts, penologists, social workers, public health officials, anthropologists, and sociologists increasingly emphasize in their work and in their writings. It is time, I submit, that political scientists also come to recognize this fact and its significance, and in this respect try to catch up with Plato and Aristotle. I am convinced that our profession will never help us to advance from our wasteful, cruel, pluralist pseudopolitics in the direction of justice and humane politics until we replace *political systems* with concepts of *human need* and *human development* as the ultimate value frameworks for our political analysis. Almond's functional approach to the study of input and output processes would by no means become obsolete by such a change in value perspective. On the contrary, it would become useful.

At times even some of our most tough-minded students of global politics seem to come within a hair's-breadth of recognizing the professional responsibility called for here.

Oskar Morgenstern has observed that "Political scientists have spent much time and effort to produce a body of knowledge that is singularly unsuited to guide us in the present dilemma of our life." This statement of fact would be hard to challenge. But what kind of knowledge would this leading American analyst of cold-war strategies like to see developed? Political scientists, Morgenstern tells us, should pay more attention to the "theory of games of strategy." He complains that so far not even Machiavelli's counsels have been abstracted "to discover whether a consistent system of rules of behavior could be constructed on that basis." Beyond this, Morgenstern recommends "tough thinking," applied to "two fields essentially: *first* to dealing with the opponent, with the uncommitted, and with our friends; and *second,* to generating the ideals we can live by, together with other nations, in the new world that is rushing toward us." The prescription is admirable. But typically, Morgenstern goes on at once to tell us it would be "ludicrous" for him to say much about these ideals. Instead, he recommends that we push for a continuing arms race, until we achieve "absolute technical certainty of immediate self-destruction for those nations who start a war" —especially, of course, for potential aggressors against the United States.[15] It would quite possibly be "ludicrous" for Morgenstern to write about "the ideals we can live by." This is not, however, because a discussion of this subject matter would necessarily be less "scientific" than the rest of his argument, but possibly because he may never have chosen to reflect deeply on these issues, in the spirit of systematic inquiry. (Though he is prepared to recommend, without such inquiry, that we push for a permanent balance of nuclear terror, rather than allowing for even the *possibility* of coming to terms politically with the aspirations of Communist nations, or of achieving sufficient disarmament or arms control to permit a politically instead of a mainly militarily competitive coexistence.)

The default which Morgenstern's thought illustrates lies, I submit, with our profession's persistent failure to develop canons of *substantive* as distinct from *formal* rationality. "Rationality" has come to be defined in terms of selection of means to given ends, rarely to the selection of ends. Talcott Parsons offers us one authoritative definition of the current usage: "An act is rational in so far as (a) it is oriented to a clearly formulated unambiguous goal, or a set of values which are clearly formulated and logically consistent; (b) the means chosen are, according to the best available knowledge, adapted to the realization of the goal."[16] This concept of rationality, which I would call "formal" rationality, is indispensable to intelligent political inquiry, or indeed almost any kind of intelligent inquiry.

But I insist that it is not sufficient. Responsible social scientists must also demand of themselves something more, which may be called *substantive rationality,* by which I mean the requirement that *ends* should be as rigorously articulated and tested as are, in political science at its current best, the proposed means to those ends, or the predictive hypotheses on which statements about means to ends rest.

Granted, the difficulties involved in what I propose are great. Indeed, it is astonishing how pervasive the notion is, even among gifted critics of our profession's "pluralistic" abdication of normative responsibility, that there can be no legitimate general purpose for politics. For example, in his fine essay "Tolerance and the Scientific Outlook," Barrington Moore, Jr., writes that one "crucial characteristic of a free society is the absence of a single overriding 'national purpose'. The attempts, never completely successful, to impose such a purpose are the stigma of the modern totalitarian state."[17] Are we to believe this to be true *regardless* of the nature of the proposed purpose, or the means with which it is advocated? Apparently even Moore will not go so far. For in the same essay he tells us that, if men are to live in society, "it may as well be with as little pain as possible." A society is bad and its social order ought to be changed, he argues, to the extent that "unnecessary suffering [is] produced by an historically specific form of government." And he appears to me to set out a fundamental objective for political science when he reflects that it possibly "is not too difficult to determine when the happiness of some people depends on the misery of others. The criterion of minimal suffering implies that such situations ought to be changed when it is possible to do so."[18]

These quotations fail to do justice to Moore's essay, in the sense that they are quite unoriginal. For as a matter of fact, even most of the full-fledged pluralists on occasion come out firmly in opposition to needless suffering. What is remarkable is that none would be so bold as to say that the overriding purpose of politics ought to be to do away with all avoidable suffering in this world of ours, and that the highest priority for political science should be to study how this can be brought about by means of social organization, including government.

It is precisely this naive view of politics that I adopt here. My position is that the proper purpose of politics is *identical with the proper purpose of medicine: to postpone death and to reduce suffering.* Political science does not prescribe drugs, for its competence is not in human physiology or body chemistry; but it should aim at prescribing the organizational innovations and social experimentation that will allow us to cultivate, in Albert Schweitzer's term, a "reverence for life."

Granted, human well-being is an elusive subject. But human suffering is far less elusive, and so are questions of life or death. Governments cannot, of course, eliminate death, but they can and should see it as their prime obligation to prevent and postpone death whenever and wherever possible. This proposition suggests any number of immediate and obvious tasks. Honorable men in government can work to eliminate capital punishment, for one thing. They can and therefore should institute—as a matter of legal right—full access to the best available medical care, regardless of the patient's ability to pay and regardless of cost to the taxpayers. The government of a truly "developed" society can and therefore should abolish poverty and slums, inferior schools, and other stymieing social institutions in the urban and rural ghettoes. And so on.

In medicine the moral commitment is clear, even if it is not always lived up to: priorities in treatment are determined not by the affluence of the various patients, but by degrees of illness, of suffering, of danger to life. There is an indisputable consensus among practitioners of medicine, at least in principle, that their commitment is to the cause of postponing death and reducing suffering; this is what their Hippocratic oath is all about, and it is not subject to revocation by the government or by a mindless public opinion which conceivably might demand, say, substandard medical treatment for communists or for ethnic or religious minorities.

There is no Hippocratic oath for politicians; nor would such an oath make any difference, given the pluralist indifference to moral imperatives in our business civilization. And here we discover an important divergence from our medical analogy. While the practice of medicine permits and often requires that first priority be given to those who are the most ill, the practice of modern pluralist politics, or pseudopolitics, almost invariably gives preferential treatment to those who are the most well-off in the sense of being least likely to suffer socioeconomic deprivation of any kind.[19] This is likely to be true to some extent in any stable social order, including a postrevolutionary communist society, on the simple sociological ground that those most privileged with affluence are likely to be disproportionately educated, articulate, and intelligent, statistically speaking, and more likely to know or have access to persons with political influence. Also, they are far more likely to have effective organizations to promote their interests.

It is precisely this state of affairs that makes the need for political scientists of maximal integrity within the academy so pressing. If a commercial society with pluralist political institutions tends to put a premium on unprincipled pragmatism, and to keep rewarding the strong at the expense of the weak, then surely our task as political scientists should not be to blend into the pluralist landscape and offer our services simply as surveyors and landscape architects, thus abandoning the ancient concern with politics as an instrument of the common good. On the contrary, I submit that our primary responsibility should be to gear our inquiry and research to the goal of prescribing the kinds of organizations and institutions that can in fact promote reverence for life.[20]

An intellectual commitment to the study of politics requires the freedom and indeed the obligation to study the fundamental normative issues with an open mind and in the scientific spirit of systematic inquiry. Yet whoever questions the legitimacy of a social order, or the assumptions by which it is habitually justified, is a radical. And radicalism can be uncomfortable and, often enough, inconvenient for career purposes. Liberalism, on the other hand, is a positive advantage nowadays within our universities, much as political conservatism is advantageous in most of the business world. Not only the training of political scientists (who nowadays are apt to refer to their *training* rather than their *education*) but the teaching that goes on at all age levels by and large aims at producing useful, pliable citizens, not free-thinking intellectuals, prone to make their own moral judgments. Every social order seeks to mold and train its young to celebrate the past and present, not to educate them to think freely and responsibly about political ideals for the future.

Nevertheless, as social scientists we must insist on speaking primarily for ourselves. Research on political aims must focus on the aims *we* want. Admittedly, we are prone to be as fallible, as selfish, as vain as the next fellow. But not more so. The comparative shelteredness of the academy and our habits of reading and writing give us at least an *opportunity* denied active politicians and those in many other careers: we *can* think disinterestedly and radically about political aims and their implications without being thrown out of our positions, at least in the better universities.

Unless larger numbers of us soon begin to take advantage of this opportunity, however, and face up to our responsibility as relatively free intellectuals, I see little hope that the social science professions will become anything better than what C. Wright Mills called them: "the utensils of history makers." Unless we learn to cultivate better our powers of substantive as well as formal rationality, and our courage to teach with candor what we know to be true, or just, our present foreign and domestic policies will remain without effective challenge. Where else but in our schools and academies can we hope to develop intelligent, principled champions of the underprivileged and the unborn?

Current prospects for American politics are indeed dismal. At home, the so-called war on poverty seems destined to remain at the minor skirmish level while the rich get richer and the poor poorer, while unemployment and crime keep rising and the explosions in the ghettoes keep getting worse. Abroad, our great liberal traditions are, especially in Vietnam, being submerged in an ooze of napalm; and in the name of liberty! It will at best take decades before America's traditional desire to be a champion of international law and of peace and human dignity becomes credible again. Those who wish this nation well must sadly observe that its present leadership seems permanently incapacitated from comprehending the realities of human aspirations and desperations in our modern world. It is surely time for our social scientists to stop cheering.

NOTES

1. Harold D. Lasswell, *Politics: Who Gets What, When, How?* (New York, McGraw-Hill Book Co., Inc., 1936).
2. Representative examples are David Easton's definition of political science as the study of "the authoritative allocation of values as it is influenced by the distribution and use of power"; and Robert A. Dahl's formulation, "A political system is any persistent pattern of human relationships that involves, to a significant extent, power, rule, or authority." See Easton, *The Political System* (New York, Alfred A. Knopf, 1953), p. 146; and Dahl, *Modern Political Analysis* (Englewood Cliffs, N.J., Prentice-Hall, Inc., 1963), p. 6.
3. Hans Morgenthau, "The Purpose of Political Science" in James

C. Charlesworth, ed., *A Design for Political Science: Scope, Objectives, Methods* (Philadelphia, American Academy of Political and Social Science, 1966), p. 73.

4. See my "Politics and Pseudopolitics: A Critical Evaluation of Some Behavioral Literature," in the *American Political Science Review*, Vol. 59 (May 1965), pp. 39–51.
5. Boston, Little, Brown and Company, 1966.
6. Among Almond's other contributions to comparative politics are Almond and Sidney Verba, *The Civic Culture* (Princeton, Princeton University Press, 1963) and "A Developmental Approach to Political Systems," *World Politics*, Vol. 17 (1965), pp. 183–214. His other studies include *The Appeals of Communism* (Princeton, Princeton University Press, 1954) and his (ed.) *The Struggle for Democracy in Germany* (New York, Russell & Russell Publishers, 1965).
7. *Comparative Politics*, pp. 13–14.
8. *Ibid.*, pp. 29–30.
9. *Ibid.*, p. 61.
10. New York, Grove Press, Inc., 1966.
11. Almond and Powell, *op. cit.*, pp. 75–76.
12. *Ibid.*, pp. 205–6.
13. But less than 2 percent are politically participative in any other way. See Lester W. Milbrath, *Political Participation* (Chicago, Rand McNally & Co., 1965).
14. The quotations from Pye come from his *Aspects of Political Development* (Boston, Little, Brown and Company, 1966), p. 45.
15. The quotations are from Morgenstern's *The Question of National Defense* (Vintage Books; New York, Random House, 1961), pp. 273, 274, 281.
16. Talcott Parsons, "Introduction" to Max Weber, *The Theory of Social and Economic Organization* (New York, Oxford University Press, 1947), p. 16.
17. See Herbert Marcuse *et al.*, *A Critique of Pure Tolerance* (Boston, Beacon Press, 1965), p. 71.
18. *Ibid.*, pp. 67, 69, and 68.
19. I am indebted to Mr. James G. Allen, one of my graduate students at the University of Alberta, for having suggested this formulation.
20. The analogy I make between medicine and political science has been developed in my paper "Beyond Pluralism," which is scheduled for publication in the *Canadian Journal of Political Science* early in 1968.

FROM THE GROVES

OF SALAMANCA...TO THE

SHORES OF TRIPOLI

↝ Gordon C. Zahn

CATHOLIC EDUCATORS AND ADMINIS-
trators frequently take great pride and satisfaction in
tracing their academic traditions back to their beginnings
in the famous medieval centers of learning. Thus the oath
ritually administered to each year's crop of graduates at
one large Midwestern Catholic university welcomes them
to the "select company" of learned men and women and
reminds them: "From the groves of Athens, from the
medieval universities of Bologna, Paris, Salamanca, and
Oxford, from our modern institutions of learning, your
predecessors have gone forth, marked by culture, zealous
for the spread of truth, trained for leadership."

What is usually not given equal emphasis, however, is
the fact that these same medieval universities were, as the

noted medievalist Raymond Schmandt describes them, "turbulent places with constant protests, secessions, demonstrations on the part of faculty and students." So too the historian Friedrich Heer has pointed out that "the universities were also oases of freedom, where all those questions which elsewhere were suppressed or forbidden were discussed with what hostile critics described as brazen impudence. One would be hard put to it to think of any thorny problem touching God, the world, the Church, Christianity and dogma, which was not posed in its basic and essential form in the universities of the thirteenth and fourteenth centuries."[1] While it may be true that this intellectual turbulence did not always carry the dominant overtones of social and political dissent associated in our time with the Berkeley uprising and other widely publicized campus protests, it is nevertheless important to note that the medieval universities were centers of ferment and that their vitality contrasts sharply with the citadels of caution which, in twentieth-century America, continue to claim them as their most revered ancestors.

For it is the unhappy fact that any discussion of the extent to which Catholic academies have been involved in public demonstrations of dissent or protest must begin with a frank confession: such occasions have been exceedingly few, and even these few have usually been limited in objective and minimal in effect. Students from Catholic institutions have not been prominent in the opposition to national military adventures in Southeast Asia or in Latin America, nor have they played much of a part in protests against conscription and its inequities. Furthermore, it cannot be said that they have shown any significant measure of support or encouragement for their fellow students from the secular colleges and universities who have carried the ball on these important issues. Moreover, the record is much the same when we shift the focus to their professors. Here the show of engagement is even less impressive, if that is possible. The battles being fought at that level—and these too are few and far between—are usually concerned with academic prerogatives and seldom reach out into the problems and controversies of the world beyond the academy.

The timidity of the Catholic university in America contrasts not only with the outspoken liveliness of its medieval predecessors, but also with many of the educational ideals and directives one would expect to have great influence on Catholic institutions. Perhaps no single work is quoted more consistently or more extensively by Catholic educators than Cardinal John Henry Newman's justly famous statement of "the idea of a university." And nothing is more certain to give a lift to the Catholic academic's heart than those passages which describe the ideal school as the place "in which the intellect may safely range and speculate, sure to find its equal in some antagonist activity, and its judge in the tribunal of truth . . . where the professor becomes eloquent and is a missionary and a preacher, displaying his science in its most complete and most winning form, pouring it forth with the zeal of enthusiasm, and lighting up his own love of it in the breasts of his hearers." These, to be sure, are intellectual activities and works; yet it is clear that Newman took it for granted that they would have their effects in the product of all the knowledge thus diffused and extended—namely, in the mind which would experience "a disgust and abhorrence, towards excesses and enormities of evil, which are often or ordinarily reached at length by those who are not careful from the first to set themselves against what is vicious and criminal."[2]

Newman's concern for a gentlemanly fastidiousness of thought and behavior admittedly is not a particularly soul-stirring call for the more activist expression of disgust and abhorrence appropriate to a world in which what Newman probably would have regarded as vicious and criminal has now become respectable.[3] However, if the basis for such activism can be found only by implication in his words, it is made a great deal more explicit in another and much more authoritative statement: the "Declaration on Christian Education" issued only within the last few years by the Second Vatican Council. This document proclaims that "while the Catholic school fittingly adjusts itself to the circumstances of advancing times, it is educating its students *to promote effectively the welfare of the earthly city*," to "become, as it were, *the saving leaven of the human family*."[4] What this means in terms of action is demonstrated throughout the Council's "Pastoral Constitution on the Church in the Modern World," and most clearly in its statement that "the obligations of justice and love are fulfilled only if each person, contributing to the common good, according to his own abilities and the needs of others, also promotes and assists the public and private institutions dedicated *to bettering the conditions of human life*."[5] For this, "efforts must be made to see that men who are capable of higher studies can pursue them" so that "they can be prepared to undertake in society those duties, offices, and services which are in harmony with their natural aptitude and with the competence they will have acquired"; in this way "all the individuals and the social groups comprising a given people will be able to attain the full development of their culture."[6]

These somewhat extended introductory remarks set

forth the necessary background to the thesis proposed in this paper: that the whole system of Catholic education is (or should be) directed toward the formation of individuals who will be ready and eager to devote their natural gifts and talents to the overriding objective of "making the family of man and its history more human."[7] By the same token—and here's the rub!—programs and policies which obstruct or otherwise threaten progress toward that objective should call forth active opposition from the Catholic student and educator. More specifically: wherever social injustice reigns, wherever men fail to serve that "special obligation" which "binds us to make ourselves the neighbor of absolutely every person and of actively helping him when he comes across our path,"[8] indeed, wherever human and natural resources are devoted systematically to that neighbor's extermination—wherever these and other "excesses and enormities" prevail, it should be possible to predict that the Catholic academy will become a leading center of resistance.

The obvious fact that this expectation would not be fulfilled in America today presents the problem this paper seeks to analyze and, if possible, explain.

One need not look far to discover some of the reasons for the default of the Catholic academy in America. The Catholic college or university, like most private schools, must find its support and students where it can. This means that it becomes extremely vulnerable to the displeasure of the wealthier and more conservative elements in the Catholic community. This is true to some extent of state-supported institutions as well; but the broader political base upon which they depend provides somewhat more of a safeguard against any threat that financial support will be totally withheld. The private university, unless it is blessed with a massive endowment, has no such protective cushion to break its fall.

So, too, with the problem of enrollment. One factor which operates to limit the amount of leftist activity on the Catholic campus is the social background of the students themselves. Drawn in great part from a middle-class population, from families which have made it only in the past generation or two, they are determined to maintain their upward movement and, even more, to preserve what their fathers and grandfathers have achieved.

The middle-class origins and higher-class aspirations of the students—and, of course, of the parents who are often paying their ever more costly way—are not the only or even the most important influence toward a conservative bias. Catholic students and parents have been quite effectively indoctrinated against the "menace" of communism, so effectively in fact that they tend to become overly sensitive to anything that might carry even the faintest taint or suspicion of Marxist ideology or objectives. It is still possible to find Catholics who oppose or question civil rights proposals and activities, efforts to achieve disarmament and peace, etc. merely because it can be shown that these have been supported by spokesmen or groups bearing the "red" label, even though the label may have been carelessly and quite unjustly applied.

It is no surprise, then, to discover that since so much of the campus activity which has stirred national notice and criticism has been directed toward such "tainted" objectives and is frankly identified with the radical New Left movements, it has made little impact on the Catholic campus. In this connection, a hasty survey recently made by this writer of the political atmosphere on twenty Catholic campuses failed to discover a single chapter of the Students for a Democratic Society, whereas six did report the presence of an active chapter of Young Americans for Freedom, regarded by many as a Birch-type student organization of the "Radical Right." Furthermore, while only one of the deans who responded to the questionnaire suspected that an application for a YAF chapter would not be approved (*neither* the SDS *nor* the YAF would be accepted on this campus), four others thought it unlikely that the SDS would pass the test (in two of these cases, the YAF was already represented).[9]

Any inference to be drawn from such limited data must be tentative in the extreme. But the response pattern does seem to reinforce the suggestion that the Catholic campus will be more on guard against the extremes of the left than of the right. This echoes to some extent the hypersensitivity to communism that has led to the scandal of Catholic support on the national or world scale for "anticommunist" dictators. In the present context, it goes far to explain the limited resistance of Catholic students to policies and situations which clearly do not meet the standards of international and national behavior set forth in the moral system to which they presumably subscribe and to the extension and perfection of which the Catholic university ought to be dedicated.

There was, however, one extremely intriguing impression which this superficial survey suggested. There would seem to be less protest activity on the Catholic campus than the administrators would be prepared to tolerate. For example, *none* of the deans queried reported that "trouble with the law for protest activities" would constitute *automatic* "grounds for serious disciplinary action"—although it should be noted that four did indicate that an ad hoc approach (which obviously could result in such reprisal action in any given instance) would be the rule. The least promising of the four commented, " 'Protest' activities is a vague term—the University does not defend the principle of civil disobedience where the law is just." One wonders if this negative statement would not allow for civil disobedience where the justice of the law is itself the matter in dispute.

In no instance did my informants state that their schools would forbid participation in off-campus demonstrations—though again most respondents did add qualifications to their permissiveness which would exclude violence, illegality, or "acting in the name of the University." Another question directed attention to current plans to organize a nation-wide "student strike for peace" and sought information as to how their students and administrations would be likely to react to this. Nine deans indicated their belief that none of their students would participate. Of the eleven who thought there might be some response, only one was willing to suggest that the proportion of interested students would approach the 5 percent level. Probably as a reflection of this assurance that the strike effort would receive little support on the Catholic campus, most of the deans felt that their administrations would take no punitive action against the few who did participate other than to record the absences and let the normal "cut" rule apply.

Now of course, this aura of unexpected permissiveness is based on verbalized estimates of what the situation *would* be; the reactions of administrators to the *actuality* of a student protest march or some similar demonstration might turn out to be far more severe than these responses would indicate. Nevertheless, taking the answers at their face value, we are brought back even more dramatically to the basic question concerning us here: Why is there so little dissent or protest on the Catholic campus?

I believe the complete answer to this question goes beyond the social background of Catholic students and their parents. The decisive factor we seek lies in the "authority complex" of the Catholic academy, a many-faceted phenomenon leading to what may be viewed as an overly submissive frame of mind.

It should be made clear at once that Catholic educational institutions are not to be dismissed as tyrannical instruments of the massive Roman Catholic monolith, the stereotype that so often has excited the fears and forebodings of suspicious non-Catholics. If anything, recent developments in the Church should make it unnecessary to affirm that this distorted image of the all-demanding hierarchical structure lording it over a helpless and totally subservient laity does not square with the facts.

But having said this much, one must make it equally clear that respect for *authority as such* still ranks high in the Catholic scale of moral and social values. Whether the stress be placed on the Pauline teachings in the New Testament or on the natural-law political philosophy developed by the great scholastics, obedience to established authority remains for Catholics the ruling principle governing relationships between subject and ruler. Though the teaching relates most directly to the obedience owed by the secular powers, the same hierarchical model of authority spills over into every structure or institution of organized society from family to universal church.

This has a direct bearing upon our problem in several distinct ways. To begin with, there is the fact that the Catholic university in its claim to stand *in loco parentis* tends to define its responsibilities in terms of the ideal family, which, in the Catholic formulation, is paternal and strongly authoritarian. Rigidity of parietal rules is not, of course, peculiar to the Catholic school. Nor should one ignore the fact that considerable relaxations of control have taken place. Required (and recorded!) attendance at religious services, curfew regulations (at least for male students), and similar restrictions seem to be on the way out. Yet the authoritarian father the Catholic administrator sees himself as replacing remains quite unwilling to permit the student-child to engage in unruly demonstrations or overtly rebellious activity.

Two other forms the Catholic authority complex takes in higher education require more discussion. They are the hierarchical order of church authority that extends by parallel (where not by actual design) into the operation of the Catholic university, and secondly and most significantly for the problem at hand, the predisposition of the Catholic student and professor toward a pattern of almost uncritical acceptance of the decisions proclaimed by his nation's leaders.

With respect to the first of these considerations, the essential institutional structure of the Catholic Church is familiar enough, with its pyramiding of spiritual authority and power from its base in the local parishes (each subject to the pastor), through the bishops, and finally culminating in its administrative center in Rome with the Pope at the very peak. The delineation of rights and obligations has been such that, in practice, the lay segment of the total community is held to clearer and more tangible manifestations of respect for clerical prerogative than the other segments (religious orders, priests, and bishops) have been required to display toward the laity.

The rationale behind the priority accorded to the

priestly, episcopal, curial, and papal judgments in that order (though there are times when curial decisions seem to override or negate the papal) finds some justification in the religious community's insistence that the requirements of the spiritual order must always be recognized as more binding than those of the temporal order. Unfortunately, the principle can be extended into areas where this choice of priorities is not involved. When it is applied out of proper context, it can operate to stifle the development and expression of a genuine and effective witness on the part of the "living" as distinguished from the purely "institutional" church.

This danger can be illustrated with respect to the Catholic educational system from the primary parochial level to the Ph.D.-awarding university. In the eyes of many, this educational enterprise is accorded a purely instrumental value; to them its *raison d'être* is to serve the parent ecclesiastical establishment and its salvational ends. So viewed, the Catholic college or university all too easily can become subject to the control, direct or indirect, of external ecclesiastical authority, thereby losing its proper autonomy as a community of free scholars. Even where this does not happen, the internal structure of the academy is such that ecclesiastical authority and its concerns, which at best can only be termed as peripheral to the functions of the academy, become an influential, even determining, factor through a kind of voluntary surrender by administrators who permit their fears of possible chancery reactions to rule decisions concerning programs, politics, and events.

At the moment a rather significant change is in the making which might ultimately serve to expand and protect the autonomy of the academic community. Most Catholic institutions of higher learning are operated by separate dioceses or a variety of religious order. It is with the bishops or designated members of the religious orders that final authority has usually remained.[10] Recently, however, this pattern has been broken in that several colleges and universities have opened membership in their governing boards—in some cases, majority membership—to laymen. It is far too early to attempt an assessment of the effects this change will bring, though the cynical observation has been voiced that the "revolution" is really a device for circumventing opposition to the participation of the church-affiliated schools in the lavish outpourings of federal money and that the laymen most likely to be chosen are those who are notoriously "safe" or even more "clerical" in their outlook than many of the clergy who have governed the schools up to now.

The change no doubt affords an opportunity to remove the overlay of ecclesiastical authority that has complicated relations between lay faculty and students on the one hand and college administration on the other. But it is clear that there has not been a corresponding advance in other areas of academic prerogative. Perhaps the greatest lag relates to rights of tenure and academic freedom. The absence of procedural safeguards in most Catholic institutions has the effect of rendering individual faculty members vulnerable to the whims or exaggerated prudence of the (almost always) clergy-staffed administration. It should be noted in this connection that this vulnerability obtains for the clerical members of the faculty as well as for the laymen; indeed, the position of the priest-scholar often proves to be the weaker in this respect.

One is tempted to go into great detail on the wealth of "atrocity" stories with which the Catholic academician is all too familiar. Not all gain the national notice and concern that brought St. John's University (of New York, not Minnesota) under formal censure of the American Association of University Professors in the spring of 1966. Others, like the Catholic University of America (on more than one occasion), the University of Dayton, St. Louis University, and Marquette University—to mention only a small selection of schools that have earned a spot on this particular roll of academic dishonor—have been torn by controversy concerning such matters as the content of courses or arbitrary administrative decisions to close the campus to speakers (sometimes world-renowned scholars!) considered "too controversial."

At times the whole sorry mess finally works out for the best. The University of Dayton's current (as of early 1967) hubbub over conservative charges that heresy was being taught in its classrooms was resolved in favor of the accused, even after the intervention of local episcopal authority seemed to favor those who brought the original charges. In this case, the university administration was able to screw its courage to the sticking-point at least to the extent of affirming its own right to hear and decide the validity of the accusations presented. On another front, it may well be that the most significant event in the history of Catholic higher education in this country was the faculty-student demonstration in protest of the summary dismissal of a "liberal" theology professor which succeeded in shutting down the entire Catholic University of America for five days or so in April 1967. The reversal of the protested decision was made all the more remarkable by the fact that it was a victory, not against an administration in the usual sense, but in effect, against the episcopal dignitaries who made up the university's board of trustees.

These accomplishments serve to give sharper focus to a

problem which, sad to say, is not always resolved in favor of academic rights and privileges. The arbitrary abuse of ecclesiastical power and authority has extended at times into the most specialized reaches of a scholar's professional activity. Thus, in the early 1950s, the University of Chicago Press was obliged to suspend publication of a multivolume work in sociology because of the author-priest's vulnerability to superior ecclesiastical authority. Some years later, during 1960, in a matter involving another work regarded as "too controversial," a nun with a Ph.D. and holding a post on the governing board of her professional society was instructed by her religious superior to vote against publishing the article in question in the official journal of that society. In fact, she was told that if the vote were to go against her and the article be accepted for publication she would have to resign her membership, not only from the governing board but from the society as well.[11]

Whether these are to be taken as exceptional cases or, as I am inclined to suspect, are more frequent than many of us realize, they testify to a general setting which is not at all conducive to political or social dissent on the part of a faculty which might also earn the designation "too controversial." And if the rights of the faculty have not yet been guaranteed full recognition within the Catholic academy, the situation is even worse as far as the students are concerned. That there has been a steadily growing measure of student self-government and responsibility is not to be denied; but the point has not yet been reached in most Catholic schools where the student body has attained anything like a defined sphere of real (i.e. absolute) autonomy. Limits, real or at least potential, always have to be recognized by students, leaders, and followers alike. These limits, it is safe to say, would not be flexible enough to permit the kind of campus protest and dissent that has taken place at, say, Berkeley.

This brings us to the second critical aspect of the authority complex prevailing in the Catholic academy. It is perhaps the most important, and certainly the most subtle, in its influence upon all segments of the Catholic academic community. I refer to the overriding respect for legitimate *secular* authority which is so crucial an element in Catholic political and social thought. It is of the utmost significance in this context that in his famous encyclical setting forth the model of the "true" Christian that is to be the anticipated product of Catholic educational endeavors, Pius XI made it explicit that confessional schools must never seek "to separate their children either from the body of the nation or its spirit, but to educate them in a perfect manner, most conducive to the prosperity of the nation. *Indeed a good Catholic, precisely because of his Catholic principles, makes the better citizen, attached to his country, and loyally submissive to constituted civil authority in every legitimate form of government.*"[12]

If we take this as the point of departure, there is more reason to marvel at the amount of dissent and protest that *does* take place on the Catholic campus than to complain of the fact that it has been so slight and ineffective. The occasional draft-card burner these schools have produced has had to come a far greater distance than one might at first suspect. To illustrate this point we can turn again to the commencement oath which inspired the title for this paper. At the school in question the lavish allusions to the traditions of learning associated with the groves of Athens and Salamanca were followed, within the body of the oath itself, by a specific pledge of loyalty "to my country and my flag." Nor was this all. Until recently the oath was administered at the end of a commencement ceremony in which the order of events moved from the traditional commencement address to the awarding of degrees in a progression of ascending dignity: first the B.A.'s, next the M.A.'s, then the Ph.D.'s, and finally the honorary degrees. But was this the crowning event of this ceremonial finish to the graduates' career? No indeed! This honor was reserved for the graduates who had completed their course-work in ROTC and who were now called forward to receive their commissions and be sworn in while the audience stood in respectful attention.

A small matter, some might think, and one which proves nothing one way or the other. On the other hand, a university which invests what is essentially a military ceremonial with such importance in what should be a purely academic event is very likely to be a setting in which conformity and obedience are valued far more than protest and dissent—a setting, in fact, in which the latter, *even when they are based on principles of morality,* risk being viewed as unwanted threats to the public image of the institution itself.

It would be unfair in the extreme to conclude this review leaving the impression that there is no evidence at all of social and political engagement on the part of students and faculties of Catholic colleges and universities. Chicago's Loyola University was placed in a rather embarrassing position a couple of years ago by some students who decided to picket its downtown classroom building because the Catholic women's club, then occupying its upper floors, was known for its racially discriminatory practices. "How can we preach racial justice on the ninth floor [i.e. in the college classrooms]," the school paper editorial-ized, "and practice racial injustice on the fourteenth [the club's dining facilities]?" The matter was complicated somewhat by the fact that the club in question was a pet project of the university's principal benefactress, and this, understandably enough, caused no little concern to the administration. But the students won their battle—and gained national notice in the process when two student nuns joined the picket line, establishing a precedent that was to be followed later and in many other settings. During the past two years, at least three Catholic colleges have found part of their student body picketing in protest against the presence of ROTC units on the campus. Students at the Catholic University of America have staged protest meetings and sit-ins to dramatize their opposition to policies and decisions of their highly conservative adminstration. In November 1966, in fact, the students went so far as to picket the assembly of American bishops held annually on their campus and were able to present a list of grievances relating to what they held to be inadequate communication between the bishops (as trustees), the administration, the faculty, and the student body.

Moreover, in assessing the social responsiveness of the Catholic university, attention should be given to the possibility that much of the dissent one would expect to find is being drawn off into other forms of activity peculiar to the Catholic campus. Thus the absence of an SDS chapter may be balanced by the presence of an active chapter of the Young Christian Students. It is estimated that there are at least a hundred such "observe, judge, and act" groups in colleges and universities around the nation with a total membership of at least two thousand "activist" students. Or one might consider the wide range of more directly "apostolic works" that engage the interest and activity of individuals or small, often informal, groups of students: tutoring grade and high school students in the inner-city slums; the Christian Appalachia Project, in which holiday and semester breaks are spent in welfare-type work in Kentucky; volunteer work with such reformist or even revolutionary groups as the Friendship House and Catholic Worker Movement.

A strong case can be made that activities of this order are more appropriate channels of protest and dissent for the Catholic students who are exposed to religion courses which stress the theological virtues of charity and social justice as these values are translated into a personal obligation to minister to the needs of the disadvantaged. The exposure may not take for the majority, but those whom it does touch might be inclined to seek what is in their eyes a more positive means of expressing their dissatisfaction with the status quo than a public demonstration of dissent or civil disobedience.

One might even advance the hypothesis that the priesthood and other forms of the religious life might be drawing off the potential Mario Savios who find their way to the Catholic academy. This is not as preposterous a notion as it might at first seem to be. Anyone who has had the opportunity to work with representatives of the deeply committed and extremely articulate new breed of Catholic priests and nuns who are responsible for so much of the ferment in the American church today will see considerable plausibility in the hypothesis. In any event, since most of these are products of Catholic education, they are evidence that the Catholic academy has not been a total failure in producing the type of socially engaged Christian one would expect in the light of its proclaimed ideals and objectives.

All things considered, however, the successes measured in terms of Catholic students who experience the awakening of a deep, personal concern for the structured inequities of the social order are greatly outnumbered by the graduates who have no difficulty at all in conforming to the demands of their not particularly Christian surroundings. Or, even worse, the dissenters are outnumbered by those who take it upon themselves to defend their best of all possible worlds against extremists (including, of course, the Catholic crank of doubtful orthodoxy) who threaten to disrupt it.

What is true of the Catholic student holds for the Catholic academician as well. For he shares many of the social and psychological characteristics which account for the lack of engagement on the part of his students. And beyond these, it is important to recognize that he is subject to all the usual limitations that beset the academic life. He too has found refuge in his chosen field of specialization and has been all too ready to ignore the social and moral concerns which should be the responsibility of that broader "community of learned men" in which he claims membership.

But for the Catholic academician this problem has an extra dimension. Experience has taught him that too open a display of moral commitment on a public issue carries with it a special risk for him. Actions which might be accepted and respected (even by those who disagree with them) when performed by the academic at a secular university are all too likely to be condemned in his case (even by those who agree) as a violation of the norms of "value-free scholarship." Perhaps he is overly sensitive to this reaction or to the likelihood of the reaction, but it is enough to deter him from taking too frequent or too obvious a moral stance on public issues. It is well known how the old nativist canard that the Catholic citizen is unreliable because he "gives first loyalty to Rome" operated to produce a defense reaction of "200 percent Americanism." In a similar way many Catholic academicians (or, as they are more likely to describe themselves, "academicians who happen to be Catholic") go out of their way to avoid actions which might seem to lend substance to the unfavorable stereotype they attribute, with much justice, to their scholarly peers. One of America's most distinguished sociologists once declared that he would never hire a Communist or a Catholic because, as far as he was concerned, the competence of both was destroyed by their prior commitment to their respective value systems. Familiar with this or similar expressions of the same point of view, the Catholic academician is perhaps to be forgiven if he prefers to think twice before taking up his placard and joining the picket line.

But here, too, a change is taking place. Perhaps the proportion of Catholic professors who do finally decide to join that line, sign the petitions, or take part in teach-ins continues to lag behind even the feeble pace being set by their students—and certainly far behind that set by their colleagues in other academic settings. Nevertheless, whether it be the effect of Pope John's *aggiornamento* or the more explicit directives of Vatican II, the fact is inescapable that the Catholic academician is beginning to recognize the opportunity and obligation to provide effective leadership within the religious community and in the society outside as well. As this awareness grows, he will necessarily find himself forced into situations where he will have to stand up and be counted, where this new sense of engagement will require him to take an open and public stand against practices and policies he previously accepted without serious question because they were not "in his street."

We may yet reach the point at which the Catholic university will rediscover its potential to produce men who are prepared to give stronger voice to Newman's "disgust and abhorrence" and to "set themselves against what is vicious and criminal" in the world about them. Those same institutions may even find it possible to provide encouragement to the student dissenter who is ready to burn his draft card in protest against the excesses and enormities of modern war—at least as much encouragement as is now given the student who completes the program of military training that, incongruous though it may seem, has somehow become a recognized part of the curriculum of the Catholic academy and, indeed, a *requirement* at fully *half* our Catholic academies.

This may strike the reader as a rather optimistic note on which to end a generally pessimistic survey. But the optimism has two things going for it. First there are the drastic changes now taking place in the Roman Catholic Church and the wide-ranging reassessment of its relevance to what Thomas Merton and others have described as our "post-Christian" era.[13] The second is related to this. The changes taking place in the secular order are giving new clarity to the essential incompatability between the ideals of a universal church created to serve the spiritual needs of all the children of the Father and the insatiable and ever more inhuman demands of racial and national particularisms which seem prepared to carry the divisions between men to the point of annihilating the world and all its inhabitants. Together these trends are forcing the Christian conscience—and the agencies responsible for instructing and forming that conscience—into a corner from which there can be no escape without a return to the patterns of protest and dissent that have always marked the prophetic mission of the Christian church. When that stage is reached, the Catholic academy will have an important role to play.

NOTES

1. Friedrich Heer, *The Medieval World* (Mentor MQ524; New York, New American Library, 1963), p. 241.
2. John Henry Newman, *The Idea of a University*, David M. O'Connell, S.J., ed. (Chicago, Loyola University Press, 1927), pp. 472–73, 207.
3. Msgr. Paul Hanly Furfey's recent book, *The Respectable Murderers* (New York, Herder & Herder, 1966), elaborates upon some of the social practices that merit this condemnatory description. Furfey, it might be well to note, has long been one of the strongest voices of dissent within the Catholic academic community.
4. "Declaration on Christian Education," in *Documents of Vatican II*, Walter J. Abbott, S.J., ed. (New York, Guild Press, Ltd., 1966), p. 646.
5. "Pastoral Constitution on the Church in the Modern World," *ibid.*, p. 228.
6. *Ibid.*, p. 266–67.
7. *Ibid.*, p. 239.
8. *Ibid.*, p. 226.
9. Brief questionnaires were sent to twenty-one deans of students selected in such a way as to give representation (matched where possible) to Catholic men's (or coeducational) and women's colleges in the major regions of the country. In addition, a selection of the larger Catholic universities was included. All deans responded, and only two failed to complete the questionnaire. Even these are not to be taken as refusals, however. One answered some of the questions and left others blank; the second missed the deadline set for return of the questionnaire and sent a note of apology (without the questionnaire) later. The schools from which responses were received were: Assumption College (Mass.); Bellarmine College; Catholic University of America; De Paul University; University of Dayton; Duquesne University; Fordham University; Georgetown University; LaSalle College;

From the Groves of Salamanca . . .

Loyola University (Chicago); Loyola University (Los Angeles); University of Notre Dame; College of St. Catherine; St. Mary's Dominican College; St. Norbert's College; College of St. Thomas; University of San Francisco; Ursuline College; Regis College (Mass.); Xavier College (New Orleans).

10. The Catholic University of America is perhaps the outstanding exception to the general form of administration outlined here. The University's Board of Trustees consists of all the Archbishops of the United States in an *ex officio* capacity, approximately 30 bishops, and a minority of lay trustees to complete the membership of 50. In a very real sense, however, the Board may be considered as representing the policies and wishes of the total episcopate in this country.

11. The vote favored publication. The issue became moot soon after, however, when the article was published by another Catholic intellectual journal. The important point is, of course, the attempted imposition of the superior's *religious* authority in an academic area in which she could claim no competence whatsoever.

12. Pius XI, "Divini Illius Magistrii," in *Seven Great Encyclicals* William J. Gibbons, S.J., ed. (Glen Rock, N.J., Paulist Press, 1963), p. 62.

13. Among recent works dealing with new currents in the Catholic university see Robert Hassenger, ed., *The Shape of Catholic Higher Education* (soon to be published by the University of Chicago Press), which contains a most perceptive foreword by David Riesman; and Edward Manier and John Houck, eds., *Academic Freedom and the Catholic University* (Notre Dame, Ind., Fides Publishers, Inc., 1967).

THE RESPONSIBILITY

OF INTELLECTUALS *

✍ Noam Chomsky

TWENTY YEARS AGO, DWIGHT MACDON-
ald published a series of articles in *Politics* on the responsibilities of peoples, and specifically, the responsibility of
intellectuals. I read them as an undergraduate, in the
years just after the war, and had occasion to read them
again a few months ago. They seem to me to have lost
none of their power or persuasiveness. Macdonald is
concerned with the question of war guilt. He asks the
question: To what extent were the German or Japanese
people responsible for the atrocities committed by
their governments? And, quite properly, he turns the
question back to us: To what extent are the British
or American people responsible for the vicious terror bombings of civilians, perfected as a technique of warfare by the Western democracies and reaching their cul-
mination in Hiroshima and Nagasaki, surely among the
most unspeakable crimes in history? To an undergraduate

in 1945–1946—to anyone whose political and moral consciousness had been formed by the horrors of the 1930s, by the war in Ethiopia, the Russian purge, the "China Incident," the Spanish Civil War, the Nazi atrocities, the Western reaction to these events and, in part, complicity in them—these questions had particular significance and poignancy.

With respect to the responsibility of intellectuals, there are still other, equally disturbing questions. Intellectuals are in a position to expose the lies of governments, to analyze actions according to their causes and motives and often hidden intentions. In the Western world, at least, they have the power that comes from political liberty, from access to information and freedom of expression. For a privileged minority, Western democracy provides the leisure, the facilities, and the training to seek the truth lying hidden behind the veil of distortion and misrepresentation, ideology and class interest, through which the events of current history are presented to us. The responsibilities of intellectuals, then, are much deeper than what Macdonald calls the "responsibility of peoples," given the unique privileges that intellectuals enjoy.

The issues that Macdonald raised are as pertinent today as they were twenty years ago. We can hardly avoid asking ourselves to what extent the American people bear responsibility for the savage American assault on a largely helpless rural population in Vietnam, still another atrocity in what Asians see as the "Vasco da Gama era" of world history. As for those of us who stood by in silence and apathy as this catastrophe slowly took shape over the past dozen years, on what page of history do we find our proper place? Only the most insensible can escape these questions. I want to return to them, later on, after a few scattered remarks about the responsibility of intellectuals and how, in practice, they go about meeting this responsibility in the mid-1960s.

It is the responsibility of intellectuals to speak the truth and to expose lies. This, at least, may seem enough of a truism to pass without comment. Not so, however. For the modern intellectual, it is not at all obvious. Thus we have Martin Heidegger writing, in a pro-Hitler declaration of 1933, that "truth is the revelation of that which makes a people certain, clear, and strong in its action and knowledge"; it is only this kind of "truth" that one has a responsibility to speak. Americans tend to be more forthright. When Arthur Schlesinger was asked by the *New York Times,* in November 1965, to explain the contradiction between his published account of the Bay of Pigs incident and the story he had given the press at the time of the attack, he simply remarked that he had lied; and a few days later, he went on to compliment the *Times* for also having suppressed information on the planned invasion, in "the national interest," as this was defined by the group of arrogant and deluded men of whom Schlesinger gives such a flattering portrait in his recent account of the Kennedy administration. It is of no particular interest that one man is quite happy to lie in behalf of a cause which he knows to be unjust; but it is significant that such events provoke so little response in the intellectual community—no feeling, for example, that there is something strange in the offer of a major chair in humanities to a historian who feels it to be his duty to persuade the world that an American-sponsored invasion of a nearby country is nothing of the sort. And what of the incredible sequence of lies on the part of our government and its spokesmen concerning such matters as negotiations in Vietnam? The facts are known to all who care to know. The press, foreign and domestic, has presented documentation to refute each falsehood as it appears. But the power of the government propaganda apparatus is such that the citizen who does not undertake a research project on the subject can hardly hope to confront government pronouncements with fact.[1]

The deceit and distortion surrounding the American invasion of Vietnam is by now so familiar that it has lost its power to shock. It is therefore well to recall that although new levels of cynicism are constantly being reached, their clear antecedents were accepted at home with quiet toleration. It is a useful exercise to compare government statements at the time of the invasion of Guatemala in 1954 with Eisenhower's admission—to be more accurate, his boast—a decade later that American planes were sent "to help the invaders."[2] Nor is it only in moments of crisis that duplicity is considered perfectly in order. "New Frontiersmen," for example, have scarcely distinguished themselves by a passionate concern for historical accuracy, even when they are not being called upon to provide a "propaganda cover" for ongoing actions. For example, Arthur Schlesinger describes the bombing of North Vietnam and the massive escalation of military commitment in early 1965 as based on a "perfectly rational argument": "so long as the Vietcong thought they were going to win the war, they obviously would not be interested in any kind of negotiated settlement."[3] The date is important. Had the statement been made six months earlier, one could attribute it to ignorance. But this statement appeared after months of front-page news reports detailing the UN, North Vietnamese, and Soviet initiatives that preceded the February 1965 escalation and that, in fact, continued for several weeks after the bombing began, after months of soul-searching by Washington correspondents who were trying desperately to find some mitigating circumstances for the startling deception that had been revealed (Chalmers Roberts, for example, wrote with unconscious irony that late February 1965 "hardly seemed to Washington to be a propitious moment for negotiations [since] Mr. Johnson . . . had just ordered the first bombing of North Vietnam in an effort to bring Hanoi to a conference table where bargaining chips on both sides would be more closely matched"[4]). Coming at this moment, Schlesinger's statement is less an example of deceit than of contempt—contempt for an audience that can be expected to tolerate such behavior with silence, if not approval.[5]

To turn to someone closer to the actual formation and implementation of policy, consider some of the reflections of Walt Rostow, a man who, according to Schlesinger, brought a "spacious historical view" to the conduct of foreign affairs in the Kennedy administration.[6] According to his analysis, the guerrilla warfare in Indochina in 1946 was launched by Stalin,[7] and Hanoi initiated the guerrilla war against South Vietnam in 1958 (*The View from the Seventh Floor*, pp. 39 and 152). Similarly, the Communist planners probed the "free world spectrum of defense" in Northern Azerbaijan and Greece (where Stalin "supported substantial guerrilla warfare"—*ibid.*, pp. 36 and 148), operating from plans carefully laid in 1945. And in Central Europe, the Soviet Union was not "prepared to accept a solution which would remove the dangerous tensions from Central Europe at the risk of even slowly staged corrosion of communism in East Germany" (*ibid.*, p. 156).

It is interesting to compare these observations with studies by scholars actually concerned with historical events. The remark about Stalin's initiating the first Vietnamese war in 1946 does not even merit refutation. As to Hanoi's purported initiative of 1958, the situation is more clouded. But even government sources[8] concede that in 1959 Hanoi received the first direct reports of what Diem referred to[9] as his own Algerian war and that only after this did they lay their plans to involve themselves in this struggle. In fact, in December 1958 Hanoi made another of its many attempts—rebuffed once again by Saigon and the United States—to establish diplomatic and commercial relations with the Saigon government on the basis of the status quo.[10] Rostow offers no evidence of Stalin's support for the Greek guerrillas; in fact, though the historical record is far from clear, it seems that Stalin was by no means pleased with the adventurism of the Greek guerrillas, who, from his point of view, were upsetting the satisfactory postwar imperialist settlement.[11]

Rostow's remarks about Germany are more interesting still. He does not see fit to mention, for example, the Russian notes of March–April 1952, which proposed unification of Germany under internationally supervised elections, with withdrawal of all troops within a year, *if* there was a guarantee that a reunified Germany would not be permitted to join a Western military alliance.[12] And he has also momentarily forgotten his own characterization of the strategy of the Truman and Eisenhower administrations: "to avoid any serious negotiation with the Soviet Union until the West could confront Moscow with German rearmament within an organized European framework, as a *fait accompli*"[13]—to be sure, in defiance of the Potsdam agreements.

But most interesting of all is Rostow's reference to Iran. The facts are that there was a Russian attempt to impose by force a pro-Soviet government in Northern Azerbaijan that would grant the Soviet Union access to Iranian oil. This was rebuffed by superior Anglo-American force in 1946, at which point the more powerful imperialism obtained full rights to Iranian oil for itself, with the installation of a pro-Western government. We recall what happened when, for a brief period in the early 1950s, the only Iranian government with something of a popular base experimented with the curious idea that Iranian oil should belong to the Iranians. What is interesting, however, is the description of Northern Azerbaijan as part of "the free world spectrum of defense." It is pointless, by now, to comment on the debasement of the phrase "free world." But by what law of nature does Iran, with its resources, fall within Western dominion? The bland assumption that it does is most revealing of deep-seated attitudes toward the conduct of foreign affairs.

In addition to this growing lack of concern for truth, we find, in recent statements, a real or feigned naiveté with regard to American actions that reaches startling proportions. For example, Arthur Schlesinger has recently characterized our Vietnamese policies of 1954 as "part of our general program of international goodwill."[14] Unless intended as irony, this remark shows either a colossal cynicism or an inability, on a scale that defies comment, to comprehend elementary phenomena of contemporary history. Similarly, what is one to make of the testimony of Thomas Schelling before the House Foreign Affairs Committee, January 27, 1966, in which he discusses the two great dangers if all Asia "goes Communist"?[15] First, this would exclude "the United States and what we call Western civilization from a large part of the world that is poor and colored and potentially hostile." Second, "a country like the United States probably cannot maintain self-confidence if just about the greatest thing it ever attempted, namely to create the basis for decency and prosperity and democratic government in the underdeveloped world, had to be acknowledged as a failure or as an attempt that we wouldn't try again." It surpasses belief that a person with even minimal acquaintance with the record of American foreign policy could produce such statements.

It surpasses belief, that is, unless we look at the matter from a more historical point of view, and place such statements in the context of the hypocritical moralism of the past; for example, of Woodrow Wilson, who was going to teach the Latin Americans the art of good government, and who wrote (1902) that it is "our peculiar duty" to teach colonial peoples "order and self-control . . . [and] . . . the drill and habit of law and obedience." Or of the missionaries of the 1840s, who described the hideous and degrading opium wars as "the result of a great design of Providence to make the wickedness of men subserve his purposes of mercy toward China, in breaking through her wall of exclusion, and bringing the empire into more immediate contact with western and Christian nations." Or, to approach the present, of A. A. Berle, who, in commenting on the Dominican intervention, has the impertinence to attribute the problems of the Caribbean countries to imperialism—*Russian* imperialism.[16]

As a final example of this failure of skepticism, consider the remarks of Henry Kissinger in concluding his presentation in a Harvard-Oxford television debate on American Vietnam policies. He observed, rather sadly, that what disturbs him most is that others question not our judgment but our motives—a remarkable comment on the part of one whose professional concern is political analysis, that is, analysis of the actions of governments in terms of motives that are unexpressed in official propaganda and perhaps only dimly perceived by those whose acts they govern. No one would be disturbed by an analysis of the political behavior of Russians, French, or Tanzanians, questioning their motives and interpreting their actions in terms of long-range interests, perhaps well concealed behind official rhetoric. But it is an article of faith that American motives are pure and not subject to analysis (see note 1). Although it is nothing new in American intellectual history—or, for that matter, in the general history of imperialist apologia—this innocence becomes increasingly distasteful as the power it serves grows more dominant in world affairs and more capable, therefore, of the unconstrained viciousness that the mass media present to us each day. We are hardly the first power in history to combine material interests, great technological capacity, and an utter disregard for the suffering and misery of the lower orders. The long tradition of naiveté and self-righteousness that disfigures our intellectual history, however, must serve as a warning to the Third World, if such a warning is needed, as to how our protestations of sincerity and benign intent are to be interpreted.

The basic assumptions of the "New Frontiersmen" should be pondered carefully by those who look forward to the involvement of academic intellectuals in politics. For example, I have referred to Arthur Schlesinger's objections to the Bay of Pigs invasion, but the reference was imprecise. True, he felt that it was a "terrible idea," but "not because the notion of sponsoring an exile attempt to overthrow Castro seemed intolerable in itself." Such a reaction would be the merest sentimentality, unthinkable to a tough-minded realist. The difficulty, rather, was that it seemed unlikely that the deception could succeed. The operation, in his view, was ill-conceived but not otherwise objectionable.[17] In a similar vein, Schlesinger quotes with approval Kennedy's "realistic" assessment of the situation resulting from Trujillo's assassination: "There are three possibilities in descending order of preference: a decent democratic regime, a continuation of the Trujillo regime or a Castro regime. We ought to aim at the first, but we really can't renounce the second until we are sure that we can avoid the third."[18] The reason why the third possibility is so intolerable is explained a few pages later: "Communist success in Latin America would deal a much harder blow to the power and influence of the United States." Of course, we can never really be sure of avoiding the third possibility; therefore, in practice, we will always settle for the second, as we are now doing in Brazil and Argentina, for example.[19]

Or consider Walt Rostow's views on American policy in Asia.[20] The basis on which we must build this policy is that "we are openly threatened and we feel menaced by Communist China." To prove that we are menaced is of course unnecessary, and the matter receives no attention; it is enough that we feel menaced. Our policy must be based on our national heritage and our national interests. Our national heritage is briefly outlined in the following terms: "Throughout the nineteenth century, in good conscience Americans could devote themselves to the extension of both their principles and their power on this continent," making use of "the somewhat elastic concept of the Monroe doctrine" and, of course, extending "the American interest to Alaska and the mid-Pacific islands. . . . Both our insistence on unconditional surrender and the idea of post-war occupation . . . represented the formulation of American security interests in Europe and Asia." So much for our heritage. As to our interests, the matter is equally simple. Fundamental is our "profound interest that societies abroad develop and strengthen those elements in their respective cultures that elevate and protect the dignity of the individual against the state." At the same time, we must counter the "ideological threat," namely "the possibility that the Chinese Communists can prove to Asians by progress in China that Communist methods are better and faster than democratic methods." Nothing is said about those people in Asian cultures to whom our "conception of the proper relation of the individual to the state" may not be the uniquely important value, people who might, for example, be concerned with preserving the "dignity of the individual" against concentrations of foreign or domestic capital, or against semifeudal structures (such as Trujillo-type dictatorships) introduced or kept in power by American arms. All of this is flavored with allusions to "our religious and ethical value systems" and to our "diffuse and complex concepts" which are to the Asian mind "so much more difficult to grasp" than Marxist dogma, and are so "disturbing to some Asians" because of "their very lack of dogmatism."

Such intellectual contributions as these suggest the need for a correction to De Gaulle's remark, in his *Memoirs,* about the American "will to power, cloaking itself in idealism." By now, this will to power is not so much cloaked in idealism as it is drowned in fatuity. And academic intellectuals have made their unique contribution to this sorry picture.

Let us, however, return to the war in Vietnam and the response that it has aroused among American intellectuals. A striking feature of the recent debate on Southeast Asian policy has been the distinction that is commonly drawn between "responsible criticism," on the one hand, and "sentimental," or "emotional," or "hysterical" criticism, on the other. There is much to be learned from a careful study of the terms in which this distinction is drawn. The "hysterical critics" are to be identified, apparently, by their irrational refusal to accept one fundamental political axiom, namely, that the United States has the right to extend its power and control without limit, insofar as is feasible. Responsible criticism does not challenge this assumption, but argues, rather, that we probably can't "get away with it" at this particular time and place.

A distinction of this sort seems to be what Irving Kristol has in mind, for example, in his analysis of the protest over Vietnam policy, in *Encounter*, August 1965. He contrasts the responsible critics, such as Walter Lippmann, the *New York Times*, and Senator Fulbright, with the "teach-in movement." "Unlike the university protesters," he maintains, "Mr. Lippmann engages in no presumptuous suppositions as to 'what the Vietnamese people really want'—he obviously doesn't much care—or in legalistic exegesis as to whether, or to what extent, there is 'aggression' or 'revolution' in South Vietnam. His is a *realpolitik* point of view; and he will apparently even contemplate the possibility of a *nuclear* war against China in extreme circumstances." This is commendable, and contrasts favorably, for Kristol, with the talk of the "unreasonable, ideological types" in the teach-in movement, who often seem to be motivated by such absurdities as "simple, virtuous 'anti-imperialism,'" who deliver "harangues on 'the power structure,'" and who even sometimes stoop so low as to read "articles and reports from the foreign press on the American presence in Vietnam." Furthermore, these nasty types are often psychologists, mathematicians, chemists, or philosophers (just as, incidentally, those most vocal in protest in the Soviet Union are generally physicists, literary intellectuals, and others remote from the exercise of power), rather than people with Washington contacts, who, of course, realize that "had they a new, good idea about Vietnam, they would get a prompt and respectful hearing" in Washington.

I am not interested here in whether Kristol's characterization of protest and dissent is accurate, but rather in the assumptions that it expresses with respect to such questions as these: Is the purity of American motives a matter that is beyond discussion, or that is irrelevant to discussion? Should decisions be left to "experts" with Washington contacts—that is, even if we assume that they command the necessary knowledge and principles to make the "best" decision, will they invariably do so? And, a logically prior question, is "expertise" applicable—that is, is there a body of theory and of relevant information, not in the public domain, that can be applied to the analysis of foreign policy or that demonstrates the correctness of present actions in some way that the psychologists, mathematicians, chemists, and philosophers are incapable of comprehending? Although Kristol does not examine these questions directly, his attitudes presuppose answers, answers which are wrong in all cases. American aggressiveness, however it may be masked in pious rhetoric, is a dominant force in world affairs and must be analyzed in terms of its causes and motives. There is no body of theory or significant body of relevant information, beyond the comprehension of the layman, which makes policy immune from criticism. To the extent that "expert knowledge" is applied to world affairs, it is surely appropriate—for a person of any integrity, quite necessary—to question its quality and the goals that it serves. These facts seem too obvious to require extended discussion.

A corrective to Kristol's curious belief in the administration's openness to new thinking about Vietnam is provided by McGeorge Bundy in a recent article.[21] As Bundy correctly observes, "on the main stage . . . the argument on Viet Nam turns on tactics, not fundamentals," although, he adds, "there are wild men in the wings." On stage center are, of course, the President (who in his recent trip to Asia had just "magisterially reaffirmed" our interest "in the progress of the people across the Pacific") and his advisers, who deserve "the understanding support of those who want restraint." It is these men who deserve the credit for the fact that "the bombing of the North has been the most accurate and the most restrained in modern warfare"—a solicitude which will be appreciated by the inhabitants, or former inhabitants, of Nam Dinh and Phu Ly and Vinh. It is these men, too, who deserve the credit for what was reported by Malcolm Browne as long ago as May 1965: "In the South, huge sectors of the nation have been declared 'free bombing zones,' in which anything that moves is a legitimate target. Tens of thousands of tons of bombs, rockets, napalm and cannon fire are poured into these vast areas each week. If only by the laws of chance, bloodshed is believed to be heavy in these raids."

Fortunately for the developing countries, Bundy assures us, "American democracy has no enduring taste for imperialism," and "taken as a whole, the stock of American experience, understanding, sympathy and simple knowledge is now much the most impressive in the world." It is true that "four-fifths of all the foreign investing in the world is now done by Americans" and that "the most admired plans and policies . . . are no better than their demonstrable relation to the American interest"—just as it is true, so we read in the same issue of *Foreign Affairs,* that the plans for armed action against Cuba were put into motion a few weeks after Mikoyan visited Havana, "invading what had so long been an almost exclusively American sphere of influence." Unfortunately, such facts as these are often taken by unsophisticated Asian intellectuals as indicating a "taste for imperialism." For example, a number of Indians have expressed their "near exasperation" at the fact that "we have done everything we can to attract foreign capital for fertilizer plants, but the American and the other Western private companies know we are over a barrel, so they demand stringent terms which we just cannot meet,"[22] while "Washington . . . doggedly insists that deals be made in the private sector with private enterprise."[23] But this reaction, no doubt, simply reveals once again how the Asian mind fails to comprehend the "diffuse and complex concepts" of Western thought.

It may be useful to study carefully the "new, good ideas about Vietnam" that are receiving a "prompt and respectful hearing" in Washington these days. The United States Government Printing Office is an endless source of insight into the moral and intellectual level of this expert advice. In its publications one can read, for example, the testimony of Professor David N. Rowe, Director of Graduate Studies in International Relations at Yale University, before the House Committee on Foreign Affairs (see note 15). Professor Rowe proposes (p. 266) that the United States buy all surplus Canadian and Australian wheat, so that there will be mass starvation in China. These are his words: "Mind you, I am not talking about this as a weapon against the Chinese people. It will be. But that is only incidental. The weapon will be a weapon against the Government because the internal stability of that country cannot be sustained by an unfriendly Government in the face of general starvation." Professor Rowe will have none of the sentimental moralism that might lead one to compare this suggestion with, say, the *Ostpolitik* of Hitler's Germany.[24] Nor does he fear the impact of such policies on other Asian nations, for example Japan. He assures us, from his "very long acquaintance with Japanese questions," that "the Japanese above all are people who respect power and determination." Hence "they will not be so much alarmed by American policy in Vietnam that takes off from a position of power and intends to seek a solution based upon the imposition of our power upon local people that we are in opposition to." What would disturb the Japanese is "a policy of indecision, a policy of refusal to face up to the problems [in China and Vietnam] and to meet our responsibilities there in a positive way," such as the way just cited. A conviction that we were "unwilling to use the power that they know we have" might "alarm the Japanese people very intensely and shake the degree of their friendly relations with us." In fact, a full use of American power would be particularly reassuring to the Japanese, because they have had a demonstration "of the tremendous power in action of the United States . . . because they have felt our power directly." This is surely a prime example of the healthy *"realpolitik* point of view" that Irving Kristol so much admires.

But, one may ask, why restrict ourselves to such indirect means as mass starvation? Why not bombing? No doubt this message is implicit in the remarks to the same committee of the Reverend R. J. de Jaegher, Regent of the Institute of Far Eastern Studies, Seton Hall University, who

explains that like all people who have lived under Communism, the North Vietnamese "would be perfectly happy
to be bombed to be free" (p. 345).

Of course, there must be those who support the Communists. But this is really a matter of small concern, as the
Honorable Walter Robertson, Assistant Secretary of
State for Far Eastern Affairs from 1953 to 1959, points
out in his testimony before the same committee. He assures us that "The Peiping regime . . . represents something less than 3 percent of the population" (p. 402).

Consider, then, how fortunate the Chinese Communist
leaders are, compared to the leaders of the Vietcong, who,
according to Arthur Goldberg, represent about "one-half
of one percent of the population of South Vietnam," that
is, about one half the number of new Southern recruits for
the Vietcong during 1965, if we can credit Pentagon statistics.[25]

In the face of such experts as these, the scientists and
philosophers of whom Kristol speaks would clearly do well
to continue to draw their circles in the sand.

Having settled the issue of the political irrelevance of
the protest movement, Kristol turns to the question of
what motivates it—more generally, what has made students
and junior faculty "go left," as he sees it, amid general
prosperity and under liberal, Welfare State administrations. This, he notes, "is a riddle to which no sociologist
has as yet come up with an answer." Since these young
people are well-off, have good futures, etc., their protest
must be irrational. It must be the result of boredom, of too
much security, or something of this sort.

Other possibilities come to mind. It might be, for example, that as honest men the students and junior faculty
are attempting to find out the truth for themselves rather

than ceding the responsibility to "experts" or to government; and it might be that they react with indignation to what they discover. These possibilities Kristol does not reject. They are simply unthinkable, unworthy of consideration. More accurately, these possibilities are inexpressible; the categories in which they are formulated (honesty, indignation) simply do not exist for the tough-minded social scientist.

In this implicit disparagement of traditional intellectual values, Kristol reflects attitudes that are fairly widespread in academic circles. I do not doubt that these attitudes are in part a consequence of the desperate attempt of the social and behavioral sciences to imitate the surface features of sciences that really have significant intellectual content. But they have other sources as well. Anyone can be a moral individual, concerned with human rights and problems; but only a college professor, a trained expert, can solve technical problems by "sophisticated" methods. Ergo, it is only problems of the latter sort that are important or real. Responsible, nonideological experts will give advice on tactical questions; irresponsible "ideological types" will "harangue" about principle and trouble themselves over moral issues and human rights, or over the traditional problems of man and society, concerning which "social and behavioral science" have nothing to offer beyond trivialities. Obviously, these emotional, ideological types are irrational, since, being well-off and having power in their grasp, they shouldn't worry about such matters.

At times this pseudoscientific posing reaches levels that are almost pathological. Consider the phenomenon of Herman Kahn, for example. Kahn has been both denounced as immoral and lauded for his courage. By people who should know better, his *On Thermonuclear War* has been described "without qualification . . . [as] . . . one of the great works of our time" (Stuart Hughes). The fact of the matter is that this is surely one of the emptiest works of our time, as can be seen by applying to it the intellectual standards of any existing discipline, by tracing some of its "well-documented conclusions" to the "objective studies" from which they derive, and by following the line of argument, where detectable. Kahn proposes no theories, no explanations, no factual assumptions that can be tested against their consequences, as do the sciences he is attempting to mimic. He simply suggests a terminology and provides a façade of rationality. When particular policy conclusions are drawn, they are supported only by *ex cathedra* remarks for which no support is even suggested (e.g., "The civil defense line probably should be drawn somewhere below $5 billion annually" to keep from provoking the Russians—why not $50 billion, or $5.00?). What is more, Kahn is quite aware of this vacuity; in his more judicious moments he claims only that "there is no reason to believe that relatively sophisticated models are more likely to be misleading than the simpler models and analogies frequently used as an aid to judgment." For those whose humor tends towards the macabre, it is easy to play the game of "strategic thinking" à la Kahn, and to prove what one wishes. For example, one of Kahn's basic assumptions is that "an all-out surprise attack in which all resources are devoted to counter-value targets would be so irrational that, barring an incredible lack of sophistication or actual insanity among Soviet decision makers, such an attack is highly unlikely." A simple argument proves the opposite. Premise 1: American decision makers think along the lines outlined by Herman Kahn. Premise 2: Kahn thinks it would be better for everyone to be red than for everyone to be dead. Premise 3: If the Americans were to respond to an all-out countervalue attack, then everyone would be dead. Conclusion: The Americans will not respond to an all-out countervalue attack, and therefore it should be launched without delay. Of course, one can carry the argument a step further. Fact: The Russians have not carried out an all-out countervalue attack. It follows that they are not rational. If they are not rational, there is no point in "strategic thinking." Therefore . . .

Of course this is all nonsense, but nonsense that differs from Kahn's only in the respect that the argument is of slightly greater complexity than anything to be discovered in his work. What is remarkable is that serious people actually pay attention to these absurdities, no doubt because of the façade of tough-mindedness and pseudo-science.

It is a curious and depressing fact that the "antiwar movement" falls prey all too often to similar confusions. In the fall of 1965, for example, there was an International Conference on Alternative Perspectives on Vietnam, which circulated a pamphlet to potential participants stating its assumptions. The plan was to set up study groups in which three "types of intellectual tradition" will be represented: (1) area specialists; (2) "social theory, with special emphasis on theories of the international system, of social change and development, of conflict and conflict resolution, or of revolution"; (3) "the analysis of public policy in terms of basic human values, rooted in various theological, philosophical and humanist traditions." The second intellectual tradition will provide "general propositions, derived from social theory and tested against historical, comparative, or experimental data"; the third "will provide the framework out of which fundamental value questions can be raised and in terms of which the moral implications of societal actions can be analyzed." The hope was that "by approaching the questions [of Vietnam policy] from the moral perspectives of all great religions and philosophical systems, we may find solutions that are more consistent with fundamental human values than current American policy in Vietnam has turned out to be."

In short, the experts on values (i.e., spokesmen for the great religions and philosophical systems) will provide fundamental insights on moral perspectives, and the experts on social theory will provide general empirically validated propositions and "general models of conflict." From this interplay, new policies will emerge, presumably from application of the canons of scientific method. The only debatable issue, it seems to me, is whether it is more ridiculous to turn to experts in social theory for general well-confirmed propositions, or to the specialists in the great religions and philosophical systems for insights into fundamental human values.

There is much more that can be said about this topic, but without continuing, I would simply like to emphasize that, as is no doubt obvious, the cult of the expert is both self-serving, for those who propound it, and fraudulent. Obviously, one must learn from social and behavioral science whatever one can; obviously, these fields should be pursued in as serious a way as is possible. But it will be quite unfortunate, and highly dangerous, if they are not accepted and judged on their merits and according to their actual, not pretended, accomplishments. In particular, if there is a body of theory, well tested and verified, that applies to the conduct of foreign affairs or the resolution of domestic or international conflict, its existence has been kept a well-guarded secret. In the case of Vietnam, if those who feel themselves to be experts have access to principles or information that would justify what the American government is doing in that unfortunate country, they have been singularly ineffective in making this fact known. To anyone who has any familiarity with the social and behavioral sciences (or the "policy sciences"), the claim that there are certain considerations and principles too deep for the outsider to comprehend is simply an absurdity, unworthy of comment.

When we consider the responsibility of intellectuals, our basic concern must be their role in the creation and analysis of ideology. And, in fact, Kristol's contrast between the unreasonable ideological types and the responsible experts is formulated in terms that immediately bring to mind Daniel Bell's interesting and influential essay on the "end of ideology,"[26] an essay which is as important for what it leaves unsaid as for its actual content. Bell presents and discusses the Marxist analysis of ideology as a mask for class interest, in particular, quoting Marx's well-known description of the belief of the bourgeoisie "that the *special* conditions of its emancipation are the *general* conditions through which alone modern society can be saved and the class struggle avoided." He then argues that the age of ideology is ended, supplanted, at least in the West, by a general agreement that each issue must be settled on its own individual terms, within the framework of a welfare state in which, presumably, experts in the conduct of public affairs will have a prominent role. Bell is quite careful, however, to characterize the precise sense of "ideology" in which "ideologies are exhausted." He is referring only to ideology as "the conversion of ideas into social levers," to ideology as "a set of beliefs, infused with passion, . . . [which] . . . seeks to transform the whole of a way of life." The crucial words are "transform" and "convert into social levers." Intellectuals in the West, he argues, have lost interest in converting ideas into social levers for the radical transformation of society. Now that we have achieved the pluralistic society of the Welfare State, they see no further need for a radical transformation of society; we may tinker with our way of life here and there, but it would be wrong to try to modify it in any significant way. With this consensus of intellectuals, ideology is dead.

There are several striking facts about Bell's essay. First, he does not point out the extent to which this consensus of the intellectuals is self-serving. He does not relate his observation that, by and large, intellectuals have lost interest in "transforming the whole of a way of life" to the fact that they play an increasingly prominent role in running the Welfare State; he does not relate their general satisfaction with the Welfare State to the fact that, as he observes elsewhere, "America has become an affluent society, offering place . . . and prestige . . . to the onetime radicals." Secondly, he offers no serious argument to show that intellectuals are somehow "right" or "objectively justified" in reaching the consensus to which he alludes, with its rejection of the notion that society should be transformed. Indeed, although Bell is fairly sharp about the empty rhetoric of the "New Left," he seems to have a quite utopian faith that technical experts will be able to come to grips with the few problems that still remain; for example, the fact that labor is treated as a commodity, and the problems of "alienation."

It seems fairly obvious that the classical problems are very much with us; one might plausibly argue that they have even been enhanced in severity and scale. For example, the classical paradox of poverty in the midst of plenty is now an ever increasing problem on an international scale. Whereas one might conceive, at least in principle, of a solution within national boundaries, a sensible idea as to how to transform international society in such a way as to cope with the vast and perhaps increasing human misery is hardly likely to develop within the framework of the intellectual consensus that Bell describes.

Thus it would seem natural to describe the consensus of Bell's intellectuals in somewhat different terms than his. Using the terminology of the first part of his essay, we might say that the Welfare State technician finds justification for his special and prominent social status in his "science," specifically, in the claim that social science can support a technology of social tinkering on a domestic or international scale. He then takes a further step, proceeding, in a familiar way, to claim universal validity for what is in fact a class interest: he argues that the special conditions on which his claims to power and authority are based are, in fact, the general conditions through which alone modern society can be saved; that social tinkering within a Welfare State framework must replace the commitment to the "total ideologies" of the past, ideologies which were concerned with a transformation of society. Having found his position of power, having achieved security and affluence, he has no further need for ideologies that look to radical change. The scholar-expert replaces the "free-floating intellectual" who "felt that the wrong values were being honored, and rejected the society," and who has now lost his political role (now, that is, that the right values are being honored).

Conceivably, it is correct that the technical experts who will (or hope to) manage the "postindustrial society" will be able to cope with the classical problems without a radical transformation of society. Just so, it is conceivably true that the bourgeoisie was right in regarding the special conditions of its emancipation as the general conditions through which alone modern society would be saved. In either case, an argument is in order, and skepticism is justified where none appears.

Within the same framework of general utopianism, Bell goes on to pose the issue between Welfare State scholar-experts and Third World ideologists in a rather curious way. He points out, quite correctly, that there is no issue of communism, the content of that doctrine having been "long forgotten by friends and foes alike." Rather, he says, "the question is an older one: whether new societies can grow by building democratic institutions and allowing people to make choices—and sacrifices—voluntarily, or whether the new elites, heady with power, will impose totalitarian means to transform their countries." The question is an interesting one; it is odd, however, to see it referred to as "an older one." Surely he cannot be suggesting that the West chose the democratic way—for example, that in England during the industrial revolution, the farmers voluntarily made the choice of leaving the land, giving up cottage industry, becoming an industrial proletariat, and voluntarily decided, within the framework of the existing democratic institutions, to make the sacrifices that are graphically described in the classic literature on nineteenth-century industrial society. One may debate the question whether authoritarian control is necessary to permit capital accumulation in the underdeveloped world, but the Western model of development is hardly one that we can point to with any pride. It is perhaps not surprising to find a Walt Rostow referring to "the more humane processes [of industrialization] that Western values would suggest."²⁷ Those who have a serious concern for the problems that face backward countries and for the role that advanced industrial societies might, in principle, play in development and modernization, must use somewhat more care in interpreting the significance of the Western experience.

Returning to the quite appropriate question, whether "new societies can grow by building democratic institutions" or only by totalitarian means, I think that honesty requires us to recognize that this question must be directed more to American intellectuals than to Third World ideologists. The backward countries have incredible, perhaps insurmountable problems, and few available options; the United States has a wide range of options, and has the economic and technological resources, though evidently neither the intellectual nor moral resources, to confront at least some of these problems. It is easy for an American intellectual to deliver homilies on the virtues of freedom and liberty, but if he is really concerned about, say, Chinese totalitarianism or the burdens imposed on the Chinese peasantry in forced industrialization, then he should face a task that is infinitely more significant and challenging—the task of creating, in the United States, the intellectual and moral climate, as well as the social and economic conditions, that would permit this country to participate in modernization and development in a way commensurate with its material wealth and technical capacity. Massive capital gifts to Cuba and China might not succeed in alleviating the authoritarianism and terror that tend to accompany early stages of capital accumulation, but they are far more likely to have this effect than lectures on democratic values. It is possible that even without "capitalist encirclement" in its varying manifestations, the truly democratic elements in revolutionary movements—in some instances, soviets and collectives, for example—might be undetermined by an "elite" of bureaucrats and technical intelligentsia; but it is a near certainty that the fact of capitalist encirclement, which all revolutionary movements now have to face, will guarantee this result. The lesson, for those who are concerned to strengthen the democratic, spontaneous, and popular elements in developing societies, is quite clear. Lectures on the two-party system, or even the really substantial democratic values that have been in part realized in Western society, are a monstrous irrelevance in the face of the effort that is required to raise the level of culture in Western society to the point where it can provide a "social lever" for both economic development and the development of true democratic institutions in the Third World—and for that matter, at home as well.

A good case can be made for the conclusion that there is indeed something of a consensus among intellectuals who have already achieved power and affluence, or who sense that they can achieve them by "accepting society" as it is and promoting the values that are "being honored" in this society. And it is also true that this consensus is most noticeable among the scholar-experts who are replacing the free-floating intellectuals of the past. In the university, these scholar-experts construct a "value-free technology" for the solution of technical problems that arise in contemporary society,[28] taking a "responsible stance" towards these problems, in the sense noted earlier. This consensus among the responsible scholar-experts is the domestic analogue to that proposed, in the international arena, by those who justify the application of American power in Asia, whatever the human cost, on the grounds that it is necessary to contain the "expansion of China" (an "expansion" which is, to be sure, hypothetical for the time being)[29]—to translate from State Department Newspeak, on the grounds that it is essential to reverse the Asian nationalist revolutions, or at least to prevent them from spreading. The analogy becomes clear when we look carefully at the ways in which this proposal is formulated. With his usual lucidity, Churchill outlined the general position in a remark to his colleague of the moment, Joseph Stalin, at Teheran in 1943: " . . . the government of the world must be entrusted to satisfied nations, who wished nothing more for themselves than what they had. If the world-government were in the hand of hungry nations, there would always be danger. But none of us had any reason to seek for anything more. The peace would be kept by peoples who lived in their own way and were not ambitious. Our power placed us above the rest. We were like rich men dwelling at peace within their habitations."[30]

For a translation of Churchill's biblical rhetoric into the jargon of contemporary social science, one may turn to the testimony of Charles Wolf, Senior Economist of the RAND Corporation, at the congressional committee hearings cited earlier:

> I am dubious that China's fears of encirclement are going to be abated, eased, relaxed in the long-term future. But I would hope that what we do in Southeast Asia would help to develop within the Chinese body politic more of a realism and willingness to live with this fear than to indulge it by support for liberation movements, which admittedly depend on a great deal more than external support . . . the operational question for American foreign-policy is not whether that fear can be eliminated or substantially alleviated, but whether China can be faced with a structure of incentives, of penalties

and rewards, of inducements that will make it willing to live with this fear.[31]

The point is further clarified by Thomas Schelling: "There is growing experience which the Chinese can profit from, that although the United States may be interested in encircling them, may be interested in defending nearby areas from them, it is, nevertheless, prepared to behave peaceably if they are."[32]

In short, we are prepared to live peaceably within our— to be sure, rather extensive—habitations. And quite naturally, we are offended by the undignified noises from the servants' quarters. If, let us say, a peasant-based revolutionary movement tries to achieve independence from foreign domination or to overthrow semifeudal structures supported by foreign powers, or if the Chinese irrationally refuse to respond properly to the schedule of reinforcement that we have prepared for them, if they object to being encircled by the benign and peace-loving "rich men" who control the territories on their borders as a natural right, then, evidently, we must respond to this belligerence with appropriate force.

It is this mentality that explains the frankness with which the United States government and its academic apologists defend the American refusal to permit a political settlement in Vietnam at a local level, a settlement based on the actual distribution of political forces. Even government experts freely admit that the NLF is the only "truly mass-based political party in South Vietnam";[33] that the NLF had "made a conscious and massive effort to extend political participation, even if it was manipulated, on the local level so as to involve the people in a self-contained, self-supporting revolution" (p. 374); and that this effort had been so successful that no political groups, "with the possible exception of the Buddhists, thought themselves equal in size and power to risk entering into a coalition, fearing that if they did the whale would swallow the minnow" (p. 362). Moreover, they concede that until the introduction of overwhelming American force, the NLF had insisted that the struggle "should be fought out at the political level and that the use of massed military might was in itself illegitimate. . . . The battleground was to be the minds and loyalties of the rural Vietnamese, the weapons were to be ideas" (pp. 91–92; cf. also pp. 93, 99–108, 155f.); and correspondingly, that until mid-1964, aid from Hanoi "was largely confined to two areas—doctrinal know-how and leadership personnel" (p. 321). Captured NLF documents contrast the enemy's "military superiority" with their own "political superiority" (p. 106), thus fully confirming the analysis of American military spokesmen who define our problem as how, "with considerable armed force but little political power, [to] contain an adversary who has enormous political force but only modest military power."[34]

Similarly, the most striking outcome of both the Honolulu conference in February and the Manila conference in October was the frank admission by high officials of the Saigon government that "they could not survive a 'peaceful settlement' that left the Vietcong *political* structure in place even if the Vietcong guerilla units were disbanded," that "they are not able to compete *politically* with the Vietnamese Communists."[35] Thus, Mohr continues, the Vietnamese demand a "pacification program" which will have as "its core . . . the destruction of the clandestine Vietcong political structure and the creation of an iron-like system of government political control over the population." And from Manila, the same correspondent, on October 23, quotes a high South Vietnamese official as saying: "Frankly, we are not strong enough now to compete with the Communists on a purely political basis. They are organized and disciplined. The non-Communist nationalists are not—we do not have any large, well-organized political parties and we do not yet have unity. We cannot leave the Vietcong in existence." Officials in Washington understand the situation very well. Thus Secretary Rusk has pointed out that "if the Vietcong come to the conference table as full partners they will, in a sense, have been victorious in the very aims that South Vietnam and the United States are pledged to prevent" (January 28, 1966). Similarly, Max Frankel reported from Washington: "Compromise has had no appeal here because the Administration concluded long ago that the non-Communist forces of South Vietnam could not long survive in a Saigon coalition with Communists. It is for that reason—and not because of an excessively rigid sense of protocol—that Washington has steadfastly refused to deal with the Vietcong or recognize them as an independent political force."[36]

In short, we will—magnanimously—permit Vietcong representatives to attend negotiations only if they will agree to identify themselves as agents of a foreign power and thus forfeit the right to participate in a coalition government, a right which they have now been demanding for a half-dozen years. We know well that in any representative coalition, our chosen delegates could not last a day without the support of American arms. Therefore, we must increase American force and resist meaningful negotiations, until the day when a client government can exert both military and political control over its own population —a day which may never dawn, for as William Bundy has pointed out, we could never be sure of the security of a Southeast Asia "from which the Western presence was effectively withdrawn." Thus if we were to "negotiate in the direction of solutions that are put under the label of neutralization," this would amount to capitulation to the Communists.[37] According to this reasoning, then, South Vietnam must remain, permanently, an American military base.

All of this is of course reasonable, so long as we accept the fundamental political axiom that the United States, with its traditional concern for the rights of the weak and downtrodden, and with its unique insight into the proper mode of development for backward countries, must have the courage and the persistence to impose its will by force until such time as other nations are prepared to accept these truths—or simply to abandon hope.

If it is the responsibility of the intellectual to insist upon the truth, it is also his duty to see events in their historical perspective. Thus one must applaud the insistence of the Secretary of State on the importance of historical analogies, the Munich analogy, for example. As Munich showed, a powerful and aggressive nation with a fanatic belief in its manifest destiny will regard each victory, each extension of its power and authority, as a prelude to the next step. The matter was very well put by Adlai Stevenson, when he spoke of "the old, old route whereby expansive powers push at more and more doors, believing they will open, until, at the ultimate door, resistance is unavoidable and major war breaks out." Herein lies the danger of appeasement, as the Chinese tirelessly point out to the Soviet Union, which they claim is playing Chamberlain to our Hitler in Vietnam. Of course, the aggressiveness of liberal imperialism is not that of Nazi Germany, though the distinction may seem rather academic to a Vietnamese peasant who is being gassed or incinerated. We do not want to occupy Asia; we merely wish, to return to Mr. Wolf, "to help the Asian countries progress toward economic modernization, as relatively 'open' and stable societies, to which our access, as a country and as individual citizens, is free and comfortable."[38] The formulation is appropriate. Recent history shows that it makes little difference to us what form of government a country has as long as it remains an "open society," in our peculiar sense of this term —a society, that is, that remains open to American economic penetration or political control. If it is necessary to approach genocide in Vietnam to achieve this objective, then this is the price we must pay in defense of freedom and the rights of man.

It is, no doubt, superflous to discuss at length the ways in which we assist other countries to progress towards open societies "to which our access is free and comfortable." One enlightening example is discussed in the recent congressional hearings from which I have now quoted several times, in the testimony of Willem Holst and Robert Meagher, representing the Standing Committee on India of the Business Council for International Understanding.[39] As Mr. Meagher points out: "If it was possible, India would probably prefer to import technicians and know-how rather than foreign corporations. Such is not possible; therefore India accepts foreign capital as a necessary evil." Of course, "the question of private capital investment in India . . . would be no more than a theoretical exercise" had the groundwork for such investment not been laid by foreign aid, and were it not that "necessity has forced a modification in India's approach to private foreign capital." But now, "India's attitude toward private foreign investment is undergoing a substantial change. From a position of resentment and ambivalence, it is evolving toward an acceptance of its necessity. As the necessity becomes more and more evident, the ambivalence will probably be replaced by a more accommodating attitude." Mr. Holst contributes what is "perhaps a typical case history," namely, "the plan under which it was proposed that the Indian Government in partnership with a United States private consortium was to have increased fertilizer production by a million tons per year, which is just double presently installed capacity in all of India. The unfortunate demise of this ambitious plan may be attributed in large part to the failure of both Government and business to find a workable and mutually acceptable solution within the framework of the well-publicized 10 business incentives." The difficulty here was in connection with the percentage of equity ownership. Obviously, "fertilizers are desperately needed in India." Equally obviously, the consortium "insisted that to get the proper kind of control majority ownership was in fact needed." But "the Indian Government officially insisted that they shall have majority ownership," and "in something so complex it was felt that it would be a self-defeating thing."

Fortunately, this particular story has a happy ending. The remarks just quoted were made in February 1966, and within a few weeks, the Indian government had seen the light, as we read in a series of reports in the *New York Times*. The criticism, inside India, that "the American Government and the World Bank would like to arrogate to themselves the right to lay down the framework in which our economy must function," was stilled (April 24); and the Indian government accepted the conditions for resumed economic aid, namely, "that India provide easier terms for foreign private investment in fertilizer plants" and that the American investors "have substantial management rights" (May 14). The development is summarized in a dispatch datelined April 28, from New Delhi, in these terms:

> There are signs of change. The Government has granted easy terms to private foreign investors in the fertilizer industry, is thinking about decontrolling several more industries and is ready to liberalize import policy if it gets sufficient foreign aid. . . . Much of what is happening now is a result of steady pressure from the United States and the International Bank for Reconstruction and Development, which for the last year have been urging a substantial freeing of the Indian economy and a greater scope for private enterprise. The United States pressure, in particular, has been highly effective here because the United States provides by far the largest part of the foreign exchange needed to finance India's development and keep the wheels of industry turning. Call them "strings," call them "conditions" or whatever one likes, India has little choice now but to agree to many of the terms that the United States, through the World Bank, is putting on its aid. For India simply has nowhere else to turn.

The heading of the article refers to this development as India's "drift from socialism to pragmatism."

Even this was not enough, however. Thus we read a few months later, in the *Christian Science Monitor* (December 5), that American entrepreneurs insist "on importing all equipment and machinery when India has a tested capacity to meet some of their requirements. They have insisted on importing liquid ammonia, a basic raw material, rather than using indigenous naphtha which is abundantly available. They have laid down restrictions about pricing, distribution, profits, and management control." The Indian reaction I have already cited (see p. 268).

In such ways as these, we help India develop towards an

open society, one which, in Walt Rostow's words, has a proper understanding of "the core of the American ideology," namely, "the sanctity of the individual in relation to the state." And in this way, too, we refute the simple-minded view of those Asians who, to continue with Rostow's phrasing, "believe or half-believe that the West has been driven to create and then to cling to its imperial holdings by the inevitable workings of capitalist economies."[40]

In fact, a major postwar scandal is developing in India as the United States, cynically capitalizing on India's current torture, applies its economic power to implement India's "drift from socialism to pragmatism."

In pursuing the aim of helping other countries to progress towards open societies, with no thought of territorial aggrandizement, we are breaking no new ground. Hans Morgenthau has aptly described our traditional policy towards China as one of favoring "what you might call freedom of competition with regard to the exploitation of China."[41] In fact, few imperialist powers have had explicit territorial ambitions. Thus in 1784, the British Parliament announced that: "to pursue schemes of conquest and extension of dominion in India are measures repugnant to the wish, honor, and policy of this nation." Shortly after, the conquest of India was in full swing. A century later, Britain announced its intentions in Egypt under the slogan "intervention, reform, withdrawal." It is unnecessary to comment on which parts of this promise were fulfilled, within the next half-century. In 1936, on the eve of hostilities in North China, the Japanese stated their Basic Principles of National Policy. These included the use of moderate and peaceful means to extend her strength, to promote social and economic development, to eradicate the menace of Communism, to correct the aggressive policies of the great powers, and to secure her position as the stabilizing power in East Asia. Even in 1937, the Japanese government had "no territorial designs upon China." In short, we follow a well-trodden path.

It is useful to remember, incidentally, that the United States was apparently quite willing, as late as 1939, to negotiate a commercial treaty with Japan and arrive at a *modus vivendi* if Japan would "change her attitude and practice towards our rights and interests in China," as Secretary Hull put it. The bombing of Chungking and the rape of Nanking were rather unpleasant, it is true, but what was really important was our rights and interests in China, as the responsible, unhysterical men of the day saw quite clearly. It was the closing of the open door by Japan that led inevitably to the Pacific war, just as it is the closing of the open door by "Communist" China itself that may very well lead to the next, and no doubt last, Pacific war.

Quite often, the statements of sincere and devoted technical experts give surprising insight into the intellectual attitudes that lie in the background of the latest savagery. Consider, for example, the following comment by economist Richard Lindholm, in 1959, expressing his frustration over the failure of economic development in "free Vietnam": "the use of American aid is determined by how the Vietnamese use their incomes and their savings. The fact that a large portion of the Vietnamese imports financed with American aid are either consumer goods or raw materials used rather directly to meet consumer demands is an indication that the Vietnamese people desire these goods, for they have shown their desire by their willingness to use their piasters to purchase them."[42]

In short, the Vietnamese *people* desire Buicks and air conditioners, rather than sugar-refining equipment or road-building machinery, as they have shown by their behavior in a free market. And however much we may deplore their free choice, we must allow the people to have their way. Of course, there are also those two-legged beasts of burden that one stumbles on in the countryside, but as any graduate student of political science can explain, they are not part of a responsible modernizing elite, and therefore have only a superficial biological resemblance to the human race.

In no small measure, it is attitudes like this that lie behind the butchery in Vietnam, and we had better face up to them with candor, or we will find our government leading us towards a "final solution" in Vietnam, and in the many Vietnams that inevitably lie ahead.

Let me finally return to Macdonald and the responsibility of intellectuals. Macdonald quotes an interview with a death-camp paymaster who bursts into tears when told that the Russians would hang him. "Why should they? What have I done?" he asked. Macdonald concludes: "Only those who are willing to resist authority themselves when it conflicts too intolerably with their personal moral code, only they have the right to condemn the death-camp paymaster." The question "What have I done?" is one that we may well ask ourselves, as we read, each day, of fresh atrocities in Vietnam—as we create, or mouth, or tolerate the deceptions that will be used to justify the next defense of freedom.

NOTES

* This is a revised version of the talk given at Harvard and published in *Mosaic,* June 1966. It appeared in substantially this form in the *New York Review of Books,* February 23, 1967.
1. Such a research project has now been undertaken and published

as a "Citizens' White Paper": F. Schurmann, P. D. Scott, R. Zelnik, *The Politics of Escalation in Vietnam* (New York, Fawcett World Library, and Boston, Beacon Press, 1966). For further evidence of American rejection of UN initiatives for diplomatic settlement, just prior to the major escalation of February 1965, see Mario Rossi, "The US Rebuff to U Thant," *New York Review of Books,* November 17, 1966. See also Theodore Draper, "How Not To Negotiate," *New York Review of Books,* May 4, 1967. There is further documentary evidence of NLF attempts to establish a coalition government and to neutralize the area, all rejected by the United States and its Saigon ally, in Douglas Pike, *Viet Cong* (Cambridge, The M.I.T. Press, 1966). In reading material of this latter sort one must be especially careful to distinguish between the evidence presented and the "conclusions" that are asserted, for reasons noted briefly below (see note 33).

It is interesting to see the first, somewhat oblique published reactions to *The Politics of Escalation,* by those who defend our right to conquer South Vietnam and institute a government of our choice. For example, Robert Scalapino (*New York Times Magazine,* December 11, 1966) argues that the thesis of the book implies that our leaders are "diabolical." Since no right-thinking person can believe this, the thesis is refuted. To assume otherwise would betray "irresponsibility," in a unique sense of this term—a sense that gives an ironic twist to the title of this chapter. He goes on to point out the alleged central weakness in the argument of the book, namely, the failure to perceive that a serious attempt on our part to pursue the possibilities for a diplomatic settlement would have been interpreted by our adversaries as a sign of weakness.

2. *New York Times,* October 14, 1965.

3. *New York Times,* February 6, 1966.

4. *Boston Globe,* November 19, 1965.

5. At other times, Schlesinger does indeed display admirable scholarly caution. For example, in his Introduction to *The Politics of Escalation* he admits that there may have been "flickers of interest in negotiations" on the part of Hanoi. As to the administration's lies about negotiations and its repeated actions undercutting tentative initiatives towards negotiations, he comments only that the authors may have underestimated military necessity and that future historians may prove them wrong. This caution and detachment must be compared with Schlesinger's attitude toward renewed study of the origins of the Cold War: in a letter to the *New York Review of Books,* October 20, 1966, he remarks that it is time to "blow the whistle" on revisionist attempts to show that the Cold War may have been

the consequence of something more than mere Communist belligerence. We are to believe, then, that the relatively straightforward matter of the origins of the Cold War is settled beyond discussion, whereas the much more complex issue of why the United States shies away from a negotiated settlement in Vietnam must be left to future historians to ponder.

It is useful to bear in mind that the United States government itself is on occasion much less diffident in explaining why it refuses to contemplate a meaningful negotiated settlement. As is freely admitted, this solution would leave it without power to control the situation. See, for example, note 37.

6. Arthur M. Schlesinger, Jr., *A Thousand Days: John F. Kennedy in the White House* (Boston, Houghton Mifflin Company, 1965), p. 421.

7. Walt W. Rostow, *The View from the Seventh Floor* (New York, Harper & Row, Publishers, 1964), p. 149. See also his *United States in the World Arena* (New York, Harper & Row, Publishers, 1960), p. 244: "Stalin, exploiting the disruption and weakness of the postwar world, pressed out from the expanded base he had won during the Second World War in an effort to gain the balance of power in Eurasia . . . turning to the East, to back Mao and to enflame the North Korean and Indochinese Communists. . . ."

8. For example, the article by CIA analyst George Carver in *Foreign Affairs*, April 1966. See also note 33.

9. Cf. Jean Lacouture, *Vietnam: Between Two Truces* (New York, Random House, 1966), p. 21. Diem's analysis of the situation was shared by Western observers at the time. See, for example, the comments of William Henderson, Far Eastern specialist and executive, Council on Foreign Relations, in R. W. Lindholm, ed., *Vietnam: The First Five Years* (East Lansing, Michigan State University Press, 1959). He notes "the growing alienation of the intelligentsia," "the renewal of armed dissidence in the South," the fact that "security has noticeably deteriorated in the last two years," all as a result of Diem's "grim dictatorship," and predicts "a steady worsening of the political climate in free Vietnam, culminating in unforeseen disasters."

10. See Bernard Fall, "Vietnam in the Balance," *Foreign Affairs*, Vol. 45 (October 1966), pp. 1–18.

11. Stalin was neither pleased by the Titoist tendencies inside the Greek Communist party, nor by the possibility that a Balkan federation might develop under Titoist leadership. It is nevertheless conceivable that Stalin supported the Greek guerrillas at some stage of the rebellion, in spite of the difficulty in obtaining firm documentary evidence. Needless to say, no elaborate study is necessary to document the British or American role in this

civil conflict, from late 1944. See D. G. Kousoulas, *The Price of Freedom* (Syracuse, Syracuse University Press, 1953), *Revolution and Defeat* (New York, Oxford University Press, 1965), for serious study of these events from a strongly anti-Communist point of view.

12. For a detailed account, see James Warburg, *Germany: Key to Peace* (Cambridge, Harvard University Press, 1953), pp. 189f. Warburg concludes that apparently "the Kremlin was now prepared to accept the creation of an All-German democracy in the Western sense of that word," whereas the Western powers, in their response, "frankly admitted their plan 'to secure the participation of Germany in a purely defensive European community'" (i.e. NATO).

13. *The United States in the World Arena*, pp. 344–45. Incidentally, those who quite rightly deplore the brutal suppression of the East German and Hungarian revolutions would do well to remember that these scandalous events might have been avoided had the United States been willing to consider proposals for neutralization of Central Europe. Some of George Kennan's recent statements provide interesting commentary on this matter, for example, his comments on the falsity, from the outset, of the assumption that the USSR intended to attack or intimidate by force the Western half of the continent and that it was deterred by American force, and his remarks on the sterility and general absurdity of the demand for unilateral Soviet withdrawal from Eastern Germany together with "the inclusion of a united Germany as a major component in a Western defense system based primarily on nuclear weaponry" (Edward Reed, ed., *Peace on Earth* [New York, Pocket Books, 1965]).

It is worth noting that historical fantasy of the sort illustrated in Rostow's remarks has become a regular State Department specialty. Thus we have Thomas Mann justifying our Dominican intervention as a response to actions of the "Sino-Soviet military bloc." Or, to take a more considered statement, we have William Bundy's analysis of stages of development of Communist ideology in his Pomona College address, February 12, 1966, in which he characterizes the Soviet Union in the 1920s and early 1930s as "in a highly militant and aggressive phase." What is frightening about fantasy, as distinct from outright falsification, is the possibility that it may be sincere and may actually serve as the basis for formation of policy.

14. *New York Times*, February 6, 1966.

15. *United States Policy Toward Asia*, Hearings before the Subcommittee on the Far East and the Pacific of the Committee on Foreign Affairs, House of Representatives (Washington, D.C., U.S. Government Printing Office, 1966), p. 89.

16. *New York Times Book Review,* November 20, 1966. Such comments call to mind the remarkable spectacle of President Kennedy counseling Cheddi Jagan on the dangers of entering into a trading relationship "which brought a country into a condition of economic dependence." The reference, of course, is to the dangers in commercial relations with the Soviet Union. See Schlesinger, *A Thousand Days,* p. 776.

17. *A Thousand Days,* p. 252.

18. *Ibid.,* p. 769.

19. Though this too is imprecise. One must recall the real character of the Trujillo regime to appreciate the full cynicism of Kennedy's "realistic" analysis.

20. W. W. Rostow and R. W. Hatch, *An American Policy in Asia* (New York, Technology Press and John Wiley & Sons, Inc., 1955).

21. "End of Either/Or," *Foreign Affairs,* Vol. 45 (January 1967), pp. 189–201.

22. *Christian Science Monitor,* November 26, 1966.

23. *Ibid.,* December 5, 1966.

24. Although, to maintain perspective, we should recall that in his wildest moments, Alfred Rosenberg spoke of the elimination of thirty million Slavs, not the imposition of mass starvation on a quarter of the human race. Incidentally, the analogy drawn here is highly "irresponsible," in the technical sense of this neologism discussed earlier. That is, it is based on the assumption that statements and actions of Americans are subject to the same standards and open to the same interpretations as those of anyone else.

25. *New York Times,* February 6, 1966. What is more, Goldberg continues, the United States is not certain that all of these are voluntary adherents. This is not the first such demonstration of Communist duplicity. Another example was seen in the year 1962, when according to United States government sources 15,000 guerrillas suffered 30,000 casualties. See Arthur Schlesinger, *A Thousand Days,* p. 982.

26. Reprinted in a collection of essays with the title *The End of Ideology: On the Exhaustion of Political Ideas in the Fifties* (New York, The Free Press, 1960). I have no intention here of entering into the full range of issues that have been raised in the discussion of the "end of ideology" for the past dozen years. It is difficult to see how a rational person could quarrel with many of the theses that have been put forth, e.g., that at a certain historical moment the "politics of civility" is appropriate, and perhaps efficacious; that one who advocates action (or inaction —a matter less frequently noted) has a responsibility to assess its social cost; that dogmatic fanaticism and "secular religions"

should be combated (or if possible, ignored); that technical solutions to problems should be implemented, where possible; that
*"le dogmatisme idéologique devait disparaître pour que les idées
reprissent vie"* (Aron); and so on. Since this is sometimes taken
to be an expression of an "anti-Marxist" position, it is worth
keeping in mind that such sentiments as these have no bearing
on non-Bolshevik Marxism, as represented, for example, by
such figures as Luxemburg, Pannekoek, Korsch, Arthur Rosenberg, and many others.

27. Rostow and Hatch, *An American Policy in Asia*, p. 10.
28. The extent to which this "technology" is value-free is hardly
very important, given the clear commitments of those who apply
it. The problems with which research is concerned are those
posed by the Pentagon or the great corporations, not, say, by
the revolutionaries of Northeast Brazil or by SNCC. Nor am I
aware of a research project devoted to the problem of how
poorly-armed guerrillas might more effectively resist a brutal
and devastating military technology—surely the kind of problem
that would have interested the free-floating intellectual who is
now hopelessly out of date.
29. In view of the unremitting propaganda barrage on "Chinese expansionism," perhaps a word of comment is in order. Typical of
American propaganda on this subject is Adlai Stevenson's assessment, shortly before his death (cf. *New York Times Magazine*, March 13, 1966): "So far, the new Communist 'dynasty' has
been very aggressive. Tibet was swallowed, India attacked, the
Malays had to fight 12 years to resist a 'national liberation' they
could receive from the British by a more peaceful route. Today,
the apparatus of infiltration and aggression is already at work
in North Thailand."

As to Malaya, Stevenson is probably confusing ethnic Chinese
with the government of China. Those concerned with the actual
events would agree with Harry Miller, in *Communist Menace
in Malaya* (New York, Frederick A. Praeger, Publishers, 1954),
that "Communist China continues to show little interest in the
Malayan affair beyond its usual fulminations via Peking Radio."
There are various harsh things that one might say about Chinese
behavior in what the Sino-Indian Treaty of 1954 refers to as
"the Tibet region of China," but it is no more proof of a
tendency towards expansionism than is the behavior of the
Indian government with regard to the Naga and Mizo tribes-
men. As to North Thailand, "the apparatus of infiltration" may
well be at work, though there is little reason to suppose it to be
Chinese—and it is surely not unrelated to the American use of
Thailand as a base for its attack on Vietnam. This reference is
the sheerest hypocrisy.

The "attack on India" grew out of a border dispute that began several years after the Chinese had completed a road from Tibet to Sinkiang in an area so remote from Indian control that the Indians learned about this operation only from the Chinese press. According to American Air Force maps, the disputed area is in Chinese territory. Cf. Alastair Lamb, *China Quarterly*, July–September, 1965. To this distinguished authority, "it seems unlikely that the Chinese have been working out some master plan . . . to take over the Indian sub-continent lock, stock and overpopulated barrel." Rather, he thinks it likely that the Chinese were probably unaware that India even claimed the territory through which the road passed. After the Chinese military victory, Chinese troops were, in most areas, withdrawn beyond the McMahon Line, a border which the British had attempted to impose on China in 1914 but which has never been recognized by China (Nationalist or Communist), the United States, or any other government.

It is remarkable that a person in a responsible position could describe all of this as Chinese expansionism. In fact, it is absurd to debate the hypothetical aggressiveness of a China surrounded by American missiles and a still expanding network of military bases backed by an enormous American expeditionary force in Southeast Asia. It is conceivable that at some future time a powerful China may be expansionist. We may speculate about such possibilities if we wish, but it is American aggressiveness that is the central fact of current politics.

30. W. S. Churchill, *Closing the Ring*, Vol. 5 of *The Second World War* (Boston, Houghton Mifflin Company, 1951), p. 382.
31. *United States Policy Toward Asia*, p. 104. See note 15.
32. *Ibid.*, p. 105.
33. Douglas Pike, *op. cit.*, p. 110. This book, written by a foreign service officer working at the Center for International Studies, MIT, poses a contrast between our side, which sympathizes with "the usual revolutionary stirrings . . . around the world because they reflect inadequate living standards or oppressive and corrupt governments," and the backers of "revolutionary guerrilla warfare," which "opposes the aspirations of people while apparently furthering them, manipulates the individual by persuading him to manipulate himself." Revolutionary guerrilla warfare is "an imported product, revolution from the outside" (other examples, besides the Vietcong, are "Stalin's exportation of armed revolution," the Haganah in Palestine, and the Irish Republican Army—see pp. 32–33). The Vietcong could not be an indigenous movement since it has "a social construction program of such scope and ambition that of necessity it must have been created in Hanoi" (p. 76—but on pp. 77–79 we

read that "organizational activity had gone on intensively and systematically for several years" before the Lao Dong party in Hanoi had made its decision "to begin building an organization"). On page 80 we find that "such an effort had to be the child of the North," even though elsewhere we read of the prominent role of the Cao Dai (p. 74), "the first major social group to begin actively opposing the Diem government" (p. 222), and of the Hoa Hao sect, "another early and major participant in the NLF" (p. 69). He takes it as proof of Communist duplicity that in the South, the party insisted it was "Marxist-Leninist," thus "indicating philosophic but not political allegiance," whereas in the North it described itself as a "Marxist-Leninist organization" thus "indicating that it was in the main-stream of the world-wide Communist movement" (p. 150). And so on. Also revealing is the contempt for "Cinderella and all the other fools [who] could still believe there was magic in the mature world if one mumbled the secret incantation: solidarity, union, concord"; for the "gullible, misled people" who were "turning the countryside into a bedlam, toppling one Saigon government after another, confounding the Americans"; for the "mighty force of people" who in their mindless innocence thought that "the meek, at last, were to inherit the earth," that "riches would be theirs and all in the name of justice and virtue." One can appreciate the chagrin with which a sophisticated Western political scientist must view this "sad and awesome spectacle."

34. Lacouture, *op. cit.,* p. 188. The same military spokesman goes on, ominously, to say that this is the problem confronting us throughout Asia, Africa, and Latin America, and that we must find the "proper response" to it.
35. Charles Mohr, *New York Times,* February 11, 1966. Italics mine.
36. *New York Times,* February 18, 1966.
37. William Bundy, in A. Buchan, ed., *China and the Peace of Asia* (New York, Frederick A. Praeger, Publishers, 1965).
38. *Op. cit.,* p. 80.
39. *United States Policy Toward Asia,* pp. 191–201, passim.
40. *An American Policy in Asia,* p. 10.
41. *United States Policy Toward Asia,* p. 128.
42. Lindholm, *op. cit.,* p. 322.

✍ The Contributors

CHRISTIAN BAY received his doctorate at the University of Oslo, where he was a law school student when the Nazis occupied Norway. During the postwar period he joined the Norwegian Labour Party and was one of the founders of the neutralist socialist magazine *Orientering*. Since coming to the United States in 1957 he has taught at Michigan State University, at the University of California-Berkeley, and at Stanford University where he held appointments in the Department of Political Science and in the Institute for the Study of Human Problems. He was active in a number of San Francisco Bay Area peace, civil rights, and anti-capital-punishment organizations before assuming his present position in 1966 as Head of the Department of Political Science at the University of Alberta. He is a contributor to the *International Encyclopedia of the Social Sciences* as well as to many professional and political journals, among them the *Journal of Conflict Resolution* (of which he is an associate editor), the *American Political Science Review*, the *Nation*, *Our Generation*, and the *Review of Politics*. He is the author of *The Structure of Freedom*.

NOAM CHOMSKY took his bachelor's degree and doctorate from the University of Pennsylvania. He has been a National Science Foundation Fellow at the Princeton Institute for Advanced Study and an American Council of Learned Societies Fellow at the Center for Cognitive Studies at Harvard, where he remains a Research Fellow. In 1966 he became the Ferrari Ward Professor of Linguistics at the Massachusetts

Institute of Technology, where he has taught since 1955. In 1965 he became a national sponsor of a citizens' committee to publicize tax refusal as a protest against the war in Vietnam. His books include *Syntactic Structures, Aspects of the Theory of Syntax, Cartesian Linguistics,* and, with Morris Halle, *The Sound Pattern of English.*

ROBERT ENGLER is Professor of Political Science at Queens College of the City University of New York and also at Sarah Lawrence College. He holds a doctorate from the University of Wisconsin. He has previously taught at the University of Wisconsin, Syracuse University, the New School for Social Research, and Columbia University, where he was on the graduate faculty in sociology.

He is the author of *The Politics of Oil: A Study of Private Power and Democratic Directions.* He has received the Sidney Hillman Prize for political writing, and is now completing a book on planning for a new society.

KATHLEEN GOUGH was educated at Girton College, Cambridge, and took her doctorate at Cambridge in 1950. She has been a visiting lecturer at several English and American universities and has taught at Brandeis University, the University of Oregon, and since 1967, at Simon Fraser University in Canada. She has held research grants from the Wenner-Gren Foundation for Anthropological Research, the Social Science Research Council, and the Ford Foundation. She was an active member of the Campaign for Nuclear Disarmament and the Direct Action Committee in England. Recently, at the University of Oregon, she has been a faculty adviser to the Students for a Democratic Society and has participated in the Faculty-Student Committee to Stop the War in Vietnam. She has contributed to many professional journals, among them the *Journal of the Royal Anthropological Institute,* the *Inter-*

national *Archives of Ethnography,* and the *American Anthropologist,* and has placed chapters in several anthropological studies, among them *Concept of Freedom in Anthropology,* edited by David Bidney. She is coeditor of and a contributor to *Matrilineal Kinship,* published by the University of California Press in 1961.

LOUIS KAMPF is Associate Professor of Humanities at the Massachusetts Institute of Technology and head of the school's Literature Section. With Noam Chomsky he teaches a special course at MIT titled "Intellectuals and Social Change." He is on the Steering Committee of the Educational Cooperative, an experimental school in Boston which seeks to introduce various social groups—students, young academics, lawyers, welfare recipients, seminarians—to the basic techniques of radical political action. He is the author of *On Modernism: The Prospects for Literature and Freedom.*

STAUGHTON LYND is Assistant Professor of History at Yale. Over the past five years he has become one of the leading figures in pacifist and New Left activities. He was a chairman of the Students for a Democratic Society-sponsored march on Washington in April 1965 and a participant in the 1965 teach-ins at Berkeley and Washington, D.C. In August of 1965 he was arrested while participating in the Assembly of Unrepresented People in Washington. Later that year he traveled to North Vietnam in order to observe the effects of the war there. As a result of the visit, he is the plaintiff in Lynd *vs.* Rusk, an American Civil Liberties Union-sponsored case which seeks to enjoin the United Stated government from withdrawing passports as punishment for travel to "unauthorized countries." He is an editor of *Liberation* and has contributed to several periodicals, including the *William and Mary Quarterly,* the *Political Science Quarterly, Labor History,* the *Journal of*

Negro History, and the *American Scholar.* His books include *Anti-Federalism in Dutchess County, New York* and, with Thomas Hayden, *The Other Side.* He has edited *Nonviolence in America: A Documentary History.* For the academic year 1967–1968, he has taken a leave of absence from Yale to work in Chicago with the School for Community Organizers.

SUMNER M. ROSEN earned his Ph.D. in economics at the Massachusetts Institute of Technology. He has taught at Northeastern University and Simmons College. His articles and book reviews have appeared in the *Correspondent, Liberation, New Politics, Studies on the Left, War/Peace Report,* and *Trans-Action.* He was a founder of Massachusetts Political Action for Peace, and has served as adviser to the Students for a Democratic Society and the Committee for Nonviolent Action. He has served as research associate with the Industrial Union Department of the AFL-CIO, and as Director of Education for the American Federation of State, County and Municipal Employees (AFL-CIO), District Council 37.

THEODORE ROSZAK received his doctorate at Princeton University and has taught at Stanford, and at California State College at Hayward, where he is Associate Professor of History and chairman of the History of Western Culture program. During 1964–1965 he served as editor of the British pacifist weekly, *Peace News.* He has returned to London for the academic year 1967–1968 to work at the Centre for Group Studies, a leading British social research organization.

JOHN WILKINSON studied physics and the philosophy of science at the Universities of Pennsylvania, Chicago, Munich, and Vienna. He has taught at the Universities of Chicago,

Istanbul, and California. In 1962 he left university teaching to become a member of the staff of the Center for the Study of Democratic Institutions. At the Center he organized the 1965 Convocation on the Technological Society. He is the translator of Jacques Ellul's *Technological Society* and the author of *The Quantitative Society or, What Are You To Do With Noodle?*, a Center Occasional Paper.

MARSHALL WINDMILLER took his doctorate in political science at the University of California-Berkeley and is presently Associate Professor of International Relations at San Francisco State College. He has held a Ford Foundation Fellowship and was research political scientist at the Center for South Asia Studies at Berkeley from 1954 to 1958. He was active in building the California Democratic Council and was, from 1960 to 1964, editor of the *liberal democrat*. For a number of years he has contributed weekly political commentaries to the Pacifica radio stations, KPFA, KPFK, and WBAI. In 1966 he visited Vietnam and Cambodia under the auspices of the Inter-University Committee for Debate on Foreign Policy. He has written for the *Nation, Progressive,* and *Ramparts* and is co-author of *Communism in India,* published by the University of California Press.

GORDON C. ZAHN was educated at St. John's University (Collegeville), the College of St. Thomas (St. Paul), and the Catholic University of America. Before assuming his present position as Professor of Sociology at the University of Massachusetts, he taught for a number of years at Loyola University in Chicago. During World War II he was a conscientious objector in civilian public service. He is a national sponsor of the National Committee for a Sane Nuclear Policy, the Catholic Peace Fellowship, and the American Pax Association. In 1967 he was elected to the National Council of the Fellowship of

Reconciliation and to the Catholic Commission on Intellectual and Cultural Affairs. He is the president of the American Catholic Sociological Society and his books include *German Catholics and Hitler's Wars, In Solitary Witness: The Life and Death of Franz Jägerstätter, What Is Society?*, and *War, Conscience and Dissent.*